COLSON

Manual of Below-Grade Waterproofing Systems

Manual of Below-Grade Waterproofing Systems

Justin Henshell
Edited by C.W. Griffin

JOHN WILEY & SONS, INC.
New York, Chichester, Weinheim, Brisbane, Singapore, Toronto

Library of Congress Cataloging-in-Publication Data:

ISBN: 0471-37730-9

Printed in the United States of America.

10 9 8 7 6 5 4 3 2 1

Contents

Preface

The topics of waterproofing and roofing sometimes appear linked like building-industry counterparts of fraternal twins. Designers experienced in both fields, however, know that this picture is badly distorted. Despite the identity of their primary functions — to prevent water intrusion into occupied spaces — waterproofing and roofing present designers with markedly different problems. The roof designer has a big advantage over the waterproofing designer. A long epidemic of low-slope roof failures involving wind blowoffs resulting from poor anchorage to insulated metal decks; two-ply, coated-felt membrane splitting and blistering; and a host of other problems resulting from a proliferation of untested roofing products taught the roofing industry a hard-learned lesson. It responded with improved guidance to designers through expanded technical literature. Suffering along with architects, contractors, and owners through a quarter century of rampant roof litigation, roofing manufacturers now provide reference details for a wide spectrum of roofing conditions. Through this improved technical literature, the roofing industry has demonstrated its commitment to providing designers with plenty of help in avoiding the monumental problems of the past.

Waterproofing manufacturers lag far behind roofing manufacturers in providing this expanded aid to designers. Like roofing, waterproofing technology has experienced an exponential proliferation of systems and materials over the past several decades. But unlike the roofing industry, the waterproofing industry has never been buried under an avalanche of litigation comparable to that experienced by the roofing industry. That lack of dismal experience may explain why, with few exceptions, waterproofing manufacturers provide so little guidance to designers in their technical literature. It is a demonstrably myopic policy, for many waterproofing failures result from designers' ignorance. And waterproofing failures make up in catastrophic cost and disruption what they lack in frequency.

The predominant defects in waterproofing manufacturer' technical literature are errors of omission. With few exceptions, waterproofing manufacturers illustrate only a few common conditions, and their details are unique for their proprietary products. On a typical waterproofing project, however, the designer may need to specify two or more generically similar systems provided by different manufacturers. The typical manufacturer's technical brochure leaves the designer totally without guidance on many conditions constantly recurring on ordinary projects. Illustrated details normally include termination at grade, expansion joints, and footing conditions.

There are, however, many conditions recurring on ordinary projects for which the typical manufacturer provides no details. These omitted details include critical transitions between foundation and mud slabs; connections at offset slabs at different elevations (e.g., at subbasements and elevator pits); and transitions from plaza waterproofing at rising walls, at steps, and at moving and static joints.

Note again that these are not extraordinary conditions, but merely the normal problems recurring on average waterproofing projects, each characterized by a unique combination of geometric, soil and climatic conditions. And a failure at any of these vulnerable joints or connections can precipitate a costly reconstruction project, which makes the typical reroofing project seem comparatively benign.

This lack of guidance on waterproofing details is, however, only one aspect of the designer ignorance at the root of many waterproofing failures. The proliferation of waterproofing systems and materials over the past several decades has surpassed the parallel growth of new roof systems and materials. Only a minority of architects have kept pace with this specialized new branch of building technology. There is widespread confusion about the proper functions and limitations of today's variegated waterproofing systems. They present the designer with a host of new challenges — from balancing the assets and liabilities of positive vs. negative-side waterproofing to the impact of new environmental protective regulations on volatile solvents and carcinogenic fumes from hot-applied bituminous systems.

This waterproofing manual is accordingly dedicated not only to filling this gap between limited technical literature and the designer's much greater needs, but also to providing a sound, fundamental approach to waterproofing problems. These problems can only grow more complex with the building industry's increasing need to exploit underground space in our crowded urban environment.

No reader should attempt to use this manual as a substitute for the professional expertise required to design a waterproofing system. In particular, the reader is cautioned against copying details without a full understanding of the limitations. The details presented in this manual were chosen to illustrate general design principles. Since most waterproofing projects have unique aspects, general details will require adaptation for use on specific projects. Moreover, information supplied by manufacturers may supersede that shown in the general details. (See Chapter 14 for expanded discussion.)

Readers should also note that the information incorporated in this manual came from many different sources. Because waterproofing technology is changing rapidly, some systems presented herein may be obsolete or replaced by others at the time of publication."

Acknowledgments

I wish to thank all those who helped me bring this book to fruition. Special thanks go to my partner Paul Buccellato who meticulously prepared and organized the illustrations and Richard Fricklas who reviewed the entire manuscript and provided thought-provoking and incisive comments.

I owe a special debt to Dorothy Lawrence of Laurenco Waterproofing Systems and Charles O. Pratt, PE, Consultant who fanned my interest in waterproofing, held my hand, offered encouragement and patiently and cheerfully tutored me with their wealth of technical and historical information.

Thanks also to my secretary Margaret Mary McCarthy, who spent countless hours in wordprocessing and proofreading the manuscript. Among the many who helped with technical input are Carl G. Cash, PE; Simpson, Gumpertz & Heger; Wayne Tobiasson, PE; Gerald Zakim, GZA; Tim Eorgin, Carlisle Coatings & Waterproofing; Donald Comerford, Waterproofing Systems of New Jersey and Alfred Kessi, Vandex Sales & Services, Inc.

Last, but not least, my sincere appreciation and gratitude to my editor, C. W. "Bill" Griffin, who organized the manuscript, put technical jargon into understandable English, challenged me at every turn and rewrote large portions of the text.

A Note on Using This Manual

This note appears in this prominent location to help readers find their way through this manual in the most efficient manner. Since no one will read this manual cover to cover (though the author graciously grants permission to do so), readers must rely on chapter headings and, more importantly, on the *Index* to locate pertinent material.

Take, as a prime example, the subject of "Failures." There is an entire chapter (12) devoted to this topic. It nonetheless contains only a fraction of the relevant information. (Failures are, after all, the manual's predominant subject; its primary purpose is to advise designers on how to avoid failure.) In addition to reading Chapter 12, the reader seeking references on a particular type of failure should search the *Index* under the entry, "Failures," and also under "Bentonite," "Liquid-applied membranes," "Modified bitumens," or whatever type of material or system (e.g., "Positive-side waterproofing") describes his particular problem.

Skillful, even imaginative, use of the *Index* is the key to exploiting the information in this manual to the fullest extent.

1

Introduction

Urban planning critics, who discuss the purely architectural aspects of plaza design with informed expertise, normally ignore the functional aspect: the unseen waterproofing system required to sustain these esthetic triumphs. The space under the street-level plaza, located on prime land sometimes priced in four digits per square foot, is inevitably dedicated to high-level occupancies in which the slightest leakage is intolerable. And unlike most building systems, the waterproofing system should ideally last the full service life of the building.

The paramount importance of durability is the first principle of waterproofing design. It will be reiterated throughout this manual. Most building systems can be designed for service lives far short of projected building service life. Airconditioning equipment, lighting, office partitions, communications, even elevators, curtain walls, and roofs can be designed for anticipated replacement as they either become obsolete or wear out under constant weathering. The waterproofing system, however, resembles the foundation and the structural framework as part of the building itself, which must last out the total anticipated service life.

The importance of durability is highlighted by industry practices. Guarantees and warranties are commonplace in the roofing industry. Few waterproofing manufacturers, however, offer guarantees or warranties. The few guarantees available are for severely limited liability, for painfully obvious reasons. Waterproofing for foundations and under slabs-on-ground is often inaccessible. And for plazas, replacement of a waterproofing system may require removal and replacement of tons of overburden or jackhammering removal of a concrete protection slab and concrete topping. Such drastic remedial action sometimes costs more than 300 times the membrane's cost.

Confronted with such catastrophic costs for failure, prudent designers ignore first-cost economy if it entails the slightest incremental risk of failure. Prudent designers select systems and materials that will do the job, regardless of a few pennies, or even dimes per-sq-ft. cost increase.

Prudent designers also require:

- Approved applicators for installing waterproofing systems
- Rigorous Quality Assurance (QA) inspection programs during installation
- Flood-testing, whenever practicable

While the problems of modern waterproofing have multiplied, advances in waterproofing technology have multiplied at an even faster rate, giving the designer a vastly expanded array of new systems and materials. More new waterproofing materials have appeared in the past three decades than in the previous three millennia, more in the past decade than in the previous century. Modern polymer chemistry simultaneously expands the waterproofing designer's arsenal of weapons against leakage as it complicates his problem of selecting the proper combination of systems or materials.

Waterproofing Unbound

The growing demand for a greater quantity and higher quality of waterproofing in building construction has a simple explanation. The rapid proliferation of airconditioning following World War II made windowless, underground spaces feasible for human occupancy. In pre-airconditioning days, underground spaces were severely limited by the practical inability to control interior temperature, humidity, and circulating air quality for comfortable, healthful habitation. The advent of airconditioning created a demand promoted by many interrelated factors:

- Space needs for expanded mechanical plants
- Space needs for windowless functions
- Trend toward water-shedding curtain walls
- Sites with poor drainage
- Incentive zoning for open, street-level plazas
- Rise in HVAC energy costs
- Rising cost of waterproofing failures

Space needs for expanded mechanical plants grew with the technological demand for sophisticated HVAC systems, electronic-data processing centers, etc., in the postwar building boom. The rudimentary building mechanical equipment preceding the 1950s seldom required deep basements. But the advent of huge chillers for office skyscrapers and other mechanical equipment created a demand for even more underground space. Basements, sub-basements, and even sub-sub-basements were excavated to accommodate this equipment.

Space needs for windowless functions include many activities best conducted in an environment usually isolated from the outside world. Since underground locations are necessarily windowless, they are prime locations for a whole spectrum of occupancies — theaters and similar audio-visual uses, archives, data-processing, electronic switch gear, parking, retailing and bowling alleys (see Fig. 1-1).

The trend toward water-shedding curtain walls aggravated building waterproofing problems. The traditional masonry walls of pre-World War II construction absorbed substantial quantities of rainwater and shed it by evaporation in a cyclical wetting-drying process. Glass and metal wall panels, however, shed this water rapidly, via vertical flow directly to the foundation soil. Accumulation of storm water at the foundation thus magnifies drainage and waterproofing problems at the building basement.

Fig. 1-1 This deep excavation, for book storage at the central branch of the New York Public Library, second only to the Library of Congress in number of volumes, exemplifies the expanded use of underground space in the nation's urban centers. This midtown Manhattan location lies only a few hundred yards west of Grand Central and a similar distance from Times Square, where land values approximate the world's highest. In the above photograph, waterproofing is being installed on a mud slab.

Sites with poor drainage became more common during the 1950s, when the accelerated tempo of postwar building made prime land scarcer. Foundation soil at previously occupied sites was sometimes contaminated, particularly in reclaimed swamps. Contaminants included acid and alkaline water, insecticides, soil poisoners, fertilizers and petroleum products discharged from vessels, refineries, and underground tanks.

Zoning regulations, promulgated to induce developers to provide more open space in city centers, magnified waterproofing problems. Incentive zoning offered developers greater building heights and floor area in return for street-level plazas. To maximize the economic potential of high-priced urban land, underground commercial space and parking garages were built below these plazas. Waterproofing of these city-center plazas requires much greater dependability and durability than the traditional membrane waterproofing of sidewalk vaults over cellar utility spaces.

The energy crises of the 1970s indirectly complicated waterproofing design. Prior to these sudden increases in energy costs, at a time when heating oil cost less than 10 cents per gal, thermal insulation was invariably omitted from waterproofing systems. Earth-covered buildings, which enjoyed a brief vogue in the early 1970s, are more energy-efficient than conventional, above-ground buildings. Increasing the underground space in a conventional building obviously increases the overall energy efficiency of the building. This bargain, however, exacts a price — i.e., a tougher waterproofing problem.

Rising costs of waterproofing failures have naturally accompanied modern building trends, as indicated by the preceding discussion. Failure may occur even without leakage of liquid moisture into the occupied space. Environmentally sensitive occupancies are routinely located underground in contemporary buildings. Electronic equipment in underground computer rooms and public assembly spaces containing audiovisual equipment requires rigorous humidity control as well as leakproof waterproofing. Auditoriums with wood floors are nearly as demanding as computer rooms. Such uses create waterproofing problems of unprecedented scope, virtually unknown to designers of pre-World War II buildings.

Historical Background

Paradoxically, the archetypal waterproofing project, the Hanging Gardens of Babylon, anticipated modern waterproofing problems nearly 26 centuries ago, six centuries before the Christian era. One of the seven wonders of the ancient world, the Hanging Gardens featured terraces ris-

Fig. 1-2   The Hanging Gardens of Babylon, built by King Nebuchardnezzar six centuries before the Christian era, is the archetypal waterproofing project. Earth-covered terraces planted with trees and other plants were supported on a series of arches rising to a height of 75 ft. Irrigation from the Euphrates watered the trees.

ing 75 ft. from a colonnade superstructure. Waterproofing consisted of bitumen and lead. Along with other plants, trees were planted in the over-burden over the deck and watered by slave-powered irrigation machines lifting water from the nearby Euphrates (see Fig. 1-2).

In the more recent past, at the beginning of the twentieth century, waterproofing projects have involved more mundane uses — primarily tunnels, dams, pools, and other water-containment structures. Cellar vaults under sidewalks were also protected, normally with built-up coal-tar pitch membranes.

These early built-up bituminous waterproofing membranes com-prised alternate layers of cotton or burlap, organic felts and coal tar pitch. The membrane was then covered with bricks dipped in hot pitch. Before World War I, built-up waterproofing was applied to building foundations, vertically to brick and tile walls, horizontally to mud slabs in hot coal tar pitch or asphalt. Standard specifications for these early built-up mem-branes comprised four to six plies for waterproofing, three to four plies for dampproofing. Concrete foundations and floor slabs were cast over these hot-applied membranes. For shallow cellars, a sub-slab drainage system was specified in conjunction with the membrane.

Because waterproofing membranes were expensive to install and difficult to repair, cementitious waterproofing was introduced nearly a century ago, as a less expensive, more convenient alternative. Cementitious waterproofing coats interior (dry) faces of walls and slabs. The most popular of several proprietary compounds was a hydrolithic metallic system containing iron fillings. (Oxidation of the filings' surfaces, in the presence of mixing water hydrating the cement, expands the iron filings' volume to several multiples of its unoxidized volume, and this expanded volume fills interstices in the concrete matrix, forming a tight, water-resistant solid.)

Two systems and two materials thus dominated traditional waterproofing: wet-face (i.e., *positive*-side) waterproofing featuring built-up membranes and dry-side (i.e., *negative*-side) waterproofing featuring cementitious coatings. Though still in use today, both of these traditional materials have declined from predominance to minor status, buried under an avalanche of improved, new materials.

Built-up coal tar pitch membranes do, however, have two survival factors at work preserving them from extinction:

- Existing coal tar pitch systems are practicably repaired by overlaying the defective old membrane with the same built-up system. (Air pollution regulations may, however, ban hot kettles.)
- A dwindling group of conservative building owners, like professionals who still wear coats and ties to the office, still swears eternal allegiance to coal-tar-pitch membranes for plaza waterproofing.

Brave New Waterproofing

The development of new materials to replace traditional built-up membranes and cementitious coatings accompanied an accelerated evolution of waterproofing that has also largely replaced drainage media and even waterstops with new, superior plastics. Supplanting hot-mopped bituminous membrane materials in use since the mid-nineteenth century is a host of modern membrane materials: rubberized-asphalt membranes, single-ply sheets of butyl and PVC, one and two-component liquid-applied membranes (LAMs) and bentonite sheets. The old cementitious coatings with iron or aluminum filings are giving way to crystalline/chemical conversion coatings capable of sealing tiny shrinkage cracks. Bentonite clay is the basis for a whole spectrum of prefabricated composite components. These bentonite-based laminates may contain one or more combinations of high-density polyethylene, geotextiles, and butyl sheets, plus several different versions of kraft paper containers.

By the 1990s, environmental constraints became a significant factor shaping the evolution of waterproofing systems and materials. With the advent of EPA and VOC (volatile organic content) regulations setting TLV (threshold level values promulgated by OSHA), systems releasing volatile solvents and potentially carcinogenic fumes fell under severe restrictions or outright bans in densely populated center cities. This trend has severely reduced the use of hot-mopped built-up bituminous membranes and promoted their replacement with environmentally harmless systems: liquid-applied membranes, cold-applied systems, water-based instead of solvent-based primers.

Prefabricated modified bitumens (i.e., rubberized asphalt) membranes, supported on HDPE (high-density polyethylene) sheets, are prominent among the replacements for traditional hot-mopped built-up membranes. In addition to reducing (or even eliminating) the polluting fumes emanating from traditional hot-mopped application, modified bitumen membranes represent a forward leap in the perennial goal of building construction: to shift as much work as practicable from field to factory. This process facilitates quality control, labor productivity, and safety. One waterproofing manufacturer, W.R. Grace, introduced a proprietary, self-adhering modified-bitumen membrane, which Grace called "rubberized asphalt," back in the 1960s. Grace's Bituthene had monopolized this market until its patents expired in the early 1990s, when several manufacturers began marketing similar products (see Fig. 1-3). All modified-bitumen waterproofing membranes marketed today contain an SBS (styrene butadiene styrene) plasticizer. Because it is unreinforced (but laminated to HDPE), SBS-modified bitumen provides superior waterproofing. The alternative roofing products, APP (atactic polypropylene) and

Fig. 1-3 Self-adhering modified bitumen membranes, with high-density polyethylene (HDPE) facer sheets, are among the most popular replacements for traditional hot-mopped, built-up membranes, increasingly banned by anti-pollution ordinances. (TC Mira DRI.)

SBS-modified bitumen sheets, are reinforced with glass or polyester felts. They have not achieved a significant market share in the waterproofing field because, at exposed edges, the reinforcement can wick water into the sheet, delaminating it and shortening its service life.

Single-ply sheets, both thermosetting (i.e., vulcanized rubber) and thermoplastic, have been vastly improved. Butyl is favored over EPDM and neoprene, which is no longer manufactured in large sheets. Butyl has much lower water absorptivity than either EPDM or neoprene, a tremendous advantage for continuously wet waterproofing membranes.

Among the thermoplastic waterproofing sheets, glass fiber-reinforced PVC, in gages up to 120 mils, has emerged as the material of choice, replacing CPE and unreinforced PVC, whose thinner cross sections often resulted in plasticizer loss and consequent embrittlement as the material aged.

Long used under slabs and for foundations, especially as blindside waterproofing, bentonite clay has become a major positive-side waterproofing material, ranking it among the most widely used waterproofing materials. It comes in a wide variety of laminates, ranging from prefabricated panels of biodegradable paper, through geotextiles filled with bentonite granules, and high-density polyethylene sheets with adhered bentonite granules. (See Chapter 10 for discussion of bentonite-based waterproofing products.)

Like built-up bituminous membranes, negative-side, cementitious coatings with iron or aluminum filings are fading away. Crystalline/chemical coatings offer greater dependability, longer service life, and a self-healing property that enhances their long term waterproofing quality. Also called *chemical conversion* or *capillary* coatings, these solutions of organic and inorganic compounds react chemically with Portland cement and free lime in the presence of moisture. They fill capillaries and shrinkage cracks with long chain molecules crystallized within the concrete. When shrinkage cracks occur after the concrete has cured, the reactivated crystallization process tends to fill the crack openings.

Synthetic materials have replaced natural materials even in ancillary components of contemporary waterproofing systems. Plastic drainage panels have begun to replace pea gravel and granular backfill on plazas and against foundations. Geotextiles serve as filters for plastic drainage panels and granular backfill and also as wrapping filters for footing drains.

These synthetic materials offer greater filtration design control than bulkier natural materials. With their thinner cross sections, they also reduce excavation volume and costs.

Like improved filtering materials, waterstops have undergone several stages of improvement. Embrittled bent metal strips were replaced by plastic and rubber-derivative dumbbells and bulb cross sections. These, in turn, have yielded to the currently popular butyl and bentonite/butyl bars. (See Appendix C). Besides greater durability, butyl and bentonite/butyl bars offer other advantages:

- Simple installation (featuring lap joints)
- Elimination of onsite welding
- Easy visual inspection of installation
- Stability during concrete casting operations
- Complete encapsulation in concrete

New Standards For Improved Design

Accompanying these improved materials introduced over the past several decades, waterproofing design has seen similar improvement with the promulgation of new industry standards. Plaza waterproofing design took a giant forward step with the 1978 publication of ASTM Standards C 898 (for liquid-applied membranes, LAMs) and C 981 (for built-up bituminous membranes), published in 1983.

These ASTM standards have revolutionized plaza design, through establishment of three vitally important design principles:

- Sloping the deck for dependable drainage
- Need for thermal insulation
- Need for drainage course above the membrane

These new standards correct several long-standing defects resulting from the perpetuation of traditional practices unsuited to modern waterproofing projects. For nearly a century, traditional waterproofing assemblies over setback terraces and sidewalk vaults consisted of four or five-ply built-up membranes, without protection boards or thermal insulation. The membrane was covered with concrete or quarry tile in a mortar setting bed. On terraces, the membrane was installed on a 1- or 2-in.-thick concrete topping underlain with cinder fill and sloped to drain. As an alternative design, the deck could be level and the setting bed sloped to drain.

Omission of insulation from these traditional assemblies kept the membrane, warmed by the heat loss from the interior space, within a relatively narrow temperature range and thus reduced thermal contraction stresses experienced by membranes with insulation located on the warm side of the membrane.

The specific defect corrected by Standard ASTM C 898 was the practice of sandwiching the waterproofing membrane between the structural concrete deck and the wearing slab. This defective detail propagated shrinkage cracks from the substrate below or movement from the topping above into the membrane (Fig. 1-4). Traditional built-up bituminous membranes are especially vulnerable to splitting. (Their breaking strains are less than 2% at low temperature, compared with 200% or more for vulcanized rubber sheets and breaking strains ranging up to 100% for modified bitumens.)

The solution to this problem was isolation of the membrane from

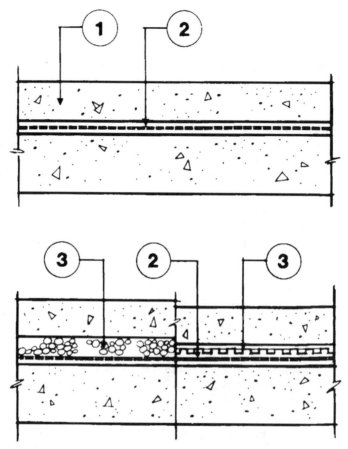

Fig. 1-4 Traditional split slab construction bonded the wearing course (1), to the membrane (2), as indicated on the top. Contemporary design divorces it with a layer of drainage composite (3), or gravel (3), as indicated on the bottom.

the paving with an intervening layer of insulation. Extruded polystyrene board has the properties required of waterproofing insulation. It has high compressive strength, required to resist traffic loads. It also has extremely low water absorptivity, required to prevent water buildup within the waterproofing assembly. Placed above a plaza waterproofing membrane, extruded polystyrene board reduces the membrane's temperature range, thereby reducing the splitting risk from thermal contraction at low temperature. Drainage fills and composite panels normally used in conjunction with this foamed insulation, also help to isolate the membrane from the paving (Fig. 1-5).

Membrane splitting from concrete cracking propagated upward from the deck is a less severe problem than movement propagated downward from the paving. The use of alternative adhered membrane materials —

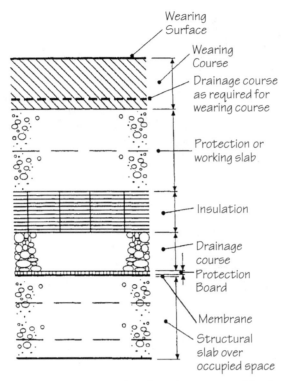

Fig. 1-5   Basic Components of Built-up Bituminous Membrane Waterproofing System with Separate Wearing Course. (American Society for Testing and Materials.)

modified bitumens, butyl, and PVC — with their much higher breaking strains, virtually eliminates the risk of membrane splitting from deck cracking. Even traditional built-up membranes are fairly safe from splitting at the narrow temperature ranges assured by locating the insulation between cold winter air and the membrane.

Another design error corrected by the new standards involved an increasing number of wearing-surface failures caused by improper drain location or improper drain installation. Drain elevation was set to carry water from the quarry tile wearing surface, with no drain for the membrane below. When drains with weep holes at the membrane elevation were installed to correct this latter defect, the weepholes were often clogged either with bitumen mopping or cement leached from the mortar setting bed. As a consequence, water was dammed in ever-widening circles around drains, causing efflorescence, popping tiles, disintegrating grout, and organic growth. These factors then combine to accelerate the failure process. Vegetation growth, for example, can ultimately result in roots penetrating the membrane (Fig. 1-6).

Fig. 1-6   Lack of weep holes in this drain dammed water at the membrane level. Dammed water can cause efflorescence, popping tiles, disintegrating grout, and organic growth.

What Is Waterproofing?

To establish the scope of this manual it is first necessary to dispel widespread confusion about the meaning of the term *waterproofing*. It has been variously, and often erroneously, construed to denote a coating applied to above-grade masonry or concrete walls; a membrane cover on spandrel beams; a membrane in split-slab construction under a mechanical or shower room; a coating on a parking garage, in a tank, or pool; as well as four different treatments of below-grade foundation walls and slabs. And to add ambiguous insult to semantic injury, waterproofing is sometimes confused with dampproofing.

In this manual, in accordance with ASTM usage, waterproofing will denote a system designed to resist hydrostatic pressure exerted by moisture in the liquid state. It is thus differentiated from dampproofing, which is designed merely to resist the flow of moisture in gaseous state — i.e., water vapor. (See Chapter 3, "Dampproofing." and Chapter 4, "Waterproofing," for detailed discussion of this distinction.)

A subtler source of semantic confusion concerns the problem of distinguishing between a waterproofing system and a low-slope roof system, when the roof system is a so-called Protected Membrane Roof (PMR) assembly. In a PMR, the membrane is placed directly on the deck below the insulation, instead of in its conventional, weather-exposed location atop the insulation. When a PMR is ballasted with concrete pavers, it resembles a waterproofed plaza. A roof plaza can, in fact, be identical to a waterproofed plaza at or below grade.

The distinguishing feature differentiating a PMR from a waterproofed plaza system is the membranes's accessibility in event of failure, and this feature is the basic determinant in manufacturers' willingness to issue guarantees. Manufacturers will generally guarantee a PMR if the pavers are installed on pedestals, in which case the membrane is accessible. Most manufacturers will guarantee PMR systems in which the pavers, serving as ballast or maintenance walkways, are loose-laid on the insulation. (In industry semantics, such a system is not considered to be plaza water-proofing.) If, on the other hand, the membrane is inaccessible — with wearing surface units (such as brick, tile or stone) installed in a mortar setting bed or in sand over a concrete protection slab — then the system is classified as waterproofing, and manufacturers will not guarantee it.

A guarantee should, however, be a secondary, not a primary consider-ation. Only if your primary goal is to provide the owner with the dubious assurance of a manufacturer's warranty should you select the PMR system. If a lower-risk system assuring long service life in a continuously moist environment over a moisture-sensitive space is your primary goal, then a waterproofing system is the more prudent selection.

Manual's Scope

In accordance with the preceding discussion of terminology, this manual will focus on waterproofing of below-grade, occupiable building spaces subject to hydrostatic pressure as well as dampproofing. It will thus be limited to covering waterproofing and dampproofing for the following underground building components:

- Structural concrete slabs with a wearing surface or earth fill
- Concrete slabs-on-ground below grade elevation
- Foundation walls

Excluded from the manual are waterproofing (and dampproofing) for the following structures:

- Water-containment vessels
- Vehicular, pipe and similar tunnels not enclosing habitable space
- Above-grade mechanical room floors (not exposed to ground water or soil chemicals)
- Traffic toppings or traffic-bearing waterproofing systems for vehicles and balconies offering short-term protection, but not resistance to hydrostatic pressure

2

Principles of
Water Management

Water management is essential to keeping the building dry. As in many other aspects of building design, a gram of prevention is worth a kilogram of cure. It is better to manage water flow, to alleviate or even eliminate leakage problems, than simply to rely on waterproofing.

There is a parallel here in the ubiquitous glass walled-office towers built in the 1960s and early 1970s, before the big increase in energy costs commanded designers' attention. Many architects ignored these buildings' tremendous solar heat loads, which ranged up to 10 times as much through single-layered glass compared with opaque insulated curtain walls. Before the energy crisis, these architects simply had their mechanical engineers design the airconditioning system to handle these heavy loads. They not only ignored the additional capital and operating costs; they also ignored the greater difficulty in assuring comfortable conditions in these heat-absorbing structures.

Good water management is analogous to good thermal design. Just as wall-shading and heat-reflective glass reduce thermal loads, so sloping below-grade structural slabs to drain can reduce hydrostatic loading of subsurface building components. Drainage panels or pervious granular backfills alleviate lateral pressure against walls. Granular fills under slabs-on-grade reduce capillary movement of moisture upward through voids in subsoil, reducing or eliminating hydrostatic pressure.

These subsurface building components must also be designed to resist corrosive chemicals present in soil. Most products are usually resistant to chemicals with pH values of 3 to 12.

Hydrostatic Pressure

Though structural design of waterproofed building components is beyond the manual's scope, the waterproofing designer requires at least an elementary understanding of hydrostatics. Below-grade structures must resist a combination of hydrostatic and soil pressures. These pressures generally range from 30 to 62.4 psf per ft. of depth. They are obviously lower for dry, granular soils, which facilitate vertical subsurface water flow, and higher for wet soils, which approach purely liquid properties. Some soils — e.g., saturated clays and silts — exert lateral pressure (psf) equal to their densities (pcf), which can exceed that of purely hydrostatic pressure. This added earth pressure, however, affects only the structural design of the wall or slab. Despite the additional lateral compressive stress on the waterproofing membrane, the leakage threat to the waterproofing component comes from liquid water pressure alone.

Hydrostatic pressure increases linearly with depth, producing a triangular horizontal loading pattern (see Fig. 2-1 and Table 2-1). At a depth of 10 ft., hydrostatic pressure is 62.4 x 10 = 624 psf, in all directions. The extreme pressures shown in Fig. 2-1 assume a ground-water level at grade elevation, a conservative assumption that nonetheless indicates the scope of the waterproofing designer's problem.

Hydrostatic pressure on a building component occurs when the water table rises above it at any point. The water table, also known as the groundwater level, free-water elevation, and the phreatic surface, is defined by Labs as the underground elevation where water is at atmospheric pressure. It may be at grade or hundreds of feet below grade. There is hydrostatic pressure on slabs-on-grade and foundation walls when they are below the ground-water line, when surface water runoff temporarily raises the groundwater level, or when there is a perched water table. This is a condition where localized bodies of water are separated from the normal free-water elevation by impervious, unsaturated soils. There is hydrostatic pressure on structural slabs below grade when they are below the ground-water level, when flash floods occur, from heavy runoff from rising walls, and from clogged drains or undersized drainage systems.

Groundwater level, and consequent hydrostatic pressure, can vary seasonally (generally highest in spring), daily, or even hourly. The resulting hydrostatic pressure may be intermittent, with groundwater level periodically rising above and falling below the waterproofed components' elevation; or it can be continuous, when groundwater level remains constantly above waterproofed components. Spectacularly rapid changes in groundwater level can occur in semi-tropical locations like Florida, which sometimes experiences rainfalls of 10 in. or more in a day. Even in arid Arizona, flooding rains can suddenly raise water-table elevations in the clay desert soil. Under such conditions, the ground is swiftly saturated. Full hydrostatic pressure can be temporarily exerted against foundation walls, slabs-on-ground, and structural slabs until the surplus

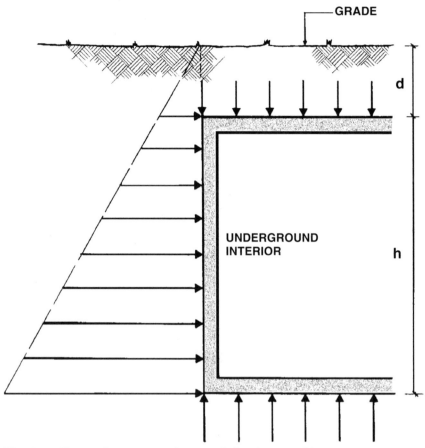

Fig. 2-1 If groundwater extends to grade level (a possible temporary state in areas struck with torrential rain), hydrostatic pressure under the worst conditions can be as follows: $p = wd$ on top slab; $p = w(d+h)$ lateral pressure at the base of the wall, and $p = w(d+h)$ upward pressure on the slab-on-ground. If $d = 2$ ft and $h = 10$ ft, the lateral pressure at the base of the wall could equal 62.4 $(2 + 10) = 749$ psf.

water drains away through the foundation soil.

Groundwater level is only the basic determinant of hydrostatic pressure. It also depends on the nature of the soil. Water rises by capillary action in most soils. This capillary rise varies from 11.5 ft in soils comprising microscopically sized particles (i.e., clay and silt) to 0 in granular soils, where the large spaces between particles nullify capillarity. The top plane of the saturation zone — i.e., the space between groundwater level and the limit of capillary rise — lies between the two. Even in coarse sand, this saturation zone can extend hydrostatic pressure more than 2 ft above groundwater elevation (see Table 2-2).

Pressure of Water Against Walls and Floors			
Hydrostatic Head Feet	Pressure per Square Inch Lbs.	Lifting Pressure per Square Foot (Under Floor) Lbs.	Average Pressure per Square Foot on Wall Surface Affected Lbs.
0.5	0.21	31.0	15.6
1.0	0.43	62.0	31.2
2.0	0.87	125.3	62.5
3.0	1.30	187.2	93.7
4.0	1.73	249.1	125.0
5.0	2.17	312.3	156.0
6.0	2.60	374.4	187.2
8.0	3.47	500.0	250.0
10.0	4.34	625.0	312.5
12.0	5.20	749.0	374.5
15.0	6.50	937.0	468.0
20.0	8.67	1248.4	624.2
25.0	10.84	1561.0	780.5
30.0	13.01	1873.4	937.0
40.0	17.34	2497.0	1248.5

Table 2-1   Hydrostatic pressure increases with depth.
(*Richey's Reference Handbook.*)

Slabs-on-ground subjected to hydrostatic pressure must be designed to resist uplift, via one or more of the following methods:

- Increased slab weight (to counterbalance upward hydrostatic pressure)
- Reinforcing the slab for flexural resistance and anchoring it to foundations or grade beams
- Tieing the slab to rock anchors

Passive resistance — i.e., prevention of hydrostatic pressure — can be accomplished by installing underslab drains and footing drains directed to the storm-water system.

In addition to designing the system for the most severe hydrostatic pressures likely to occur, the waterproofing designer must also consider other hazards when selecting the system. Swiftly flowing underground water can wash away bentonite, leaving the foundation wall defenseless. High hydrostatic pressure can force a waterproofing membrane into voids

Table 2-2   Capillary Rise

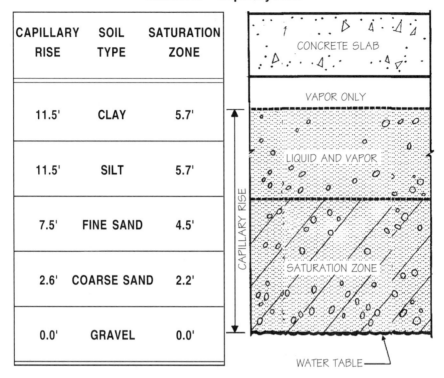

CAPILLARY RISE	SOIL TYPE	SATURATION ZONE
11.5'	CLAY	5.7'
11.5'	SILT	5.7'
7.5'	FINE SAND	4.5'
2.6'	COARSE SAND	2.2'
0.0'	GRAVEL	0.0'

Table 2-2 Water rises in all soils except gravel via capillary action, with the results tabulated above. In clay and silt, the saturation zone extends nearly 6 ft. above the groundwater table. Liquid moisture in the saturation zone exerts hydrostatic pressure that must be resisted of the waterproofed components. Data from *Construction Principles, Materials and Methods, Second Ed., 1972*, The Institute of Financial Education, Chicago, IL.

in its concrete substrate, causing shearing and flexural rupture. Hydrostatic pressure can also increase the membrane's water absorption, with consequent swelling. Membrane swelling can break the membrane's bond with its substrate, forming wrinkles vulnerable to flexural cracking and eventual leakage through local weak spots.

On negative-side waterproofing systems (see Chapter 6), hydrostatic pressure promotes water penetration into concrete walls and slabs through tie-rod holes, cold joints, and rock pockets. Other potential leak sources occur at buried conduit, tieback blockouts, and where soda cans, beer bottles, and other debris thrown into the formwork prior to casting operations create cavities in the concrete.

Site Planning and Landscaping

The most rudimentary solution to relieving water pressure in open areas with high water tables is to raise the building above it and use the excavated earth to grade away from it. Passive water and moisture control can be achieved via several methods, including:

- Proper grading to control surface runoff.
- Foundation planting.
- Providing a layer of impervious soil or paving adjacent to foundations.
- Extending downspouts to discharge drainwater well away from foundations.
- Connecting downspouts to stormwater sewers.
- Backfilling with pervious material and installing footing drains.
- Providing under-slab drainage blankets and drains.
- Providing intercepting drains (uphill on hilly sites).
- Draining impermeable surfaces around a hill-sided building (which can dam water).

Grading to control surface runoff should be sloped away from the foundation at 5% or greater slope for the first 10 ft. The BOCA code is even more conservative, requiring a 1 in 12 (8.7%) slope.

Foundation planting reduces hydrostatic pressure by absorbing groundwater via plant roots.

Impervious soil layer or paving adjacent to the foundation diverts water flowing down the exterior wall from creating hydrostatic pressure against the foundation.

Extending downspouts away from the building reduces the quantity of water that can percolate downward through the soil adjacent to foundation walls and slabs, where it can exert hydrostatic pressure.

Connecting downspouts to stormwater sewers is even more effective than extending downspouts away from the building as a means of relieving subsurface hydrostatic pressure. Unless the drainage system fails, this strategy removes 100% (or nearly so) of surface water from the building perimeter.

Backfilling with porous material and installing footing drains reduces hydrostatic pressure. In conjunction with previously listed remedies, porous backfill allows subsurface water to flow vertically to footing drains, which preferably discharge at some lower surface elevation. (See Figures 2-2 and 2-3). Footing and underslab drains serve to

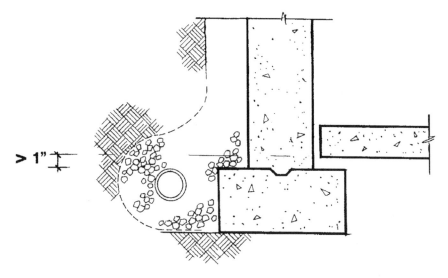

Fig. 2-2   Detail of footing drain shows minimum aggregate blanket and minimum dimension from bottom of slab-on-ground to top of pipe. Pipe is usually 4 in. or 6 in. diameter and may be level, but a 0.4% to 1% slope is preferred.

draw down surrounding ground water to relieve walls and floors from hydrostatic pressure. They also collect rain water and snow melt that percolates through the backfill.

Drain Pipe Materials

Drain pipe is manufactured in two basic types: rigid and flexible. Rigid pipe is either porous concrete or clay tile. Flexible pipe is made of corrugated polyethylene, PVC (corrugated and smooth-bore), and bituminized fibers, and styrene rubber. Flexible pipe offers a major advantage over rigid pipe in its ability to accommodate differential settlement without cracking under flexural stress and silting up from soil penetration through the cracks.

Clay tile illustrates the liabilities of rigid pipe. Until the 1960s clay tile was the most prevalent drainage pipe material. Its defects then became manifest. Its short, uncoupled sections were easily dislodged during backfill operations. Felt strips over open joints often failed and promoted silting, and so did cracks in the brittle tile from flexural stress caused by settling and heaving.

Porous concrete, corrugated PVC, and corrugated polyethylene are currently the most popular drainage materials, having demonstrated their superiority. Despite its rigidity, porous concrete seldom cracks from differential settlement, because of its superior flexural strength. It also

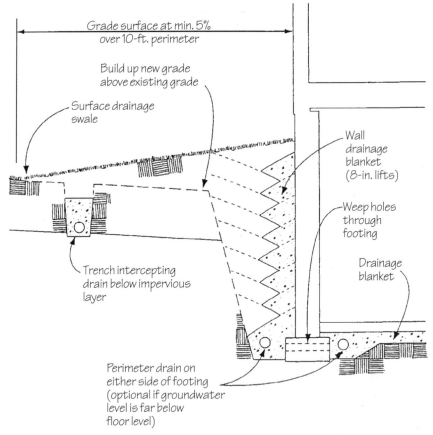

Fig. 2-3 Cross section through basement wall depicts overall water-management strategy for relieving hydrostatic pressure against waterproofing or dampproofing membrane. (The University of Minnesota.)

has a unique advantage, in allowing water infiltration around its entire perimeter. All other pipes are limited, for an obvious reason, to infiltration through perforations and slots in the bottom half of their cross sections. Porous concrete is less vulnerable to silting than perforated or slotted pipes. Its microscopically sized openings permit less intrusion by silt particles than the much larger openings in alternative materials.

The superiority of corrugated over smooth-bore plastic pipe stems from a balancing of assets and liabilities. Smooth-bore pipe offers reduced resistance to water flow, better self-flushing, and less deflection than corrugated pipe. Its reduced flexibility, however, makes smooth-bore pipe more vulnerable to cracking from differential settlement. Slotted, smooth-bore, corrugated PVC pipe (smooth-bore on its interior surface, corrugated on its exterior surface) combines the best properties of both types.

Basic Drainage Design

Drainage pipes are located at the toe of the footing or under the slab. At its highest elevation, the top of the pipe must be *below* the underside of the floor slab. And at its lowest elevation, the bottom of the pipe must be *above* the bottom of the footing (see Fig. 2-4). These rules prevent two deleterious effects:

- Hydrostatic pressure underneath the slab.
- Undermining of bearing soil by drain water seeping below the soil-bearing elevation.

To assure compliance with these requirements, the designer must coordinate the drainage plan with the foundation plan. In some instances, the structural engineer may need to drop the footing elevation below the stratum determined satisfactory for bearing capacity.

On expansive soils, the footing may be cast on a drainage bed or a void form, with the pipe invert level with the bottom of the footing (see Fig. 3-9). On unstable soils, corrugated plastic tubing may be placed on top of the footing, which must then be at a lower elevation with respect to the slab. Placement inboard of the footing is not as effective as outboard, where it receives percolation from the grade directly.

Pipes should bear on a 4-in. minimum gravel bed surrounded with 6 in. of gravel. Gravel must be encased with a filter fabric. Positive drainage and scouring cannot be assured when drains are level. A pitch of 1% ($^1/_{10}$) is desirable, but can be reduced to 0.4 - 0.5% ($^1/_{17}$ - $^1/_{20}$). Drainage systems under the slab should be connected to perimeter drains with 2-in. minimum weep tubes spaced 8 ft through the footing.

Providing intercepting drains on hill sites prevents water from flowing against foundation walls and exerting hydrostatic (and even some minor hydrodynamic) pressure (see Fig. 2-5).

Draining impermeable surfaces around a hill-sided building also relieves the foundation of subsurface hydrostatic pressure, by diverting surface water harmlessly away from the building.

Draining water under slabs-on-ground by aggregate blankets and drainage fields conducts accumulated water to daylight or drainage systems. Where intermittent water is present, from heavy rain storms or the occasional seasonal rise of the water table, gravel or combined gravel and under-slab pipe drainage systems may suffice to reduce the frequency, duration and intensity of hydrostatic pressure. Drainage backfills of gravel or sand, sometimes in concert with geocomposite panels, are also used to relieve intermittent pressure and ground-water accumulation.

Subsurface drains under slabs-on-ground, installed in a gravel drain-

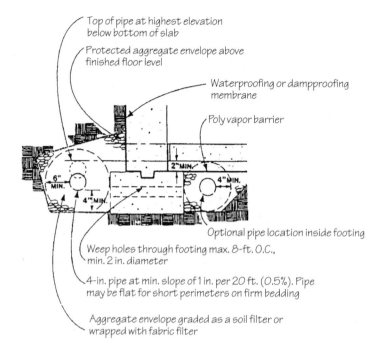

Top of pipe at highest elevation below bottom of slab

Protected aggregate envelope above finished floor level

Waterproofing or dampproofing membrane

Poly vapor barrier

2" MIN.

6" MIN.

4" MIN.

4" MIN.

Optional pipe location inside footing

Weep holes through footing max. 8-ft. O.C., min. 2 in. diameter

4-in. pipe at min. slope of 1 in. per 20 ft. (0.5%). Pipe may be flat for short perimeters on firm bedding

Aggregate envelope graded as a soil filter or wrapped with fabric filter

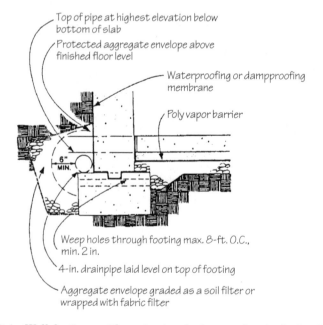

Top of pipe at highest elevation below bottom of slab

Protected aggregate envelope above finished floor level

Waterproofing or dampproofing membrane

Poly vapor barrier

6" MIN.

Weep holes through footing max. 8-ft. O.C., min. 2 in.

4-in. drainpipe laid level on top of footing

Aggregate envelope graded as a soil filter or wrapped with fabric filter

Fig. 2-4 Wall footings with perimeter drains can locate drain pipes inside or outside footings. Inside location is less likely to clog drain, but requires much more disruptive repair operations if it does clog. (The University of Minnesota.)

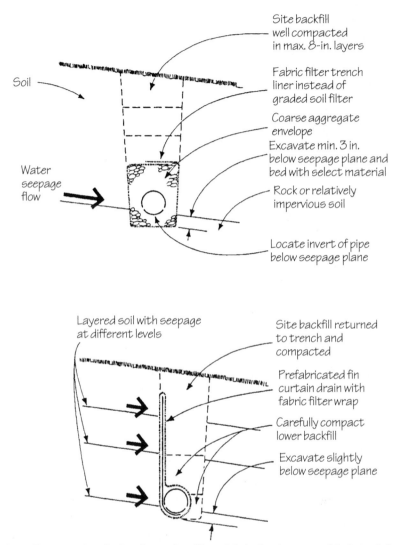

Site backfill
well compacted
in max. 8-in. layers

Fabric filter trench
liner instead of
graded soil filter

Coarse aggregate
envelope

Excavate min. 3 in.
below seepage plane and
bed with select material

Rock or relatively
impervious soil

Locate invert of pipe
below seepage plane

Soil

Water
seepage
flow

Layered soil with seepage
at different levels

Site backfill returned
to trench and
compacted

Prefabricated fin
curtain drain with
fabric filter wrap

Carefully compact
lower backfill

Excavate slightly
below seepage plane

Fig. 2-5 Intercepting drains featuring filter fabric (top) or a prefabricated fin curtain drain (bottom) can relieve hydrostatic pressure on sites where a water-proofed structure is downhill from subsurface water flow. (The University of Minnesota.)

age bed, can reduce the need to waterproof slabs exposed to intermittent water pressure. To be effective, this system should be designed to extend the drains to daylight.

Dependence on a pumping system to discharge the water can be risky, unless back-up pumps and generators are provided. Moreover, many urban sewer authorities may not permit the discharge of subsurface water into what may be an already overloaded storm drainage system. When the sewer system combines both storm water and sewage, adding subsurface drainage increases the load on a wastewater treatment plant. There is also the danger of subsurface drainage systems drawing down the water table and causing settlement of nearby buildings.

If seasonally high water levels are anticipated, the designer and owner may accept the risk of installing an underslab drainage system in lieu of waterproofing. The system can be either a thick drainage blanket or a thinner one with drain pipes in gravel-lined trenches. The thick blanket discharges water at a higher level than the piped system. The design of the gravel blanket thickness and pipe spacing is based on the permeability of the soil and drainage blanket and the height of the ground-water. Pipe sizes and spacing can be varied as dictated by cost.[1]

Subsurface Drainage

As a major factor in water management, subsurface drains require expanded discussion. Once water is induced to flow, it must be provided with a pervious material to permit it to drain freely for harmless disposal, usually via subsurface drains. Common drainage media include:

- Drainage composites and insulating drainage panels, covered on one or both sides with geotextiles
- Insulating drainage panels
- Graded pea gravel
- Coarse sand
- Coarse gravel

Drainage composites and panels are inserted between the wall waterproofing membrane and backfill and on waterproofing over horizonal membranes. Marketed in a variety of forms, the most popular are three-dimensional sheets and fused plastic filaments laminated to geotextiles and filter fabrics. Boards or panels of grooved extruded polystyrene, coated expanded polystyrene and 6-pcf fiberglass are also used for drainage, although the latter two lack sufficient compressive strength for horizontal orientation. They are all covered on one (or both) faces with geotextiles (filter fabrics). One manufacturer markets a combination insulation/drainage board comprising medium-density glass fiber as part of a liquid-applied membrane (LAM) system restricted to residential foundations only.

---

1.   The design is beyond the scope of this manual. For further information see Cedergen, H.R. 1962, "Seepage Requirements of Filters and Pervious Bases" Paper 3363, ASCE Transactions, vol. 127, part 1, pp 1099-1113 and 1967 "Seepage, Drainage and Flow Net" New York, John Wiley & Sons.

Three-dimensional plastic drainage composites are an alternative to granular backfill. They are composed of three-dimensional drainage cores of plastic sheets or mats of fused filaments. Sheets are deformed and filaments interlaced to form a geomatrix that provides multi-directional water flow. In one product the filaments are rectilinear. In the other, the filaments are non-directional. To reduce silting, both deformed plastic and filament cores are laminated to a filter fabric on one or both sides. These composite products range in thickness from 0.4 in. to 0.8 in. Despite their higher material cost, the reduced labor cost for installing plastic drainage composites can offer lesser total cost than granular fill. They eliminate the need to install a separate filter fabric between the earth and granular fill, since the filter fabric is laminated to the panel. Manufacturers also claim a reduction in costs by elimination of protection board placed against the membrane. But this may be false economy. Membrane waterproofing requires prompt protection and drainage panels are not always installed in a timely fashion. Further benefits of plastic drainage composites accrue from their thinner cross sections, which reduce the quantity of filter material. They also provide drainage at lagging and lot lines.

Different geotextiles are used for horizontal and vertical application, so care must be taken to select the appropriate type. Composites are manufactured with a range of compressive strengths depending on the application. For horizontal surfaces, specify a high compressive strength of 9,000 psf. On foundations, a 6,000-psf panel is usually sufficient.

Their thinner cross-section dimension make drainage composites the preferred drainage medium on plazas where there are design restrictions on thickness and where traditional 2-in. or 3-in.-thick sand and gravel would be unacceptable. However, the designer should anticipate a permanent initial deflection of approximately 10% under initial loading. Details should provide for this permanent deformation.

Plastic panels are spot-adhered to vertical waterproofing or loose laid on horizontal membranes. Panels function well on suspended slabs, but may distort and disbond from vertical surfaces when exposed to sunlight before backfilling.

Waterproofing on both horizonal and vertical surfaces should be covered with protection board before the panels are installed. This will prevent sharp filaments or panel edges from puncturing the waterproofing membrane. Improperly installed backfill may settle and dislodge the sheets.

Graded pea-gravel aggregate, also referred to as aggregate drainage blankets, consist of sand, gravel, crushed stone, blast furnace slag, crushed shell and coral. These aggregates are specified under ASTM D 2487 for strength and stability. Note, however, that conformance to this specification does not ensure adequate drainage properties for backfill. Pea gravel refers to a naturally rounded stone falling between $3/16$ in.

(sieve size No. 8) and ³/₈ in. roughly corresponding to ASTM C 33, No. 8. Drainage aggregate is often required to provide a permeability of at least 25 times that of the surrounding soil.

Coarse sand is a finer form of aggregate drainage material, varying from roughly a No. 30 to a No. 8 sieve. In addition to its primary function of facilitating downward water flow adjacent to foundation walls, it also reduces vibration in seismic areas, harmlessly dissipating seismic forces via frictional forces between adjacent grains. Sharp sand is much more effective than rounded bank-run sand. Gap-graded sand — i.e., sand of nearly uniform grain size — accelerates the drainage rate. The smaller size, faster drainage rates, and limited availability often make it more expensive than pea gravel. (See Fig. 2-6 and Table 2-3.)

Aggregate blankets and drainage fields under slabs-on-ground consist of aggregate placed along a wall, around a drain pipe or under slabs to facilitate the flow of water from the backfill or subsurface grade into a drainage system for disposal above grade or into a sewer. They are composed of a 6-in. to 8-in.-thick bed of ³/₄-in., single-size graded gravel usually enclosed in a filter fabric. The size and gap grading prevent capillarity and retard silting. Pipe drains are installed in shallow trenches lined with aggregate and arranged to drain intermittent rises in the water table. If the subsoil contains excessive fines, consider installation of a filter fabric under the blanket. Aggregate blankets do not relieve vapor transmission, so an underslab vapor retarder, or suitable substitute, is still required.

Geotextile Filter Fabrics

Aggregate and coarse sand backfill against foundation walls were traditionally isolated from adjacent soil backfill by a layer of fine aggregate that impeded the infiltration of soil particles conveyed laterally by subsurface water flow. Filling the interstices between aggregate or coarse sand grains, fines impede the downward flow of water through the aggregate, with the obviously harmful effect of increasing hydrostatic pressure against the walls.

As a general rule, fine aggregate filters have been replaced with geotextile filter fabrics. With today's readily available factory-manufactured filter fabrics, it is difficult to justify the use of graded soil filters. Filter fabrics, with their finite permeability and soil-retention qualities, allow the designer to precisely match the fabric to the drainage requirements. Moreover, they are lightweight, easily handled, simply installed and readily visible for quality control.

Geotextiles are fabricated from polypropylene, polyester or nylon fabrics, either woven or non-woven (spun-bonded), and designed for a

PERCENT PASSING, BY WEIGHT

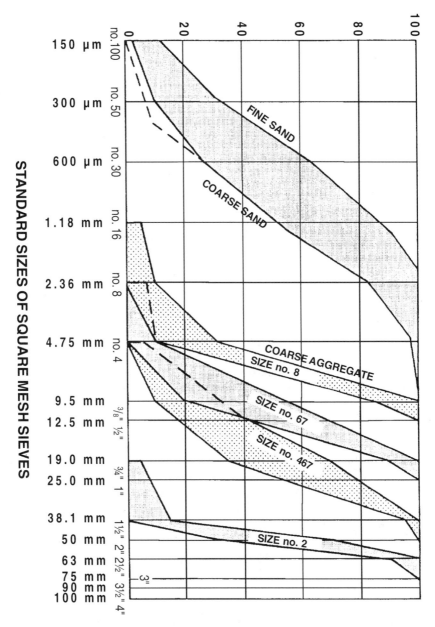

Fig. 2-6 Distribution of soil grain sizes. Soils lacking a significant group of particle sizes between the largest and smallest are termed "gap-graded". Fairly uniform particle sizes are termed "open-graded". The permeability of soils is a function of the void area. Highly permeable soils have a small percentage of fines. (The University of Minnesota.)

SOIL TYPE	K = COEFFICIENT OF PERMEABILITY (cm/sec)
Clean Fine to Coarse Gravel	10
Uniform Fine Gravel	5
Coarse Sand (2mm)	0.4
Fine Sand (.25 mm)	40×10^{-4}
Silt	0.05×10^{-4}
Clay	0.001×10^{-4}

Table 2-3 Coefficient of Permeability, K (cm/sec) is an index of vertical flow speeds of water flow through various types of soil. The major determinant of soil permeability is particle size: the larger the particles, the more permeable the soil. Large grain size creates large voids in horizontal cross sections through the soil, thus reducing frictional resistance to water flow through the soil. Uniformity of grain size also promotes vertical water flow, because heterogeneous mixtures of graded particles allow smaller particles to fill in voids between larger particles. As a consequence, the combination of size and percentage of fines is usually more important than the predominant particle size range in determining permeability. (Simpson, Gumpertz & Heger)

narrow range of permeability. There is no universally accepted guideline or standard for selecting filter fabrics. Some manufacturers determine the coefficient of permeability in cm/sec. (usually .02 to .08, "moderately slow") by measuring the rate of water transfer through the fabric at some constant head. Others measure permeance in gal/min/sq ft for a lower constant head. The U.S. Army Corps of Engineers rates filters by the Equivalent Opening Size (EOS), approximately the sieve size closest to the filter fabrics' openings. The maximum EOS is 70 (.0083 in.), which is not greater than 10% open area; the minimum is 100 (.0059 in.) which is not smaller than 4% open area.

Filter fabrics laminated to plastic drainage composites are used to encapsulate porous backfill and pipe drains. None of the fabrics are designed to withstand prolonged exposure to ultraviolet radiation.

Water Management System Failures

The most common failures of aggregate drainage systems are infiltration of fines clogging percolating aggregate and roots clogging drainage pipes. Clogged drains located on the outside of the footings are more common, but are more easily cleared by root clearing snakes and flushing. Drains under slabs inside the footings are less likely to clog from either fines or roots. They are, however, much more difficult to clear, because of their relative inaccessibility.

The most likely causes of filter-cloth failure are (a) a failure to lap the cloth sufficiently to prevent infiltration of fines, or (b) tearing of the cloth during backfilling operations. There is, however, little recorded on this subject.

Drainage composites may be dragged down when backfill is improperly placed or consolidated. When protection board has been omitted, the edges of some products can cut into or displace the membrane.

Alerts

1. Consider exploiting the building site's potential for alleviating waterproofing problems by raising the building and using excavated soil to grade the site to promote surface runoff.

2. Check building code for minimum grade slope to promote runoff. If building code requirement is less stringent than 5%, use this slope as a minimum.

3. Coordinate drainage plan with foundation plan, to assure proper elevation of drainage pipes.

4. Slope below-grade structures to drain, with minimum 2% slope.

5. Check soil for chemical contaminants that can attack waterproofing materials.

6. Discharge downspouts into a storm sewer or dry well located some distance away from the foundation.

7. Consider aggregate blankets under slabs-on-ground for hillside sites.

8. Specify gap-graded sand and gravel to increase porosity.

3

Dampproofing

Dampproofing differs from waterproofing in the following way: Waterproofing resists hydrostatic (and even minor hydrodynamic) pressures that can reach considerable magnitude: i.e., 1,000 psf for walls or slabs 16 ft. below the water table. Dampproofing, in contrast, merely resists the flow of water vapor through a building component. ASTM defines dampproofing as the treatment of a surface or structure to block the passage of water in the absence of hydrostatic pressure. In summary, then, positive-side membrane waterproofing resists both vapor migration and hydrostatic pressure from liquid moisture. Dampproofing, on the other hand, merely resists vapor migration.

Regardless of construction material — cast-in-place, reinforced concrete, concrete or brick masonry — dampproofing or waterproofing is required for slabs-on-ground and foundation retaining walls. Though well constructed reinforced concrete is inherently waterproof, concrete inevitably cracks — from plastic or drying shrinkage; from live-load deflection resulting from traffic, mechanical vibration, seismic movement, building settlement; or from frost damage. Water can penetrate tie-rod holes, "cold" (i.e., construction) joints, expansion joints, and through inadequately vibrated, honeycombed voids within the concrete. For these reasons, underground structures require either dampproofing or waterproofing. And, as indicated in the waterproofing chapter, elevated structural slabs over underground spaces always require waterproofing. This requirement holds both for structural slabs below grade as well as structural slabs above grade, either earth-covered or with separate wearing surfaces — e.g., for plazas, terraces, or promenades. These slabs require waterproofing because there is always a threat of some liquid moisture above them, exerting downward hydrostatic pressure.

Other components requiring dampproofing or waterproofing include planters and retaining walls, where water penetration might stain or deteriorate exterior finishes.

Preliminary Investigation

As preliminary steps in his or her decision between waterproofing and dampproofing, the designer must consult the building code and conduct a site survey.

Consulting the building code is the obvious first step, as building-code requirements pre-empt the designer's choice with mandatory minimum requirements that take legal precedence over the designer's judgment. It is wasted effort for the designer to produce a solution that fails to comply with the minimum requirements of the building code. By first determining the governing code's requirements, the designer can then proceed efficiently toward his solution.

Dampproofing and waterproofing are covered under Section 1800 in all three model building codes: BOCA, UBC and SBCCI (Southern/ Standard) which collectively serve as a basis for the vast majority of the nations's state and local codes[1]. They require waterproofing or dampproofing where walls or portions thereof retain earth and enclose interior spaces and floors below grade. All require:

- A subsoil investigation to determine whether hydrostatic pressure is present or will exist during intermittent groundwater
- UBC and BOCA require dampproofing where ground water-table is lowered and maintained at an elevation not less than 6 in. below the bottom of the slab on ground. UBC requires dampproofing where hydrostatic pressure will not occur
- Perimeter drains where walls are dampproofed

See Table 3-1 for code sections that specify dampproofing materials.

There will soon be code unanimity on dampproofing, as well as other aspects of building design, when the three model codes are combined into the *International Building Code 2000*, with its millennial target date. Here, from this code's final draft, is the relevant section:

> *1806.1.3 Ground water control. Where the ground water table is lowered and maintained at an elevation not less*

---

1.   The three model codes will be combined as the International Building Code. The target date is 2000. The requirements are taken from the Final Draft July, 1998.

than 6 inches (152 mm) below the bottom of the lowest floor, the floor and walls shall be dampproofed in accordance with Section 1806.2. The design of the system to lower the ground water table shall be based upon accepted principles of engineering which shall consider, but not necessarily be limited to: permeability of the soil; rate at which water enters the drainage system; rated capacity of pumps; head against which pumps are to pump; and the rated capacity of the disposal area of the system.

The designer's next task, conducting a site survey, should focus on determining the presence of the following hazards:

- Water levels (as an index of hydrostatic pressure)
- Flowing underground water
- Corrosive soil chemicals or petroleum pollutants

The discovery of any of the above hazards obviously eliminates dampproofing as an alternative to waterproofing.

After completing these two steps, the designer must consider several other factors — involving risks, costs, and benefits — before making a decision. Additional construction work (e.g. pervious backfill and drains) needed to qualify a project for dampproofing instead of more expensive waterproofing may raise project costs. Drainage piping must be increased in size and complexity. Pumps and backup pumps, with standby generators, must be a cost-effective tradeoff for eliminating the risks and costs of waterproofing. The municipality must permit drainage into its

Model Code	Date	Section	Dampproofing Materials
BOCA	1993	1813.3.3.1.1 1813.3.3.2.2	Floors Walls
UBC	1994	1822.2 1822.3	Floors Walls
SBCCI	1996	1814.3.3 1814.3.5	Floors Walls
IBC	2000	1806.2.1 1806.2.2	Floors Walls

Table 3-1 Dampproofing materials specified in the Model Codes.

storm-sewer system, which may already be operating at capacity, without excessive charges.

Water-Vapor Migration

Diffusion of water vapor is roughly analogous to thermal conduction in heat-energy transfer. Whenever there is a difference in vapor pressure on opposite sides of a building component, the vapor naturally tends to flow from the higher toward the lower pressure side. This pressure-equalizing phenomenon is a consequence of the kinetic theory of gases, according to which the random motion of molecules in a mixture tends to disperse these molecules in equal proportions throughout the mixture. In the atmosphere, water vapor is only one of several gases — predominantly nitrogen and oxygen — but also including argon, carbon dioxide, and several other even rarer gases.

Vapor pressure depends on two variables: temperature and relative humidity (RH). As shown in the curves of Fig. 3-1, vapor pressure increases exponentially with increasing temperature. The inevitable presence of liquid moisture in soil, sand and aggregate backfill will maintain its RH, at or close to 100%, whereas the desired RH of the underground interior space will normally be substantially less than 100%. Vapor flow will thus be impelled toward the interior. This normally inward vapor comes from all directions — horizontally through foundation walls, vertically downward from plaza or earth-covered structual slabs, vertically upward from slabs-on-ground. If, however, the occupied space is at a significantly higher temperature, this normally inward direction of vapor flow may be reversed. (At 76°F, 50% RH, vapor pressure roughly equals the vapor pressure at 55°F, 100% RH.) Earth temperatures vary much less than air temperatures, because of the insulating value and the heat capacity of the soil. Temperature of soil near the surface thus varies much more than temperatures at greater depths, which even in climates with occasional subzero temperatures, remain above the freezing level. Thus the vapor-pressure gradient will normally be directed from the outside toward the inside. Moreover, when the underground space must be maintained at relatively constant low RH — say 25%-30% — dampproofing, at a minimum, becomes mandatory.

Water vapor flow through a building component poses a threat of condensation either within that building component or within the interior space when it contacts a surface at the dew-point temperature (i.e., the temperature representing 100% RH).

Condensation is more likely in underground spaces than in above-grade spaces for two reasons:

• Unconditioned underground spaces tend to be cooler in summer because of the insulating effect of surrounding backfill and foundation soil.

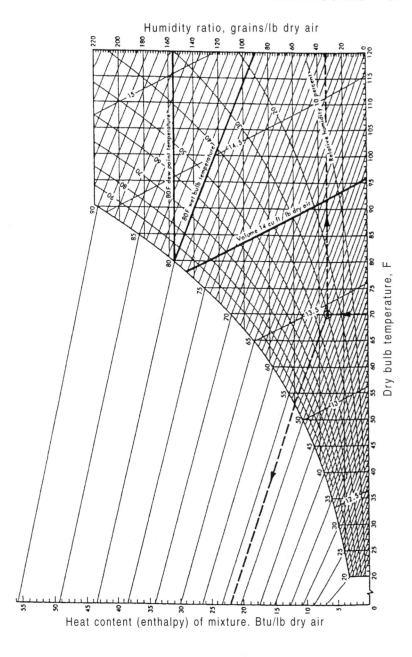

Fig. 3-1 This chart indicates vapor pressure for a given temperature and relative humidity (RH). Underground vapor pressure, represented by the vertical scale, can be assumed to be the intersection of the 100% RH curve with the temperature (horizontal scale). Interior vapor pressure will vary much more than underground vapor pressure, which is stable because of virtually unchanging underground temperature.

- Air circulation, which helps to disperse water vapor and prevent condensation, is generally diminished in underground spaces, especially in unairconditioned spaces, because there are no windows or joints for air to leak through and thus convey water vapor out of the space.

Higher soil temperatures in summer tend to make dampproofing, at a minimum, mandatory for interiors with humidity limitations. Since the soil RH can be assumed at 100%, summer soil temperatures around 70°F near the surface create a strong vapor drive toward an interior space maintained at 70°F, 30% RH (see Fig. 3-1). Even though vapor drive may reverse direction during the winter in most continental U.S. locations, the situation nevertheless calls for dampproofing. This demand for dampproofing during summer conditions makes vapor control a more demanding problem for the waterproofing designer than for the low-slope roof designer. In cold, even temperate climates, the biggest vapor problem for roof designers is upward vapor flow into the roof assembly, a consequence of higher vapor pressure in the warm interior during the winter. During spring and summer, however, solar heating of the roof surface reverses vapor-flow direction. Moisture accumulated within the roof assembly during cold weather tends to be driven back into the building interior. This "self-drying" roof mechanism has been rigorously investigated by Tobiasson and others.[1] There is no analogous "self-drying" mechanism for underground spaces. Unlike roof systems, below-grade waterproofing systems may be subjected to perpetual inward vapor pressure (see Fig. 3-2).

Dampproofing Or Waterproofing?

The decision between waterproofing and dampproofing is one of the simplest decisions confronting the designer. As stated in the preceding discussion, the only components for which you can consider dampproofing are foundations walls and slabs-on-ground. Structurally supported slabs inevitably run the risk of hydrostatic pressure and thus require waterproofing. To determine whether foundation walls and slabs-on-ground require only dampproofing you can consult the flow chart depicted in Fig. 4-2.

In Fig. 4-2, the key question, "Is a slight leak risk acceptable?" can be stated more technically: Is there any threat of hydrostatic pressure accompanying capillary rise? If so, there is increased risk of water

---

1. Wayne Tobiasson, "General Considerations for Roofs," *Moisture Control in Buildings: ASTM Manual Series,* 1994.

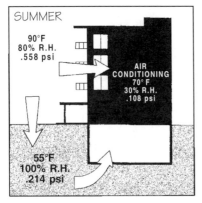 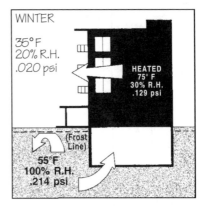

Fig. 3-2 These diagrams (Summer conditions on left, Winter on right) show how underground interiors may be subjected to perpetual, year-round inward vapor pressure, whereas the superstructure typically experiences a seasonal reversal of vapor-pressure direction. (Concrete Construction Publications, Inc.)

leakage. In an underground garage, more risk can be tolerated than in an auditorium, where even a slight risk is of concern. For such an occupancy, you could not, in fact, tolerate dampness on the interior face of the exterior walls.

As a rule of thumb, dampproofing is required on all subgrade foundations and slabs-on-ground not subject to continuous, or even intermittent, hydrostatic pressure (in which event they require waterproofing, see Chapter 2, "Water Management"). Whenever melting snow or heavy rainfall may occur in poorly drained soils or on flood plains, foundation walls should be waterproofed where interior dampness cannot be tolerated. Slabs-on-ground under gymnasiums or other uses with water-sensitive flooring similarly require waterproofing, except under subsequently discussed conditions.

If the designer eliminates the need for waterproofing, and thereby establishes the suitability of dampproofing, he can then proceed to the next step — i.e., determining when you can eliminate dampproofing. These conditions are limited to the following:

- Sites with exceedingly dry soil
- Where the bottom of a slab-on-ground is above an adjacent grade

Note again, however, that most building codes require dampproofing as a minimum moisture protection, thus pre-empting the designer's option to eliminate dampproofing. And waterproofing is required if the ground-water level cannot be maintained at least 6 in. below the bottom of the slab-on-ground. (See Fig. 3-3).

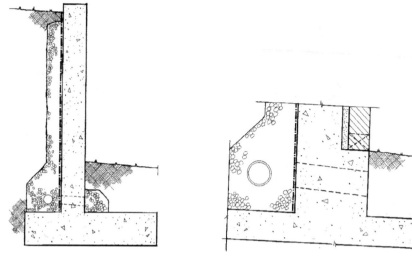

Fig. 3-3 Retaining walls are dampproofed to prevent efflorescence on the exposed face. Brick facing is detailed on insert. Pervious fill and a collector drain are mandatory.

Dampproofing is applied to the following components:

- Slabs-on-ground
- Foundation walls
- Retaining walls with finish bonded to wall
  (but not for concrete walls with cavity and brick facing).

Dampproofing Walls

Dampproofing is required for foundation and retaining walls, with one notable exception — i.e., foundation walls with a vertical cavity through which water can flow down and discharge through weepholes (See Fig. 3-3).

Dampproofing of foundation and retaining walls is always applied to the exterior (wet) face (see Fig. 3-4). Planters are similarly dampproofed on the wet — in this instance, interior — face (see Fig. 3-4). Dampproofing of the inside (dry) face of retaining or foundation walls is banned because of potential blistering from vapor pressure exerted in small chambers formed between the inside wall face and the dampproofing membrane. (Negative-side — i.e., dry-side — waterproofing requires some vapor permeability to alleviate the hazards of blistering; see Chapter 6.)

The most common dampproofing material for walls is a bituminous coating, either solvent-based (cutback asphalt) or emulsion, brushed,

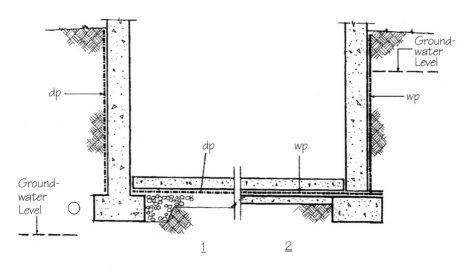

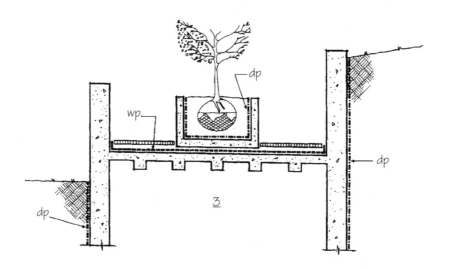

Fig. 3-4 Cross section (1) shows condition permitting dampproofing of foundation and slab-on-ground, when highest groundwater level is at least 6 in. below the bottom of the slab-on-ground. When the groundwater level is above the slab-on-ground, waterproofing is required for both foundation wall and slab-on-ground, as shown in (2). Even where the groundwater level is below the slab-on-ground, waterproofing is required for a structural plaza slab and a planter supported on it, as shown in (3) above. (Note that drainage courses on the wall are ommitted for clarity.)

sprayed, roller-coated or troweled onto the substrate. It may be liquid or mastic, reinforced with organic (plastic) or inorganic (glass) fibers.

Emulsions have several disadvantages. Being water-based, they cannot be stored or applied at freezing temperatures. If not fully set before backfilling is completed, the carrier water may not escape. This prevents formation of a uniform film and thus produces an ineffective vapor retarder.

Dampproofing membranes often feature the same materials and application techniques as waterproofing membranes. The dividing line between dampproofing and waterproofing has been set at 10-mil (0.25-mm) film thickness by Maslow.

The thicker the coating, the longer the service life. In thin coatings, the essential oils, which prevent embrittlement of the coating, may hydrolyze or migrate into the backfill soil.

Masonry foundation walls require a ¾-in. to 1-in.-thick cement parge coat, prior to application of the dampproofing, according to most authorities. It provides a smooth substrate instead of the rough masonry surface. It also tightens mortar joints and adds moisture resistance to the foundation wall.

Dampproofing Slabs-On-Ground

Slabs-on-ground require dampproofing or waterproofing except in a few instances — e.g., in arid regions with no soil or drainage problems and no irrigation (provided, of course, that the governing building code does not require them.) ACI 302.IR-89 also suggests that you can omit a vapor retarder on well drained home sites, subject to these additional conditions:

- Water table is perpetually below the ground surface
- Installation of a freely draining substratum of coarse granular fill
- Use of a floor covering unaffected by moisture

Slabs-on-ground can be dampproofed either above or below. The most common, and generally better, is the below-slab location. Plastic film vapor retarders are the most common below-slab dampproofing. The above-slab location is better in spaces where moisture control is most critical — the zero tolerance situation. These generally involve gymnasium or dance floors, where the wood flooring spans sleepers separating it from the concrete slab's top surface (see Fig. 3-5). Note, however, that this top-of-slab dampproofing is acceptable only under the following conditions:

- Water table perpetually (i.e., normal and intermittent) at least 12 in. below the slab.
- Footing drains (or footing drains plus under drains)

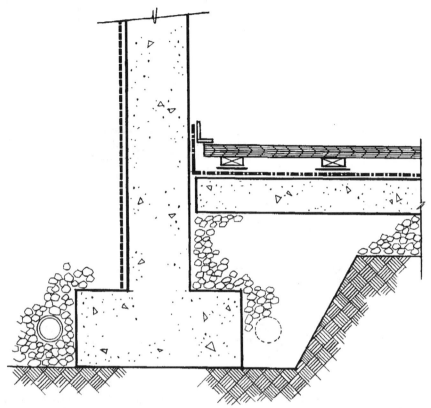

Fig. 3-5 When slabs-on-ground are covered with wood gymnasium or dance floors, where wood flooring spans sleepers separating it from the slab, dampproofing can sometimes be applied to the slab's surface, but only under certain subsoil conditions. The air space intercepted between slab and flooring should be vented at junctions with the wall at the expansion joint, as shown in the above detail. This is an additional precaution to avoid moisture damage to the floor from water vapor migration penetrating the vapor retarder. The goal is to maintain equal vapor pressures below and above the wood floor.

Unless these two conditions are satisfied, under-slab waterproofing is required for slabs-on-ground topped with wood floors or other moisture sensitive finishes.

Still another limitation imposed on top-surface dampproofing of slabs-on-ground is the presence of partitions or columns, which interrupt the vapor retarder and thus violate the dampproofing's integrity (see Fig. 3-6). In such instances, under-slab dampproofing or waterproofing is a safer alternative.

Substituting a vapor retarder for waterproofing normally entails risks. A vapor retarder depends on the integrity of the film and its seams.

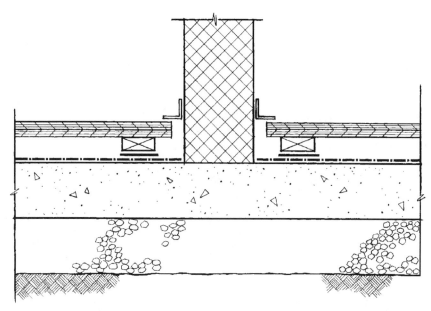

Fig. 3-6   Partitions or columns can interrupt a vapor retarder on top of a concrete slab-on-ground. Under these conditions, below-slab location for the vapor retarder is preferable. And normally waterproofing would be required.

Field conditions for a vapor retarder for slab-on-ground normally make it more difficult to maintain field-seam integrity than for a wall or roof system.

Wood and some vinyl floor coverings and their water sensitive adhesives make vapor retarders especially risky. Under these conditions, the additional expense of heavy-duty panels or waterproofing is well worth the price to avoid the expense of replacing a moisture-damaged floor covering.

Sleepers for a wood floor covering on a slab-on-ground with top-surface dampproofing should be attached to the slab with water resistant adhesives rather than mechanical anchors. Nails and other mechanical anchors puncture a vapor retarder located on a slab's top surface. If mechanical anchors are nonetheless specified, they should be installed in accordance with the detail shown in Fig. 3-7, or some other dependable method of preventing vapor leakage through the punctured vapor retarder.

When the top of the slab is dampproofed, a substratum of granular material should be placed below the slab, with aggregate properly graded to prevent moisture rise (and consequent hydrostatic pressure) via capillary action.

A designer committed to top-surface dampproofing should also

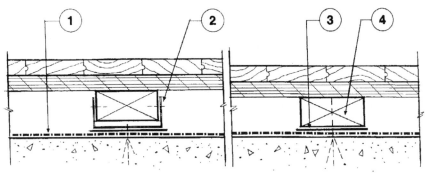

Fig 3-7 Detail showing method of sealing mechanically fastened sleepers supporting flooring above SOG with top-surface vapor retarder. (1) Vapor retarder (i.e., dampproofing); (2) lightgage metal clip; (3) butyl tape; (4) wood sleeper.

resist any temptation to use the belt-and-suspenders' approach of adding another vapor retarder below the slab. Vapor pressure from residual moisture in the concrete slab, denied any means of venting via either the top or bottom slab surface, can disbond the top vapor retarder and ultimately rupture it.

Installed before instead of after concrete casting, under-slab vapor retarders must obviously be tougher than above-slab vapor retarders. They are available in polyethylene sheets, asphalt/polyethylene composite sheets, coated granular-surfaced roofing felts or polymer-modified bitumen sheets. Polyethylene should be high density (HDPE), which is relatively inert and resistant to many different chemicals. Polyethylene sheets are marketed in clear and black, reinforced and unreinforced. One proprietary sheet consists of two sheets of kraft paper laminated with asphalt, reinforced with glass fibers and covered on both sides with polyethylene. Another consists of an asphalt core board with a PVC sheet bonded to coated asphalt felts.

Under-slab vapor retarders should be selected for their low permeance, resistance to tearing and puncture and to degradation from soil chemicals and bacteria. ASTM C 755 recommends a perm rating of less than 1, but, in fact, most vapor retarders on the market have permeances well below 0.5 and a permeance of even 0.1 perm is not unusual. Polyethylene is commonly specified in 6 to 10-mil thickness. Use of two 6-mil sheets, to reduce puncturing and provide seam redundancy, is a prudent practice.

Slab-On-Ground Installation Details

Installation of vapor retarders under slabs-on-ground should follow recommendations in ACI Document 302.IR-89 and ASTM E 1643 *Standard Practice for Installation of Water Vapor Retarders Used in Contact with Soil or Granular Fill Under Concrete Slabs.* These documents recommend a substratum of ¾-in., single-size, graded gravel under the vapor retarder, which is then covered with a 3-in.-thick layer of ungraded sand. The gravel prevents capillarity. The sand reduces the risk of damage during concrete casting operations and, prior to casting, from punctures in the vapor retarder from welded wire fabric, reinforcing bars, and supporting chairs. It also allows the concrete to vent excess moisture downward, a process that reduces slab shrinkage and curling. (These hazards are noted in ACI 301.IR's warning against use of vapor retarders directly under slabs-on-ground, see Fig. 3-8).

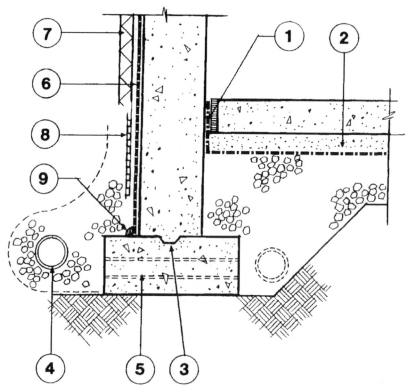

Fig. 3-8   In this detail, with the top of the wall footing at least 1 ft below the bottom of the slab-on-ground, the under-slab vapor retarder is returned to the top of the slab (1). Other components in this detail are as follows:

2. sand fill
3. key
4. footing drain 4" to 6" diameter
5. 2-in.-dia drains through footing
6. waterproofing membrane with protection board, or
7. low-density insulation as protection layer
8. drainage composite or gravel drainage fill
9. liquid component of waterproofing system

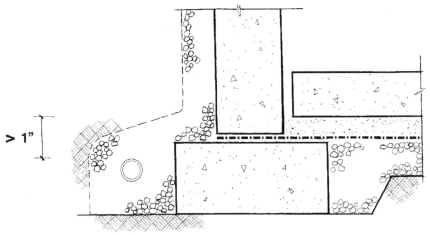

Fig. 3-9 When the bottom of the footing is located below the ground-water level, the vapor retarder should be extended across the top of the footing.

The concrete slab must be cast within 24 hours of the sand placement. This scheduling is essential to prevent displacement of the sand from construction traffic and to reduce ponding.

Footing drains are always required when the vapor retarder is below adjacent grade. Footing drains *and* underslab drainage are required when the vapor retarder is below the adjacent grade and the highest intermittent ground-water elevation is within 6 in. of the bottom of the slab. The subsurface drains should be conducted to daylight, for gravity flow, or connected to a pump. And when the bottom of the footing is located below the ground-water level, to prevent "rising damp", (the capillary rise of water in the wall from the normally wet footing), the vapor retarder should be extended across the footing, as shown in Fig. 3-9. Where the top of the wall footing is more than 1 ft below the bottom of the slab-on-ground, an alternative method is shown in Fig. 3-8, with the vapor retarder returned to the top of the slab-on-ground.

Alerts

1. Be sure to check building code requirements before considering dampproofing instead of waterproofing, or elimination of dampproofing.

2. Note that dampproofing is an option only for slabs-on-ground, walls, and planters. (Structural slabs are always designed to resist hydrostatic pressure and thus always require waterproofing.)

3. If in doubt, choose the most conservative option: i.e., water-proofing instead of dampproofing, below-slab rather than top-surface dampproofing.

4. Never apply dampproofing to both sides of a slab-on-ground. (It can cause disbonding of the top dampproofing membrane.)

Chapter

4

Waterproofing

Waterproofing can be defined as a material or system capable of preventing leakage of water through a subsurface building component under hydrostatic pressure. Dampproofing, on the other hand, has a less rigorous function: to resist the flow of water vapor through subsurface building components.

Waterproofing can be considered as dampproofing-plus. Wherever hydrostatic pressure is exerted against a building component, it is almost always accompanied by water-vapor pressure in the same direction — i.e., from the wet toward the dry side of the building component. As a consequence, waterproofing must resist both pressure from liquid water and water vapor flow, whereas dampproofing must resist vapor flow only.

Right from the start, the designer must recognize these drastically more rigorous requirements for waterproofing. The decision between waterproofing and dampproofing can be simplified by simply considering dampproofing as the alternative to waterproofing for subsurface building components. If subsurface components are subjected to hydrostatic pressure, they require waterproofing. If not, they normally require dampproofing. The only exceptions would be made for unoccupied interiors — e.g., an underground parking garage — where relatively high RH, even condensation, could be tolerated. At a minimum, dampproofing is generally required by code. The only exception may be blindside application — e.g., a subbasement cast against rock where waterproofing is not required and dampproofing cannot be installed.

This manual focuses only on waterproofing or dampproofing of subsurface building components that enclose habitable or occupiable spaces below grade. The three subsurface building components that may require waterproofing are:

- Structural concrete slabs covered by earth fill or wearing surface
- Foundation retaining walls
- Concrete slabs-on-ground serving as floors for underground space (See Fig. 4-1).

As a practical matter, framed concrete slabs over occupied below-grade spaces should always be waterproofed, as they are constantly under the threat of at least temporary hydrostatic pressure. Foundation retaining walls and concrete slabs-on-ground may require only damp-proofing. (See flow chart, Fig. 4-2).

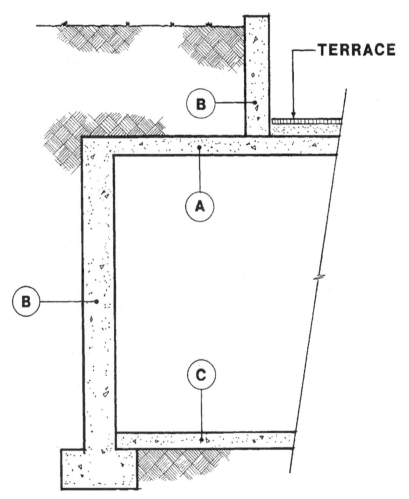

Fig. 4-1 Basic waterproofed (or dampproofed) components are (A) framed slabs (always waterproofed), retaining walls (B), and slabs-on-ground (C). Components (B) and (C) may be dampproofed, if a slight leak-risk factor is acceptable.

Waterproofing systems, in descending order of popularity, come in three basic types:

- Positive-side
- Negative-side
- Integral

Positive-side waterproofing is applied to the outside (wet) face of subsurface building components. It is the predominant type of waterproofing for new construction, solving a much greater variety of waterproofing problems than negative-side waterproofing. It comes in a tremendous variety of subsystems and materials, thus giving the designer vastly expanded opportunities for solving difficult waterproofing problems (See Fig. 4-3).

Simplified algorithm for deciding on waterproofing vs. dampproofing

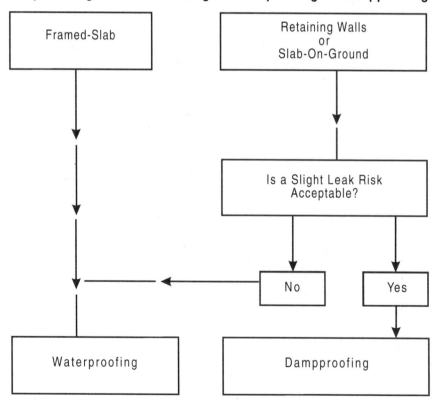

Fig. 4-2   The simplified algorithm depicted above decrees (a) waterproofing for all framed subsurface slabs or (b) for retaining walls and slabs-on-ground through which a risk of leakage is unacceptable. Dampproofing is thus a residual choice, i.e., when a slight risk is acceptable.

Negative-side waterproofing is applied to the inside (dry) face of underground building components. Easy access to the dry side of waterproofed building components makes negative-side waterproofing the first choice for remedial waterproofing projects. In new construction, it offers its greatest advantages where blindside application would otherwise be required. As in remedial waterproofing, negative-side waterproofing's major advantage in blindside waterproofing is easy access to the waterproofed surface.

Integral waterproofing consists of superplasticizers and other additives enhancing the concrete's workability. By increasing the hydration of the cement, superplasticizers reduce porosity and increase concrete density. Additives have been used for nearly a century to improve concrete's waterproofing quality. Alum and soap were the earliest, followed by fillers of diatomaceous earth, fly ash, bentonite clay, and pumice.

Despite these physical improvements to the concrete, integral waterproofing has nonetheless proven so undependable that it does not qualify as a practicable waterproofing technique meriting extended discussion in this manual. Admixtures reduce the passage of moisture through the concrete, but they are only as good as the concrete itself. Pre-curing and post-curing stresses — from drying shrinkage, temperature change, and structural loading — inevitably crack the concrete and create paths for the passage of water. Since concrete cracking of some degree is inevitable, integral waterproofing is inherently undependable.

Site Survey

As one of the earliest tasks in the design process, second only to a perusal of the governing building code, the designer should conduct a site survey, its findings based on test samples from soil borings and test pits to determine:

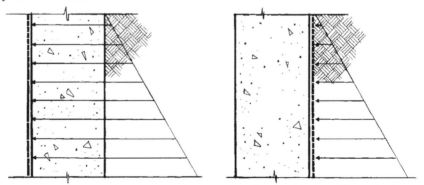

Fig. 4-3 Positive-side waterproofing goes on the outside (wet) free of subsurface building components, whereas negative-side waterproofing goes on the inside (dry) surface.

- Water table elevation (and presence of underground streams), tidal and perched watertables
- Deleterious soil chemicals, salt water, petroleum derivatives
- Other hazardous conditions, soil stability

Determination of the ground-water level is obviously required for the designer's basic decision between waterproofing and dampproofing. Depending on the date when these borings are taken, the water-table elevation used for design will probably require correction for seasonal variation. The water-table elevation in early April is likely to be at a maximum in a northern region, where late winter snow melts saturate the ground. Conversely, in October, the water table will normally be low, after summer heat and solar radiation have evaporated much surface water. Soil type is another factor to be considered. Sandy, granular soils will normally have higher water-table elevation than less permeable, clayey soils.

Detecting the presence of underground water flows requires supplementary measures in addition to soil borings. Ground of relatively low permeability — e.g., clay — often limits hydrostatic pressure to exceptional circumstances. Conversely, in highly permeable soils — e.g., gravel — you can anticipate more durable "worst-case" conditions.

Corrosive soil chemicals can occur in gaseous, liquid, or solid state. Among the hazardous gases are methane, hydrogen sulfide, and carbon dioxide. Liquids and solids include hydrocarbons, solvents, phenols, and industrial wastes.

Sulfates are a major hazard. They react chemically with Portland cement to form compounds of expanded volume, and this expanded volume can spall concrete and mortar, with progressive cracking and delamination. This destructive process continues while there is a continuing supply of sulfates. The worst situation combines soil sulfates with permeable soils and flowing underground water (see Table 4-1).

Systems And Materials

Positive-side materials and systems come in an extremely broad spectrum of materials (discussed in greater detail in subsequent chapters). Generically, these systems can be classified as follows:

- Built-up bituminous membranes
- Modified bitumen sheets
- Prefabricated elastomeric sheets
- Prefabricated thermoplastic sheets
- Bentonite
- Liquid-applied membranes (LAMs)

Balancing the unique combination of advantages and disadvantages

Classification Rank ------------------- Criteria	Mild	Moderate	Severe	Extreme
Hydrostatic Pressure (Head/Ft)	< 3Ft	3-16	16-32	> 32
Total Acid Soluble, SO_4, (%) in soil or fill	< 0.24			

Table 4-1 Classification of Subsoil Hazards

of these materials requires the designer's consideration of a long list of factors, beginning with code limitations and ending with ease of application and feasibility of quality assurance (QA). (See subsequent section in this chapter, and Chapter 5 for expanded discussion of the design process for positive-side waterproofing.)

Negative-side materials come in a very narrow range, suited to a much narrower range of suitable uses — normally limited to repair, remedial work, and blindside waterproofing, where the wet, exterior face of a foundation wall or slab-on-ground is inaccessible.

Negative-side waterproofing features coatings that seal the interior surface of the concrete rather than separate membranes applied to the exterior face. All contemporary negative-side waterproofing systems can be mixed with water and often with sand and trowelled, brushed, or sprayed as a slurry. Crystalline coatings have largely replaced traditional metallic-oxide cementitious coatings, because of their greater dependability and durability. These solutions of organic and inorganic compounds react chemically with unhydrated Portland cement and free lime, filling capillaries and shrinkage cracks with long chain molecules that crystallize within the concrete. Their superior durability stems from a self-healing property. (When cured concrete cracks, the crystalline materials are chemically reactivated and seal the concrete openings and passages.)

Positive vs. Negative-Side Waterproofing

Positive-side waterproofing has many advantages over negative-side waterproofing, as indicated by its far greater range of materials. In fact, positive-side waterproofing — i.e., waterproofing on the exterior (wet) side of the building component — includes the cementitious/crystalline coatings to which negative-side waterproofing is limited. Under some circumstances, these normally negative-side materials can serve as positive-side waterproofing.

As a major advantage of positive-side waterproofing, it protects against corrosive soils, which can attack masonry, concrete, and even reinforcing bars. Because of its location on the inside face of walls and slabs-on-ground, negative-side waterproofing obviously offers no protection against corrosive soil. Even when used as positive-side waterproofing, thus posing a barrier between the soil and the waterproofed component, cementitious/crystalline coatings provide less protection against corrosive soils than membranes.

As one of its major general advantages, positive-side waterproofing is applicable to all subsurface building components, whereas negative-side waterproofing is impractical for structural concrete slabs. The unsuitability for structural slabs creates another problem for negative-side waterproofing, as it requires a transition between positive-side and negative-side waterproofing at slab-wall intersections. (As a subsequent section will show, combinations of generically different waterproofing systems are normally impracticable.)

Negative-side waterproofing obviously offers far fewer advantages than positive-side waterproofing; it is normally a second choice. Easier application makes it the obvious first choice for remedial work where positive-side waterproofing failed. In addition to easier application, it also offers easier maintenance than positive-side waterproofing. Easy leak detection is another asset, since the leak generally occurs at or near the same location as the defective coating material. Removal of defective material and reapplication of new coating is also easy with negative-side waterproofing. And because it retains moisture within the concrete wall, in effect sandwiching the concrete between a wet (exterior) face and a water-resistant interior face, negative-side waterproofing promotes superior concrete curing. (Concrete thrives in the presence of liquid moisture, which promotes continuing strength-producing, solidifying hydration.)

Offsetting these assets are important liabilities. Higher vapor permeability than positive-side membranes limits negative-side coatings to occupancies that can tolerate high interior humidity. Negative-side coatings are also more vulnerable to substrate cracking and fastener damage. And, as previously noted, they provide no protection to concrete components from corrosive soils.

Waterproofed Combinations

There are only a limited number of combinations of building components — a total of six — requiring waterproofing and dampproofing.

These combinations are a logical consequence of several basic rules concerning their use. Before considering these rules, let's first note the two basic configurations of waterproofed components. They can consist of "boxes" — i.e., structural slab on top, foundation wall on sides, slab-on-ground (or earth-supported structural slab) on bottom. Alternatively, they can consist of "Ls" — i.e., foundation and slab-on-ground with no structural slab (see Fig. 4-4).

The rules for determining these possible combinations are as follows:

1. You must waterproof a structural slab
2. If you waterproof the slab-on-ground, you must waterproof the foundation wall
3. You must either dampproof or waterproof both the foundation wall and the slab-on-ground.

The first rule stems from the inevitability of a structural slab being subjected to some hydrostatic pressure from surface runoff. The second rule is dictated by the possibility of a fluctuating water table. The third rule is a practical concession to conservative principles, amply demonstrated in practice, to which the exceptions are so rare that they should not be allowed to complicate the discussion.

As depicted in Fig. 4-4, these permissible combinations can be classified as follows:

1. Waterproofed structural slab, plus dampproofed wall and slab-on-ground
2. Waterproofed structural slab, walls, and slab-on-ground
3. Waterproofed structural slab and walls, plus dampproofed slab-on-ground
4. Dampproofed foundation wall and slab-on-ground
5. Waterproofed wall and slab-on-ground
6. Waterproofed wall, dampproofed slab-on-ground

Single-System Superiority

For items 1 and 2 above, the designer should specify the same generic system for all components, with only rare exceptions. It is occasionally tempting to combine two (or more) systems with complementary properties, to exploit the best qualities of each material. This is almost always a bad idea. Discontinuities at slab-foundation wall intersections can produce vulnerable joints. Incompatible materials can also create problems. As one notably disastrous combination, specifying a plastic sheet membrane for a structural slab and a bituminous membrane for the intersecting foundation wall creates an extremely difficult joint-sealing problem. Lack of a positive seal between the two incompatible

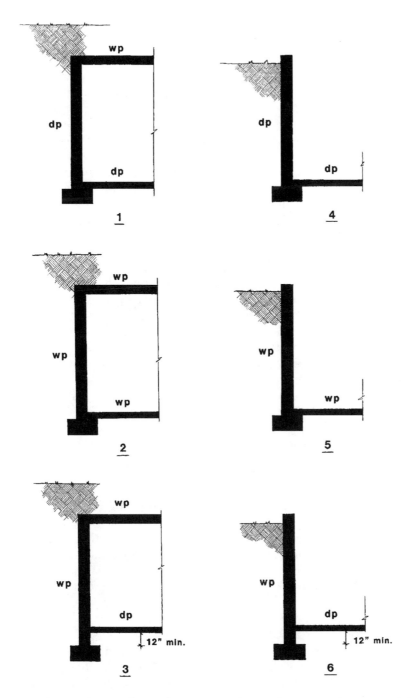

Fig. 4-4 The six figures above include all possible combinations of waterproofed components, except in extremely rare instances where dampproofing is not required for foundations walls or slabs-on-ground.

materials can compromise the waterproofing integrity of the entire project.

Equally risky is combining a waterproofing system with a dampproofing system in the same plane. It is appropriate to extend a plaza waterproofing membrane over the edge and down, lapping a dampproofing foundation wall well above the ground-water level. But extending a waterproofed membrane up from the footing to some pre-determined point below grade — say, 2 ft above the ground-water level — and then switching to dampproofing is inviting trouble, for two reasons:

- The possibility of water infiltration through the dampproofing and then migrating downward behind the waterproofing, which may be consequently disbonded
- The risk of a fluctuating water table rising above the elevation of the terminated waterproofing

Among the few exceptions to the general rule against multiple systems is the use of negative-side waterproofing (i.e., cementitious/crystalline coatings) on elevator pits (and other small pits) where waterproofing is installed under a slab-on-ground. Negative-side coatings are also occasionally combined with positive-side waterproofing membranes on structural slabs when the structural slab is above grade. And there are a few other instances where the advantages of exploiting complementary advantages of different materials or systems does work.

As one such example, a liquid-membrane applied directly on a structural concrete slab and then covered with a loose-laid rubber sheet proved to be a successful belt-and-suspenders approach on one water-proofing project. The loose-laid rubber sheet serves as the primary line of waterproofing defense, backed up by the LAM. This complementary combination of a rubber sheet, vulnerable to possibly one major rupture, with a LAM, vulnerable to a larger number of tiny defects — notably, pinholing — drastically reduces the probability of a leak.

Most belt-and-suspenders approaches are, however, highly risky. The most dangerous practice is to apply vapor-impermeable membranes on both sides of a concrete foundation wall. Entrapped moisture will vaporize and delaminate one or both membranes with blisters formed by the expanding vapor trapped at the membrane-wall interfaces.

Blindside Waterproofing

Blindside waterproofing systems are required where the exterior faces of foundation walls are inaccessible, thus requiring application of the waterproofing system to the formwork surface facing the excavation. This results in the waterproofing's final location on the outside (i.e., blind side) of the foundation wall. A common situation dictating blindside waterproofing is the proximity of adjacent property lines, which preclude excavation outside the foundation walls. Even when excavation is not barred outside the foundation perimeter, it may nonetheless be more convenient or economical to use blindside waterproofing — for example, where sheetpiling lines an excavation with a high watertable, in surrounding rock (see Fig. 4-5).

Note also that the phrase, "blindside waterproofing," is sometimes used in the broad sense of denoting the problem rather than the solution. Strictly defined, blindside waterproofing is positive-side waterproofing. But a blindside waterproofing problem is sometimes solved by negative-side waterproofing.

Blindside waterproofing is required when concrete foundations are cast against soldier piles and lagging, steel or wood sheet piling, concrete caisson retaining walls, and slurry or shotcreted rock. It is also used in pits.

Blindside waterproofing systems have their own special problems. Substrates for blindside waterproofing — wood-plank lagging, shotcrete or cement-slurry surfaces, or even masonry walls — provide poor substrates for application of membranes. Steel piling and lagging may require "boarding out" with plywood to provide plane substrates for waterproofing membranes (see Fig. 4-6). Blockouts in walls for tieback

Fig. 4-5 A typical situation requiring blindside waterproofing is created by an excavation with earth pressure retained by soldier piles anchored by tiebacks and wood lagging spanning horizontally between soldier-pile flanges. Note irregular surface of lagging must be boarded out with plywood or drainage composite.

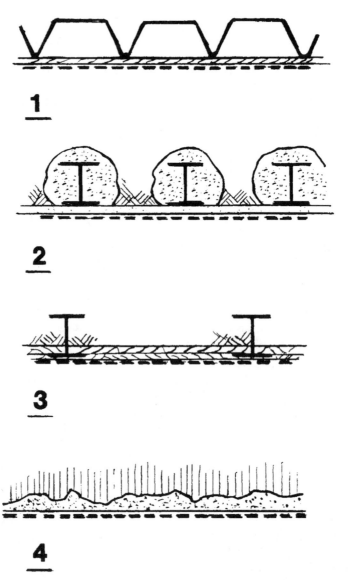

Fig. 4-6 Blindside waterproofing techniques for (1) sheetpiling; (2) caissons; (3) soldier piles are shown above; (4) shotcrete on rock. Note that plywood is preferred over lagging as a substrate for blind-side waterproofing membranes, for its obvious benefits in providing a smooth substrate.

plates or rakers must be carefully detailed to maintain continuity of the waterproofing system (see Fig. 10-9).

Bentonite panels and sheets, are usually the system of choice because of easy installation (see Chapter 10). Geotextile-laminated sheets and panels can be inexpensively installed directly against the earth-retention system. Lack of vapor control may rule out bentonite. The problem with some sheet systems is the lack of positive adhesion with the concrete. Positive adhesion is advantageous because it facilitates leak detection by limiting the migration of leakwater between the sheet and the concrete. This, in turn, localizes the area to be repaired with injection methods.

Some bituminous systems, such as one of cold-applied, chloroprene-modified asphalt, are reputed to bond to the concrete foundation as the heat of hydration softens the asphalt. Another recently introduced system consists of a specially surfaced-modified bitumen sheet that is designed to bond to the freshly cast concrete mechanically.

Designer's Checklist

The selection of a waterproofing system should proceed through an algorithmic process, formalized to the greatest practicable extent. This process should start with resistance to a common temptation: i.e., to select a system merely on the basis of past experience. (For guideline flow charts from a U.S. Navy manual on earth-sheltered buildings, see Appendix F.)

As a standard approach, the designer should prepare a checklist for each waterproofed building component. On an item-by-item basis, consider all the conditions affecting each component. Assign a weight to each item. (A chemically corrosive soil may outweigh ease of application, thus tilting a decision away from negative-side waterproofing.) Some systems can be eliminated from the start — e.g. by anti-pollution ordinances banning hot kettles used for built-up membrane application. This narrows the range of systems eligible for further investigation, thereby facilitating the design process. For the final selection, the design process then becomes a tallying of assets and liabilities, analogous to a financial statement.

The designer should be warned at the outset, however, that this process cannot be made purely mechanical at our current state of knowledge. Countless combinations of factors that make each project unique are simply too complex to reduce waterproofing design to a simple algorithmic process. It should, nonetheless, be formalized to the greatest practicable extent. As one way to proceed, the author offers the following list:

1. Code requirements
2. Occupancy
3. Hydrostatic pressure
4. Water table
5. Soil characteristics
6. Substrate stability
7. Construction sequence

8. Track record
9. Ease of application
10. Risk vs. cost

(1) **Code requirements** set mandatory parameters that narrow the designer's options. As a notable example, the Uniform Building Code (1997) contains the following provision: "1837.4 Waterproofing Materials ..shall consist of rubberized asphalt, polymer-modified asphalt, butyl rubber or other approved materials capable of bridging nonstructural cracks." As stated, this clause effectively rules out bentonite, negative-side crystalline/cementitious coatings, and even conventional built-up membranes. The vague phrase, "other approved materials," does, however, leave the door open for the designer to seek code officials' approval for a material outside of the stated scope. All codes contain provisions permitting the exercise of code officials' discretionary approval, which the designer must seek if his system selection is not explicitly approved by the code.

Closely related to code requirements are VOC (volatile organic content) regulations set by many states (and spreading). These regulations can eliminate the choice of some waterproofing materials — notably, solvent-based adhesives and primers — from consideration right at the start. Pollution regulations thus require investigation early in the design process. Retaining a VOC-banned system among the design options unnecessarily complicates an already complicated process.

(2) **Occupancy** is a vitally important design factor. Leak-risk tolerance and humidity sensitivity are two system-eliminating factors that can rapidly reduce an initially broad spectrum of choices. Low-risk occupancies include book storage, computer rooms, electrical switchgear, and medical facilities. Leakage into underground spaces with these occupancies is intolerable. These same occupancies often require tight humidity control as well. Occupancies with audio-visual equipment, art storage or exhibition, virtually eliminate negative-side waterproofing from consideration and put bentonite at a similar, if less severe disadvantage. Humidity-sensitive occupancies require positive-side membranes with low vapor permeance.

(3) **Hydrostatic pressure** is, by definition, the basic factor in the choice of a waterproofing system. Aspects demanding consideration are intensity, duration, and nature of hydrostatic pressure — i.e., whether the pressure is continuous or intermittent and whether the water is stationary or flowing. A fast-flowing underground stream eliminates bentonite. Like asphalt, bentonite deteriorates from the erosive action of flowing water, but much more rapidly.

The nature of the hydrostatic pressure is also an important factor.

Under intense, continuous hydrostatic pressure, membranes of low moisture absorptance (e.g., butyl rubber) perform well. High moisture absorptance causes membrane swelling, disbonding, and consequent wrinkling, as the expanding sheet buckles under compressive stress. Without substrate support, a wrinkled sheet membrane is subjected to a vastly increased risk of puncture. With its relatively higher absorptance, roughly double that of butyl, EPDM is a less suitable choice on projects with intense, continuous hydrostatic pressure.

Intense hydrostatic pressure poses other hazards. It can force membranes into voids in the concrete, where cracking under flexural stress can ultimately rupture the membrane and admit leak water. Because its material depends upon a constant supply of water, making it a good material where hydrostatic pressure is constant, bentonite is a poor choice where hydrostatic pressure is intermittent. (See Chapter 10 for explanation).

On negative-side waterproofing, intense hydrostatic pressure forces water into voids formed by tie-rod holes, cold joints, and rock pockets, from which it exerts pressure on the negative-side coatings. This intensified pressure turns minor imperfections into more probable sources of leakage. (These defects can, however, be readily repaired from the inside.)

Where hydrostatic pressure is intermittent and fast-flowing underground streams can erode bentonite clay systems, negative-side waterproofing may prove the best choice — but only if the occupied space is insensitive to high humidity — e.g., a parking garage or mechanical room. (For expanded discussion of hydrostatic pressure, see Chapter 2, "Principles of Water Management.")

(4)   Water-table level must be determined by accurate soil borings and results corrected for seasonal variation. In the Northern hemisphere, the water table is normally highest around the vernal equinox (after spring thaws have saturated the ground). Conversely, the water table is normally lowest around the autumnal equinox (following the summer evaporation of surface moisture). The designer must thus beware that soil borings taken in July, August, or December may not accurately depict the most severe water table elevation.

(5)   Soil characteristics include both chemical and physical properties that affect waterproofing. For negative-side systems, which leave foundation walls unprotected, pH values must be determined to assess the acidity or alkalinity of the soil. Acids or alkalis in ground water can accelerate deterioration of concrete and steel reinforcing bars. Other corrosive soil chemicals include salt water, salts, sulfates, calcium hydroxides, oils, and tars. Salt water corrodes reinforcing bars in concrete.

Sulfates are especially hazardous in concrete. They react with Portland cement to form chemical compounds of expanded volume. The resulting internal compressive and shearing stresses can spall the concrete, often exposing steel reinforcement to corrosive attack from acids and other soil contaminants. The most corrosive of these sulfates are magnesium, sodium, and ammonium. Though ammonium sulfate does not occur naturally in soil, it may be present in farmland, where it is used as a fertilizer.

Physical soil conditions also concern the designer. Clay soils of low permeability tend to limit underground hydrostatic pressure, whereas highly permeable granular or sandy soils, like Florida's, maximize hydrostatic pressure.

(6)   Substrate stability refers to the propensity for cracking in underlying masonry or other waterproofed components with many construction joints. Expansive soils encountered in the West and Southwest, and peaty soils, can produce rising or settling footings, and the induced stresses that crack the footings themselves and the foundation walls above. Over substrates vulnerable to cracking from any source, the membrane must be capable of elastically elongating or resealing. Elastomeric and modified-bitumen sheets with high breaking strains are best over unstable substrates.

(7)   Construction sequence requires close attention to prevent the exposure of vulnerable materials to the elements when long delays occur in the construction schedule. Bentonite clay panels must be shielded from rain and construction water. During cold-weather construction schedules, waterproofing systems must be capable of resisting subfreezing temperatures when exposed for more than a week. Membranes with low resistance to ultraviolet radiation can deteriorate if exposed to sunlight for intervals as short as a month on brick shelves before they are shielded by the bricks.

Construction sequence can sometimes put waterproofing under unanticipated stress. A deep foundation wall for a two-level basement may rely on the lateral support of an intermediate structural slab, shear walls or shafts. If the foundation wall is waterproofed before these structural elements are cast, the foundation wall may deflect excessively, with disastrous consequences for the membrane. (See Chapter 12 for more discussion on sequencing problems.)

(8)   The track record of each system under the designer's consideration is an obviously important factor, along with the manufacturer's reputation and warranty provisions. In assessing the system's history, the designer should ask these questions:

- Is the product manufactured by the seller or is the seller merely a distributor? (Dun & Bradstreet can provide this information if direct query fails.)
- What is the manufacturer's track record? (Satisfactory on

previous product introductions or changes? Supportive of owner if new product's performance declines?)

- Does the product have a history of successful performance under comparable conditions for at least 15-20 years?
- Has the waterproofing component maintained a consistent (or "improved") formulation for at least 10 years? (The meaning of "improved" in this context is ineluctably elusive.)

(9)   Ease of application is a relatively minor factor compared with others. Facilitating the application may, however, result in better workmanship. Application of modified-bitumen membranes is, for example, easier than dependable application of liquid-applied membranes (LAMs). On a project where other factors are roughly in balance, ease of installation could tip the decision toward modified bitumen in competition with a LAM.

(10)   Risk vs. Cost, the final design factor, is probably the easiest to apply. As this manual constantly repeats, the designer should always minimize risk despite any reasonable — and possibly what may seem unreasonable — costs. If the building owner must cut construction costs, the waterproofing system is among the last places to look for economy. The prudent designer knows that he cannot design a system with zero probability of failure. But he should err on the conservative side when evaluating design factors, matching them against the manufacturer's claims before committing himself to a less expensive system.

As an example of prudent design, the waterproofing designer of an underground space housing computers or rare books should recognize the possibility of flash floods and water-main or sewer-line breaks. They can load the waterproofing system more severely than normally anticipated hydrostatic pressure from ground water or perched water tables. Water-main breaks are quickly reported and repaired. Sewer-line breaks, on the other hand, may be either tardily repaired, or never repaired. (Whereas water-line breaks signal an immediate problem, sewer-line breaks and their consequent leakage may not be signaled with a clear message, beyond lightening the load on the treatment plant.)

Alerts

Positive-side Waterproofing

1. Check soil analysis report for chemicals and groundwater level. Require waterproofing manufacturer to certify that he has read the soils report.
2. Verify the applicator's credentials.

3. Determine if the groundwater level will be maintained sufficiently below the slab on grade to eliminate under-slab waterproofing.

4. If loose-laid sheets are used, compartmentalize them.

5. Specify substrate preparation in the concrete division.

6. Select positive-side waterproofing for corrosive soils and salt-water environments.

7. For foundation waterproofing, select self-adhering or cold-applied modified bitumen membranes over built-up, rubber, or PVC single-ply sheets.

8. Limit water absorption of membrane materials to 2% if practical; and in no case higher than 5% (per ASTM Test Method D 95).

Blindside Waterproofing

1. For blindside waterproofing where vapor control is critical, select a system that will bond to the concrete foundation.

Negative-Side Waterproofing

1. On new construction, ban installation of negative-side waterproofing under any of the following conditions:

   • Presence of corrosive soil chemicals
   • Exposure to freeze-thaw cycling
   • Low interior-humidity requirement

2. Require manufacturer's approval of applicator.

3. Require pre-installation inspection of substrate surfaces.

4. Cite surface preparation requirements.

5

Positive-side Waterproofing Systems

Positive-side waterproofing is applied to the outside (wet) face of subsurface building components, in contrast with negative-side waterproofing applied to the inside (dry) face of subsurface walls and slabs (see Fig.4-3). For new construction, positive-side waterproofing is much more widely specified than negative-side waterproofing, the most popular system for remedial work.

Additional uses for positive-side waterproofing include the inside faces of water-containment structures — e.g., planters, swimming pools, tanks, fountains, and dams.

Waterproofing materials were formerly limited to built-up bituminous membranes and negative-side cementitious coatings. In the past 20 to 30 years, newer systems — notably, liquid-applied membranes (LAMs), self-adhering sheets and bentonite — have become more popular in building waterproofing. Negative-side waterproofing is the primary system for vehicular and utility tunnels where the outside is inaccessible, and also for liquid storage and swimming pool structures.

Positive-side waterproofing solves a much greater variety of waterproofing problems, with fewer limitations, than negative-side waterproofing. It also comes in an overwhelming variety of subsystems and materials, thus giving the designer a broad spectrum of vastly expanded opportunities for solving special waterproofing problems.

In addition to the cementitious coatings used for negative-side waterproofing, positive-side waterproofing materials include bentonite, several generic categories of single-ply sheets (elastomeric, thermoplastics, modified bitumen); built-up membranes comprising felts and fabrics, and liquid-applied membranes. (See succeeding chapters for detailed discussion of each membrane type.)

Positive-side waterproofing offers several notable advantages. Unlike negative-side waterproofing, positive-side waterproofing is applicable to all subsurface components. As noted in Chapter 6, negative-side waterproofing is impractical for framed structural slabs. This disqualification spoils the continuity of negative-side waterproofing as a total system. It always requires a transition between positive-side and negative-side waterproofing at joints between walls and structural slabs. (As subsequent discussion will demonstrate, combinations of generically different waterproofing systems or materials are generally inadvisable.)

As a second advantage, positive-side waterproofing protects against corrosive soils, which can attack masonry and concrete, and even steel reinforcing bars. Corrosive soils can thus pose a threat to the system's structural integrity. With negative-side waterproofing, the designer implicitly accepts these risks. (See Fig. 5-1 for algorithmic flow chart for preliminary system selection.)

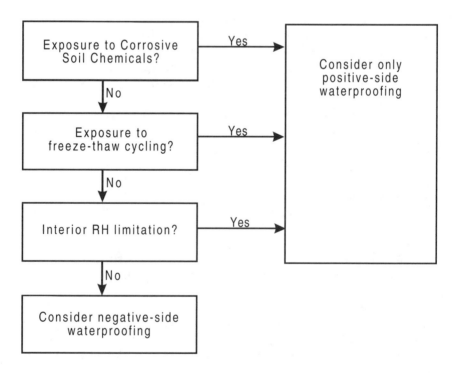

Fig. 5-1 Algorithm diagram shows preliminary design elimination process for choosing between negative-side and positive-side waterproofing systems for new construction. For remedial work, where positive-side waterproofing is impracticable, there is obviously a stronger case for negative-side waterproofing than is indicated by the algorithmic procedure depicted above.

Positive-Side Design Factors

Positive-side waterproofing comes in a bewildering variety of materials:

- Bentonite clay
- Modified bitumen sheets
- Liquid-applied membranes (LAMs)
- Built-up bituminous membranes
- Prefabricated elastomeric sheets
- Prefabricated thermoplastic sheets
- Cementitious or crystalline coatings

These materials come with their own unique combination of assets and liabilities. Their selection requires delicate balancing of numerous design factors, notably the following:

- Code limitations
- Specifier's past experience (with a particular system)
- Geometric complexity
- Feasibility of Quality Assurance (QA)
- Resistance to soil chemicals
- Ease of application
- Resistance to design hydrostatic pressure
- Vapor permeance
- Substrate Stability

Code limitations, for both pollutants and safety, are the first obstacle considered in an efficient design process. It is obviously wasteful to consider the advantages of a system barred by pollution or safety requirements. Hot-applied built-up systems, traditionally the most popular, are increasingly banned by pollution regulations in major metropolitan areas plagued by air pollution. The most effective built-up waterproofing membrane, coal tar pitch, is unfortunately the most heavily polluting.

Eliminating a hot-applied built-up system still leaves the designer with the alternative of a cold-applied built-up membrane. Yet even here, the designer confronts the possibility of a ban. Solvent-based asphalt cutbacks, used as the primer or adhesive in many cold-applied built-up membranes, may violate VOC regulations in the more rigorously regulated jurisdictions.

The specifier's past experience with a system ranks high as a design factor for obvious reasons. There are, however, additional considerations requiring the designer's attention. He should consider no system that has not provided minimum 10-year service, unless the owner expresses (in writing) his willingness to accept the additional risk associated with a newer system. On projects designed to resist high hydrostatic pressure, no material should even be considered unless it satisfies the above referenced 10-year minimum service-life criterion. And in specifying waterproofing material, even material that has performed satisfactorily in the past, the designer should assure himself that the formulation has remained essentially unchanged. (If it has not, the designer should investigate the reformulated material as an essentially new material, or system.)

Geometric complexity can pose problems for some waterproofing systems — notably, the felt-laying, hot-mopping operations of built-up membrane application. With their more readily adaptable application techniques — rolling, brushing, squeegeeing, or trowelling — LAMs are readily installed on irregular substrates. Judged by this adaptability criterion, prefabricated, single-ply sheet membranes fall somewhere between built-up and liquid-applied membranes.

Feasibility of Quality Assurance (QA) is closely correlated with the previously discussed factor. QA denotes measures undertaken by the *owner*, as opposed to the *contractor*, to assure correct system installation. But the feasibility of dependable QA obviously requires an established set of well defined application procedures empirically proven to produce waterproof components. It is highly improbable that a new, experimental waterproofing system would have such proven, well defined procedures. It is, moreover, obvious that rigorous QA programs are still lacking on many waterproofing projects. Some waterproofing failures result from such inexcusable lapses as omission of protection boards shielding waterproofing membranes from damage during backfill operations and subsequent construction above. These projects evidently had *no* QA program, at least one worthy of the name.

Quality Control (QC) (measures taken by the contractor to assure correct system installation) should also be investigated by the designer prior to application. Two agents looking for flaws in construction practice are obviously better than one. QA is, however, much more important than QC, as the owner has a greater stake in good construction practice than the contractor.

Waterproofing installers should be certified or approved by the manufacturer. Shop drawings and a pre-application conference are mandatory. The first day's work should be inspected by a technically qualified manufacturer's representative rather than a salesman. Depending on project complexity, periodic inspections should be made and a final inspection, if practicable. Each lift of wall waterproofing should be inspected before it is backfilled. The manufacturer's representative should also witness flood-testing and repairs.

Resistance to soil chemicals is another obvious design factor that can focus the designer's attention more intensely on feasible solutions early in the design process by eliminating some systems and materials. Laboratory analysis of site soil samples can identify the hazardous chemicals. The presence of corrosive chemicals may eliminate one of the most popular positive-side waterproofing material — bentonite clay — which breaks down in the presence of some soil contaminants. Consultation with the manufacturer about his system's vulnerabilities is required in such situations.

Chemical contaminants that may be present in varying concentrations include:

- Soil poisoners, (usually petroleum based)
- Fertilizers
- Toxic wastes
- Salt water (including de-icing salts)
- Waste oil

Ease of application is an obviously important factor that may have decisive local implications. In a large metropolitan area, the prospect of finding competent local contractors for any system is obviously greater than in smaller, more isolated areas where specialized expertise for applying some waterproofing systems — for example, LAMs — may not exist.

The last three of the nine previously listed design factors — hydrostatic pressure, vapor permeance, and substrate stability — require little discussion. Low vapor permeance may be an exception. It may require some designer research for suitable materials if the waterproofed space requires a controlled humidity — e.g., for rooms housing computers or other electronic equipment and even carpeting, which can be damaged by high humidity. As one notorious example, bentonite manufacturers' literature generally contains scant guidance on the vapor permeance of bentonite products. The designer may have to make specific requests for this information.

Single vs. Dual Systems

As a general rule, designers should specify a single generic waterproofing system. There are, however, conditions that may favor a combination of systems as the best design solution. Some membrane materials are more suitable for horizontal than for vertical substrates. This is especially true for LAM, coal tar pitch built-up bituminous membranes, rubber, and PVC sheets. As a consequence, a combination of two different membrane materials may provide the best design solution, allowing the designer to exploit the complementary properties of two different materials.

As one example of the advantages of combination, on projects with positive-side membrane waterproofing under slabs-on-ground, elevator pits and other small pits can be waterproofed with negative-side, cementitious or crystalline coatings. Unlike most combinations, which require an awkward transition joint between two dissimilar materials or an incompatibility between these materials, this system features a practicable overlap of the two different waterproofing systems (see Fig. 5-2).

Normally, however, the difficulty of detailing a dependable transition joint between two generically different materials — especially at wall-slab junctures — weighs against a dual system. For optimal material selection, a combination of butyl-bentonite membrane on a structural slab, combined with bentonite panels on peripheral foundation walls would provide an excellent solution to a typical design problem. But a detail for a positive seal of the joint at the wall-slab intersection is questionable, and this deficiency would compromise the watertight integrity of the entire project.

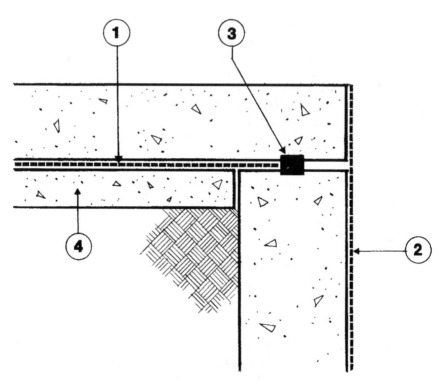

Fig. 5-2   Elevator pits and other small pits offer a rare opportunity for successful combination of positive-side and negative-side waterproofing. A method of waterproofing pits with positive-side waterproofing for slab-on-ground and negative-side waterproofing for the pit, is shown in the above detail: (1) waterproofing membrane, (2) crystalline slurry coat, (3) water stop, (4) mud slab.

Combining a waterproofing system with a dampproofing system in the same wall plane can be equally risky. If the materials are generically compatible, a plaza slab membrane can be extended over the edge of a foundation and down the wall, lapping a dampproofed foundation wall well above the ground water level. But it is inviting trouble to extend a waterproofing membrane up from a footing to some predetermined height — say, 2 ft above the ground-water table for a transition to dampproofing.

The most dangerous combination, however, is the belt-and-suspenders' approach of applying vapor-impermeable membrane systems to both sides of a concrete wall or slab. When the entrapped moisture evaporates, it can create blisters, delaminating one or both membranes from the wall. In an equally disastrous combination, a designer might apply bentonite panels against a membrane-waterproofed wall. The nails anchoring the bentonite panels will eventually corrode and admit leakwater through the nail holes in the perforated membrane.

The belt-and-suspenders' approach can work on high-risk projects by simply overlaying one system with another, to provide harmless redundancy. As one example of such redundancy, the designer might cover a fully adhered membrane with a loose-laid membrane on a below-grade structural slab.

Adhered vs. Unadhered

As his most important decision, the designer must choose between two basic concepts: fully adhered or nonadhered (i.e., loose-laid or spot-bonded) membranes. Many prefabricated membrane materials — butyl, PVC and other thermoplastic materials — can be loose laid and compartmented, spot-bonded (i.e., partially adhered), or fully adhered to the substrate. All other membranes must be fully adhered.

Compared with fully adhered waterproofing systems, loose-laid or spot-bonded systems offer the following advantages:

- Less dependence on substrate preparation
- Reduced (or eliminated) membrane-splitting risk
- Superior joint seams on thermoplastic sheets
- Less sensitivity to climatic conditions

Less dependence on substrate preparation is an obvious benefit of loose-laid or spot-bonded systems. To assure high bond strength at the membrane-substrate interface of an adhered system requires not only a smoother more uniform finish, but also a much cleaner and drier surface than a non-adhered system. Membrane adhesion to the deck can be impaired by dust, grease, liquid moisture, and some curing and form-release agents. Liquid moisture on a concrete deck boils when hit with hot bitumen, and the resulting voids in the mopping layer can permit lateral movement of water. Some curing agents, particularly sodium silicate, can also spoil adhesion. They form a crystalline molecular structure that not only fills the concrete pores, but glazes the surface. This glaze is often visually undetectable. Unlike some acrylic and alkyd resin-based curing agents, which flake off in 14 to 28 days, sodium silicate requires sand blasting to provide an acceptable surface. Pinholing and complete loss of adhesion of liquid-applied membranes can often be traced to the presence of sodium silicate curing agents.

Adhered membranes require priming of concrete (or parged masonry) surfaces to provide tack and absorb dust, which can also impair adhesion (see Fig. 5-3). VOC regulations have forced many waterproofing manufacturers to abandon solvent-based coatings and primers in favor of water-based coatings and primers. Water-based products do not "wet" or penetrate the surface as well as solvent-based materials. Since water-based products are not as "forgiving" as solvent-based materials, they must be applied to cleaner, smoother surfaces, which require more rigorous preparation.

Specifications for preparing and repairing concrete to be waterproofed can be found in ASTM D 5295 and ACI 515. Tie rod holes, static and dynamic cracks, honeycombing, rock pockets, ridges created by formwork kickouts and similar surface irregularities require correction.

Fig. 5-3 Adhered membranes (built-up, modified-bitumen, etc.) require priming of concrete substrates to absorb dust and provide a tacky surface assuring tight adhesive bond at the membrane-concrete interface. (TC Mira DRI.)

Irregularities are remedied by grinding or chipping. Avoid sanding, because it polishes the concrete and closes the pores to primers and coatings. Select form release oils that do not inhibit bonding or proper penetration of waterproofing constituents.

Cracks must be filled or detailed by stripping as required by the membrane manufacturer. According to some authorities, 60% of drying-shrinkage cracks will occur in the first 28 days

On masonry foundations the Brick Institute of America and National Concrete Manufacturers Association recommend that waterproofing and dampproofing should be applied to a cement mortar parge coat rather than directly to the masonry. These parge coats are required because mortar joints are not always full or struck flush, and broken corners of CMU are not always patched. A parge coat provides a smooth surface for the waterproofing or dampproofing. It also adds some water resistance to the foundation.

Some waterproofing systems require cementitious cants, coves or fillets at reentrant angles. Some require bevels at external edges. Include these in the concrete trade construction documents or they may pop up as an extra.

Reduced splitting risk is an obvious benefit of loose-laid or partially adhered (i.e., spot-bonded) waterproofing membranes. Adhered membranes carry a greater splitting risk than unadhered membranes because substrate cracking is propagated directly up into the membrane. If, for example, a $1/8$-in. crack occurs in a concrete substrate topped with an adhered membrane, the strain (elongation divided by length) may be 100% or more. A loose membrane can bridge over the crack, experiencing a strain of 1% or less, well within the breaking strain of any common waterproofing membrane. (Vulcanized rubber membranes generally have breaking strains of 300% or more. Built-up membranes, however, have breaking strains around 2%.)

Because of their vulnerability to splitting, adhered waterproofing membranes should be selected for their ability to accommodate substrate cracking. There are two mechanisms through which membranes can accommodate substrate cracking: by (a) "bridging" the crack without rupturing, or (b) self-healing if ruptured. (Bentonite clay offers a unique, self-healing solution to this problem; see Chapter 10.)

The superiority of joint seams, sometimes claimed for nonadhered systems is limited to thermoplastic sheets, which are predominantly PVC. The heat-welding of seams in a thermoplastic sheet produces a joint as strong as the sheet material itself. This advantage for nonadhered systems does not, however, apply to butyl, the only other material suitable for loose-laid membranes. The adhesive-based seams used for butyl membranes generally lack the strength of the sheet material.

This argument for superiority of nonadhered systems is further weakened by adhered system alternatives, which included polymer-modified bitumen as well as PVC and butyl. As one such alternative, a two-ply system with self-adhered modified-bitumen sheets, laid one-on-one with staggered joints, virtually nullifies the claimed superiority of thermoplastic loose-laid systems. A two-ply adhered system thus constructed offers redundancy. In contrast, loose-laid, single-ply membranes require greater care during installation to assure the integrity of their seams, which simultaneously provide the first and only line of defense.

Less sensitivity to climatic conditions is an irrefutable advantage for nonadhered membranes. Moreover, large plastic and rubber sheets are readily installed on horizontal surfaces, but are less practical for vertical surfaces.

Compared with unadhered membranes, adhered membranes offer two big advantages:

- Easier leak detection
- Less probability of membrane slippage during backfilling operations or subsequent settlement of poorly compacted fill.

Easier leak detection is the good-news aspect of adhered membranes' greater splitting risk. When water leaks through a crack in a slab or wall with an adhered membrane, you can reasonably assume that the membrane rupture closely coincides with the crack's locations.

In a loose-laid membrane, however, the appearance of the leak in a structural slab soffit or slab-on-ground may tell you little about the location of the water-admitting membrane defect. It may be located 30 ft or more from the interior leak location. Knowing the location of the membrane defect normally facilitates remedial work. The detective work in locating a leak of unknown source in a membrane area of 1,000 sq ft can take more time than the repair itself.

Easier leak detection is accomplished by compartmentalization, at least on horizontal surfaces. The substrate is divided into squares by applying adhesive bands in a 10-ft grid. With the membrane adhered to the bands, leaks are confined to the gridded compartments. Where a LAM is called for by other design factors, a system suggested by Parise, combining LAM with a loose-laid rubber sheet, exploits the unique advantages of each system.

On one hand, the compartmentalized adhered membrane facilitates detection of the leak's location by confining it to an area much smaller than the area that must be investigated when a loose-laid membrane leaks. On the other hand, the loose-laid membrane reduces the probability of a leak's occurrence. A loose-laid system not only reduces the number of seams, the most vulnerable spots in a waterproofing membrane; it also exploits the superior dependability of welded seams, at least when PVC sheets are specified. (For detailed discussion of seaming techniques, see Chapter 8.)

Note that even fully adhered systems can pose leak-detection problems for foundation walls constructed of concrete masonry units. A leak at the top shows up at the floor below. Negative-side waterproofing can alleviate this leak-detection problem for walls and slabs-on-ground. It does, however, create a new problem if the project has intersecting walls or slabs, which leave portions of the waterproofed space unprotected.

An adhered system's greater resistance to slippage is attributable to its greater frictional resistance to gravitational force parallel to the wall surface. Perpetual gravitational force stretching a partially adhered membrane can exert gradually increasing concentrated stresses that can ultimately result in adhesion failure at spot-bonded locations. Fully adhered membranes are subjected to lighter, uniform shearing stresses in the adhesive layer. Built-up membranes are usually installed in 6-ft to 8-ft strips laid vertically and backnailed to wood nailers to prevent slippage or sagging.

Even more important than gravitational force on wall membranes is the downward frictional force exerted by settling backfill adjacent to the wall (and transmitted through the protection boards or drainage composites sandwiched between backfill and membrane). This frictional force results from the shrinkage of the backfill materials and the natural consolidation of soils as they progress from their less-dense condition as backfill to a permanent, "undisturbed" condition. (This soil consolidation itself is, of course, a consequence of gravitational force.)

Another controversy between proponents of adhered vs. nonadhered membranes concerns membrane adhesion to lot-line walls and mud slabs. According to proponents of unadhered single-ply membranes, adhered membranes applied to lagging, lot-line slurry walls or mud slabs fail to bond to concrete cast against them. As a consequence, they allegedly share the same untraceable leak problem of loose laid membranes.

Proponents of adhered systems counter this claim with the following argument: When concrete is cast against some types of bituminous membranes, the heat of hydration liberated by the hardening concrete softens the bitumen enough to create a bond. Membranes benefitting from this phenomenon are built-up membranes (with both coal tar pitch and soft asphalt) and modified bitumen sheets without polyethylene facer films.

One method of exploiting this phenomenon, and thus reducing the probability of lateral leak water flow between built-up membranes on mud slabs and slabs-on-ground above, is proposed by Lawrence, who claims perennial success from its use. It comprises the following steps:

1. Install the first ply on the dry, unprimed mud slab.

(Use adhesives in spot locations to hold the ply in place during subsequent installation operations.)

2. Install the remaining plies in the normal manner (i.e., hot-mopped or cold-adhered, depending on the specified system).
3. Cover completed membrane with protection boards bonded to the membrane. (Orient protection boards with polyethylene slip sheet on top and lap edges. Omit protection boards on vertical surfaces.)
4. Immediately before casting of slab-on-ground, remove polyethylene film and prime protection board surface.
5. Place welded wire fabric or other slab reinforcement.
6. Cast concrete.

Because the first ply is isolated from continuous contact with the mud slab, this method minimizes chances of mud-slab cracks propagating upward into the membrane. Subsequent saturation of the mud-slab will disbond the membrane. But the hardening concrete's heat of hydration should raise the bitumen temperature enough to adhere the protection board-membrane laminate to the slab above.

Continuity in the adhesive layer between membrane and substrate is essential in an adhered system to prevent entrapment of water between the two surfaces, where it can work destructive mischief. Entrapped water can be absorbed by both membrane and substrate material with consequent swelling of the materials and expansion of disbonded areas. This degenerative process can ultimately produce blisters in some membranes, and these blisters can destroy the system's waterproofing integrity.

To prevent this degenerative process, designers should specify membrane materials with low water absorption. Adler/Ruggerio recommend a limit of 2% maximum. Systems with 2% to 5% water absorption are generally satisfactory. They suggest that materials with absorption over 5% are unsuitable for waterproofing.

Algorithmic Initiation

Because of the tremendous variety of waterproofing materials, the designer should initiate the material selection process with an informal — or perhaps with a formal — algorithmic process. It should start with elimination of ineligible materials, banned by regulation or unavailability. This step can narrow the range of alternatives to manageable proportions. Environmental regulations, for example, may exclude both hot - and cold-applied membranes, and some LAMS. (See Table 5-1 for other design factors that eliminate, weigh against, or favor certain systems.)

The following chapters expand in greater detail the particular advantages and disadvantages of the various positive-side waterproofing materials cited in this general introductory chapter.

PRELIMINARY SYSTEM SELECTION PROCESS

DESIGN FACTOR	EFFECT ON SYSTEM SELECTION
Rapidly flowing water	Eliminate bentonite
Corrosive soils	Eliminate negative-side waterproofing, bentonite
Blindside waterproofing	Eliminate LAM, PVC, butyl
Subfreezing temperatures	Eliminate negative-side waterproofing and cold-applied emulsions; extreme temperatures make built-up and self-adhering systems doubtful
Tight construction schedule	May eliminate LAM, which requires very dry substrate
Constricted work site, small building elements, VOC compliance	Eliminates hot-mopped built-up membranes. Favors LAM

Table 5-1 Waterproofing designer can narrow his range of practicable system selection by eliminating unsuitable systems early in the design process.

Alerts

1. Check soil-analysis report for chemicals and groundwater level. Require waterproofing manufacturer to certify that he has read the soils report.

2. Verify the applicator's credentials.

3. Determine if the groundwater level is sufficiently below the slab-on-grade to eliminate under-slab waterproofing.

4. If loose-laid sheets are used, compartmentalize them.

5. For blindside waterproofing where vapor control is critical, select a system that will bond to the concrete foundation.

6. Specify substrate preparation in the concrete division.

7. Select positive-side waterproofing for corrosive soils.

8. For foundation waterproofing, favor self-adhering membranes over built-up, rubber, or PVC single-ply sheets.

9. Limit water absorption of membrane materials to 2% if practical; and in no case higher than 5% (per ASTM Test Method D 95).

6

Negative-side Waterproofing

Negative-side waterproofing is applied to the inside (dry) subsurface space, in contrast with positive-side waterproofing, which is applied to the outside (wet) face of the subsurface building components (see Fig. 4-3). Because of its ready access to the dry side of waterproofed building components, negative-side waterproofing obviously finds its greatest use in remedial work. Several limitations — e.g.,concrete's vulnerability to corrosive soil chemicals — restrict use of negative-side systems for new construction, which is dominated by positive-side systems.

Negative-side waterproofing offers its greatest advantages on projects that would otherwise require positive-side solutions to blindside waterproofing problems — i.e., where lot lines or other impediments make the outside face of a foundation wall inaccessible. Pits and shafts exemplify similar blindside problems appropriate for negative-side solutions.

The primary use of negative-side waterproofing is remedial work on existing buildings, where access to the outside face of walls and slabs is, to say the least, difficult. Use of negative-side waterproofing is seldom justified for new building construction, except in instances where positive-side waterproofing is inconvenient. Although it is effective as a waterproofing coating, the higher vapor permeability of negative-side waterproofing is a drawback in underground structures with occupancies and materials sensitive to high humidity — e.g., libraries and gymnasium wood floors.

Its success in stopping leaks where other systems fail, make negative-side waterproofing the system of choice in repair and remedial work. Probably 75% of the applications are for remediation and only 25% for new construction. Of the latter 5% or more is applied on the positive-side of foundations and slabs-on-ground.

Negative-side waterproofing materials can be applied to either side of a waterproofed component. Viewed in a strictly logical light, this normally negative-side waterproofing becomes positive-side waterproofing when applied to the exterior (wet) side of a waterproofed component. But when negative-side waterproofing materials (discussed under the next subhead) are switched to the positive side of the waterproofed component, the waterproofing industry follows a convention of still calling it negative-side waterproofing.

Superior durability and repairability give negative-side waterproofing a big advantage over positive-side waterproofing. As an integral part of the construction, negative-side waterproofing will normally last the life of a wall.

Because of its virtual inaccessibility, positive-side waterproofing must last for the service life of the structure or else. The alternative is either (a) negative-side remedial system, or (b) a very difficult and expensive positive-side re-waterproofing project. Negative-side waterproofing, however, can be readily repaired in most instances. The crystalline systems will reactivate when minor leakage occurs, and major cracking from seismic forces or settlement can be repaired by reapplication of the material.

Materials

Negative-side waterproofing generally comprises coatings that seal the interior surface of the concrete rather than separate membranes applied to the exterior face. Membrane waterproofing is obviously unsuitable for negative-side waterproofing because the external water pressure can easily disbond the membrane from the wall. Bentonite is also unsuitable, because it requires continuous hydrostatic pressure to maintain intimate contact with the substrate.

In rare instances, mechanically adhered membranes have been used for negative-side remedial waterproofing, where existing walls are leaking, and it is necessary to restore waterproofing and provide a vapor-resistant system. These uses are best restricted to locations where hydrostatic pressure is intermittent — i.e., occurring only during periods of unusually high water table. In such situations, the waterproofing membrane can be installed during the normal dry period. (Alternatively, you can specify a membrane tolerant of damp substrates.) After the membrane is installed, closely spaced, powder-actuated clips are driven through self-sealing butyl pads. Heavy-duty wire mesh is secured to the clips and the wall covered with a minimum 2 in. thickness of gunite.

This system must be used judiciously. It is vulnerable at terminations, particularly at joints between walls and floors, where careful detailing is required to maintain the watertight continuity.

All contemporary negative-side waterproofing systems may be mixed with sand and trowelled on or brushed or sprayed as a slurry (see Fig. 6-1). The basic materials come in three generic types:

Fig. 6-1 Sprayed negative-side waterproofing coatings can be troweled for smooth finish. (Vandex Sales & Service, Inc.)

- Crystalline coatings
- Cementitious coatings with metallic oxide
- Cementitious coatings with various densifying additives

Crystalline coatings have to a great extent replaced metallic-oxide coatings because of their greater dependability, longer service life, and self-healing property. (They are also called *chemical conversion* or *capillary coatings.*)

These solutions of organic and inorganic compounds react chemically with unhydrated Portland cement and free lime in the presence of moisture. They fill capillaries and shrinkage cracks with long chain molecules that crystallize within the concrete. According to one manufacturer, his proprietary material features a mixture of Portland cement, silica sand, and active proprietary chemicals. Mixed with water and applied as a cementitious coating, this material promotes a catalytic reaction that generates a non-soluble crystalline formation of dendritic (i.e., branching) fibers within the pores and capillaries in concrete. By filling the fine pores of concrete, the material impedes the infiltration of water. When the concrete cures and shrinkage cracks occur, the crystalline materials are reactivated and seal the passages.

These products were compounded in 1946 in Denmark and later in Canada around 1968. They were introduced in the United States in the 1960s, primarily as remedial systems for waterproofing failures.

Oxidized metallic cementitious coatings, introduced a century ago, dominated negative-side waterproofing until recently. But during the past decade, they have been declining. Metallic oxide cementitious coatings comprise Portland cement mixed with finely divided iron or aluminum particles with ammonium or acid-based oxidation catalysts and sand in a 1:1:1 (by volume) mix. Oxidized iron particles expand several times as they corrode, thereby compacting the coating and enhancing its waterproofing properties. Where iron rust stains are objectionable, aluminum particles can be substituted in the coating. Aluminum reacts with Portland cement, releasing hydrogen-gas bubbles. Smaller than the water molecules, these hydrogen molecules disperse through the concrete matrix and make it resistant to the passage of liquid moisture.

Proprietary-densified Portland cement systems are representative of the third generic type of negative-side waterproofing. Some manufacturers claim superior waterproofing qualities against high hydrostatic heads.

Negative Vs. Positive

Compared with positive-side waterproofing, negative-side waterproofing offers several notable advantages:

- Easier application
- Easy leak detection
- Easy maintenance
- High resistance to hydrostatic pressure
- Superior concrete curing

Ease of application makes negative-side waterproofing the obvious first choice for remedial work where positive-side waterproofing has failed. Positive-side waterproofing is more inconvenient and costly even for new construction. For remedial work, it is obviously vastly more inconvenient and costly. Except for crystalline chemical conversion coatings, negative-side waterproofing requires little or no substrate preparation. And in some situations, notably for foundations cast against rock, negative-side waterproofing is usually the most practicable solution. As ancillary benefits, negative-side waterproofing cannot be damaged by backfilling operations, and it can be inspected and repaired after backfilling is completed.

Early leak detection is another advantage of negative-side waterproofing. With the coating on the inside of the wall or slab-on-ground, the leak generally occurs at the same location at (or very close to) the defective waterproofing material. With positive-side waterproofing, however, the defect in the waterproofing membrane can be located some distance from the leak appearance in the interior space.

Easy maintenance results from the convenient location of negative-side waterproofing: i.e., directly at the interior surface. Defective material can be readily removed, followed by reapplication of the waterproofing coating. Reapplication of crystalline type waterproofing will generally stop subsequent leakage after initial application. However, if the concrete dries and the chemical reactions stop, it can be reactivated by the presence of water.

Resistance to high hydrostatic pressure is another advantage of negative-side waterproofing, though many positive-side waterproofing systems can provide equal resistance. Crystalline and densified cementitious negative-side waterproofing coatings can satisfy the U.S. Army Corps of Engineers' CRD48 REF, which requires resistance to 200 psi hydrostatic pressure (equivalent to a 461-ft head of water). A liquid permeability in the range of 10^{-12} to 10^{-14} cm/sec is required for classification as waterproof.

Superior concrete curing is a final advantage of negative-side waterproofing. Since concrete thrives in the presence of liquid moisture, which continues for months to promote hydration of the cement and its consequent strengthening and densification, negative-side waterproofing promotes permanently ideal curing conditions. (With the concrete sandwiched between water on one side and an impermeable barrier on the other, you have the optimum conditions for healthy concrete. In the constant presence of moisture, concrete can continue gaining strength for years, though at a decreasing rate.) These conditions also impede the formation of cracks from drying shrinkage, which occurs in concrete surfaces exposed to the atmosphere.

In accordance with the no-free-lunch law that rules construction as well as economics, negative-side waterproofing has notable disadvantages:

- Vulnerability to substrate cracking
- Impractability for structurally framed slabs and intersecting walls
- Lack of protection against corrosive soils
- Higher vapor permeability than positive-side membranes
- Vulnerability to fastener damage

Vulnerability to substrate cracking is the most serious liability of negative-side waterproofing. This is true despite manufacturers' claims that the chemical reaction is continuous as long as there is moisture in the concrete and that cracks are sealed as the chemicals close the pores. If applied when the concrete is fresh, the crystalline and densifying systems permit the concrete to continue curing, thus reducing cracking. Crystalline coatings can close hairline cracks — i.e., cracks up to .012 in. (0.3 mm) wide. Moisture reactivation of the sealing process gives the coatings the ability to self-seal, according to manufacturers. But no negative-side waterproofing system can bridge dynamic cracks and reseal ruptures.

Impracticability for structural slabs and intersecting walls restricts negative-side waterproofing to a fairly narrow range of applications. Readily applied to vertical surfaces or to the top side of horizontal surfaces — i.e., on slab-on-ground surfaces — negative-side waterproofing is generally unsuitable for ceiling application — i.e., the soffits of framed structural slabs. The difficulty of brushing, troweling, or even spraying these coatings onto ceilings, against the perpetual force of gravity, is generally too great. Cracks can produce catastrophic leaks, and penetration for ceiling and pipe hangers, etc., will damage the waterproofing. (There is, however, at least one manufacturer who attests to successful sprayed application of his negative-side product onto a ceiling.)

Application of crystalline coatings to repair cracks is generally successful. Repaired cracks can, however, create a secondary leakage problem. The sealing of a relatively large leak hole can increase hydrostatic pressure relieved by the original leak. This increased hydrostatic pressure can then produce leaks at smaller holes, thereby necessitating further repair.

Negative-side waterproofing is also difficult to apply to foundation walls intersected by structural slabs or cast-in-place shear walls. Piers cast in with the foundations can be readily treated with the coating, but intersecting walls and elevated structural slabs cast into notches in the wall block off the area of treatment. Negative-side waterproofing on walls cannot be readily connected to positive-side waterproofing because of the loss of continuity. Positive-side waterproofing membranes carried across elevated structurally supported slabs and down a short section of the foundation cannot be practically joined to the negative-side system.

Lack of protection against corrosive soils is an obvious disadvantage of negative-side waterproofing. Epoxy coatings can protect reinforcing bars, but only positive-side waterproofing can protect concrete from corrosive soils.

High vapor permeability disqualifies negative-side waterproofing where interior humidity must be closely controlled. Positive-side membrane waterproofing, which can combine a liquid barrier with an efficient vapor retarder as well, is required when interior humidity control is vital (see Fig. 4-2). Negative-side waterproofing is thus ruled out for underground spaces containing computer or audio-visual equipment, wood or carpeted floors, and other humidity-sensitive items.

Application

Negative-side waterproofing coatings are applied to damp or green concrete substrates, by brushing, spraying in a slurry, or troweling (in one or more coats). Slabs-on-ground can be coated in this way or by broadcasting the dry powder by shake over the wet concrete surface, followed by power troweling (see Fig 6-2).

Slurries of dry powder and water are used in the first coat in new

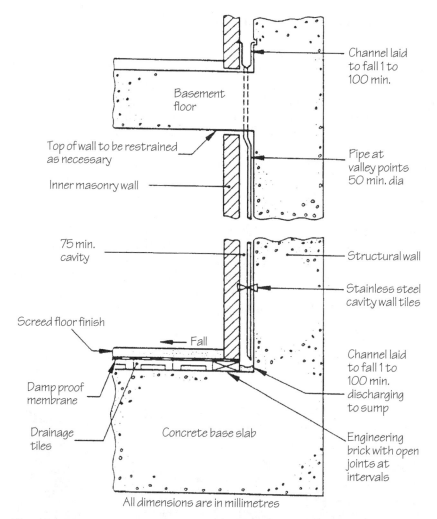

Channel laid to fall 1 to 100 min.

Basement floor

Top of wall to be restrained as necessary

Inner masonry wall

Pipe at valley points 50 min. dia

75 min. cavity

Structural wall

Stainless steel cavity wall tiles

Screed floor finish

Fall

Channel laid to fall 1 to 100 min. discharging to sump

Damp proof membrane

Drainage tiles

Concrete base slab

Engineering brick with open joints at intervals

All dimensions are in millimetres

Fig. 6-2 "Drained-cavity" construction poses many hazards despite its recommendation by British proponents as the "most effective and trouble-free" solution to the blind-side waterproofing problem. See text for a description of its many liabilities. (British Standards Institution) Extracts from BS 8102 : 1990 are reproduced with the permission of BSI under license no. PD\1998 1273. Complete editions of the standards can be obtained by post from national standards bodies.

and remedial work and as secondary applications when the first coat requires additional treatment. These coats range in thickness from 1/16 in. to 1/8 in. Powder and water are mixed with quartz sand to a mortar consistency, and applied in corners to seal cracks, form-tie holes, honeycombed areas, and construction joints. Exposed waterproofing may be finished with a parge coat or cement topping for decorative or protective surfacing. Parging is required on metallic oxide and cement topping for traffic areas.

The concrete substrate should be uncured or damp concrete or cement parging. Good adhesion is paramount in these systems. Early application of negative-side waterproofing does not create the risk of drying shrinkage cracks that would occur in positive-side waterproofing. As previously noted, negative-side waterproofing helps prevent premature drying of the concrete. It thus minimizes the hazards of shrinkage cracking.

Coatings adhere best when the concrete pores are opened by sand-blasting or mechanical chipping. Acid etching is sometimes specified, but it has two liabilities: (a) possible exposure of reinforcing bars to chloride-ion corrosion and (b) generally less effective preparation of the concrete substrate. Sandblasting wet or dry or mechanical chipping is generally required to open the pores. Grinding and sanding are ineffective, for they polish surfaces and inhibit penetration of the coatings. Wet and dry sandblasting are equally effective, but wet sandblasting is more ecologically acceptable. Dry sandblasting is sometimes prohibited by ordinances, because of particulate pollution. Wet sandblasting tends to be more expensive. Water blasting is generally unsuitable for interior spaces (see Fig. 6-3).

Despite their higher cost, these more dependable substrate preparation techniques are justifiable, in keeping with the general principle of

Fig. 6-3 Broadcasting dry powder and trowelling. (Vandex Sales & Service, Inc.)

waterproofing benefit/cost analysis. Cutting construction cost is seldom, if ever, justified for even a slight increase in leakage risk. The high cost of remedial waterproofing work should deter any owner, and his designer, from endorsing any risk-increasing first-cost economies.

Preparation for negative-side waterproofing application requires care to assure that preliminary work has been completed before application of the waterproofing coating. All cutouts for electrical boxes, floor enclosures, and other recessed items must be installed before application. Furring must be free-standing or adhered to foundation walls. Conduit and pipes must be surface-mounted. Mechanical equipment should be installed on concrete pads cast atop waterproofed slabs-on-ground to avoid penetrations from anchor bolts.

The contractor must take extreme care to avoid damage to coatings by fasteners installed after coating application. This damage can be avoided by several methods:

- Eliminating fasteners and substituting adhesives
- Use of free-standing furring
- Driving fasteners through butyl washers or pads

Because they are mixed with water and applied wet, negative-side waterproofing coatings cannot be applied in subfreezing temperatures or exposed to such temperatures before they are cured. Painting of crystalline-treated surfaces risks deterioration of the paint by continuing crystalline growth.

The Blindside "Drained-Cavity" Approach

A system originated in Great Britain, known as a "drained cavity," offers a basically negative-side approach to the blindside waterproofing problem and will, accordingly, be discussed in this chapter. It consists of a thick cast-in-place slab-on-ground and foundation wall, with cavities at the inside faces of both wall and slab. The wall cavity is created by a free-standing masonry wall. At the floor, a series of parallel cavities is created by a layer of inverted channel tiles, topped with a wearing course. A dampproofing membrane is recommended on the masonry wall and under the wearing course. Vertical cavities are drained to a sloped gutter. The cavity under the floor is sloped to drain and drained to a sump (see Fig 6-4).

According to the system's proponents, infiltrating water can be conducted to one of more sumps and discharged through pipes to daylight or to a storm drainage system. The cavities can be ventilated, either passively or mechanically, in which case the air should be exhausted to the exterior.

Despite praise from the British Standard RS8012, *Code of Practice*

Fig. 6-4   Water blasting surfaces prior to applying crystalline waterproofing. (Waterproofing Systems of New Jersey, Inc.)

for Protection of Structures Against Water From the Ground," (1990), as "most effective and trouble-free," the author considers its design liabilities as far outweighing its assets, for it combines all the liabilities of negative-side waterproofing with some of the liabilities of positive-side waterproofing. Among these liabilities are the following:

- Drainage water can promote organic growth, odors, and insect infestation, plus introduction of crystallizing salts ultimately blocking drainage and obstructing flow in the wall cavity, drainage troughs, and piping.
- Exhaust-air difficulties include a requirement for introduction of make-up air at the bottom of the wall cavity, with consequent penetration of the vapor retarder, plus limitations on both gravity and mechanical ventilation.
- Sumps require a pump, possibly a back-up pump, and a generator (since power delivery may be interrupted by the flash floods requiring sumps in the first place).
- Serious leaks will be extremely difficult to locate, and repair will require major demolition or walls and tiles.
- As previously indicated, the drained-cavity system shares all the listed deficiencies of negative-side waterproofing — notably, uselessness where soil contains chemical contaminants, where discontinuities occur at projecting columns or shear walls, and where interior humidity must be controlled.

The few advantages of the drained-cavity system — adaptability to lot-line waterproofing, ability to stop water infiltration through the foundation and slab before inner walls and floor are constructed — fail to compensate for its many disadvantages.

Performance Criterion

Manufacturers of crystalline and high-density waterproofing systems rate them by water permeability, determined via US Army Corps of Engineers CRD C48-73, Permeability of Concrete (see Appendix). In this test concrete samples, 6-in. dia., 6-in.-high cylinders, coated with .05 in. thick waterproof coatings, are subjected to hydrostatic pressure of 200 psi (=461-ft head). Two treated and two untreated samples are tested. Untreated samples should exhibit a maximum 10^{-8} cm/sec. psi or less. Treated samples should not exhibit permeability exceeding 10^{-12} and 10^{-14} cm/sec.

Alerts

1. On new construction, ban installation of negative-side waterproofing under any of the following conditions:

   - Presence of corrosive soil chemicals
   - Exposure to freeze-thaw cycling
   - Low interior-humidity requirement

2. Require manufacturer's approval of applicator.

3. Require pre-installation inspection of substrate surfaces.

4. Cite surface preparation requirements.

5. Waterstops are an integral component of negative-side waterproofing.

7

Built-Up Bituminous Waterproofing Membranes

Built-up bituminous waterproofing membranes have been fading for several decades, supplanted by a panoply of new materials and systems. There are, however, several reasons for discussing them in detail disproportionate to their current popularity. First, there is the historical experience gained through a century-plus of use. Failures encountered with built-up membranes contain lessons applicable to newer materials. As one example, slippage of built-up membranes on vertical surfaces, a result of gravity plus aggravating frictional forces exerted by settling backfill, can pose a similar problem for other wall-waterproofing membranes. There is also the conservatism of some building owners, who, despite the problems and obstacles posed by traditional built-up membranes, still swear allegiance to them. And then there is the vast number of existing waterproofing projects with these materials in place. This lingering historical usage gives built-up membranes — especially coal tar pitch — an importance greater than is indicated by their currently diminished popularity. Remedial work involving an existing built-up membrane requires more than superficial acquaintance with these materials, even when the remedial material is modified bitumen or some other contemporary membrane.

Built-up waterproofing membranes are semi-flexible laminates, comprising alternating layers of normally hot-applied bitumen and felt (or fabric) reinforcement. As positive-side waterproofing components, they are fully adhered to walls, mud slabs, below-grade structural slabs, and under slabs-on-ground.

Bitumen, the most important element, serves a dual function as waterproofing agent and adhesive. Reinforcing felts and fabrics function like veneers in a sheet of plywood. They provide at least 90% of the membrane's tensile strength. Reinforcement also stabilizes the membrane, acting as a sort of matrix. And by isolating the multiple layers of waterproofing bitumen during installation, reinforcement plies promote uniform thickness in the adhesive films that bond the membrane into a structural unit.

As their chief advantage over other types of waterproofing membranes, built-up membranes exploit a property known as *redundancy*. It denotes the built-up membrane's multiple defense lines, with each of the normally three-to-five plies of reinforcement adding an extra plane of waterproofing bitumen. Redundancy accounts for the extraordinary durability of well constructed, built-up membranes.

Like their counterpart built-up roofing (BUR) membranes on low-sloped roofs, built-up membranes are the oldest waterproofing system, introduced sometime back in the nineteenth century. (As a matter of historical fact, they are the modern evolutionary progeny of the archetypal waterproofing project, the Hanging Gardens of Babylon, which exploited the waterproofing property of bitumen more than 25 centuries ago.) Also, like their roofing counterparts, built-up waterproofing membranes have steadily declined from their overwhelming predominance as the most popular waterproofing system until the past several decades. Their many competitors — prefabricated modified bitumens, prefabricated elastomeric and thermoplastic sheets, and liquid-applied coatings — have gained at built-up membranes' expense. Built-up membranes still retain a significant share of the waterproofing market because of their long record of durable service. But the relentless march of air-pollution regulations into ever growing areas continues to reduce their use.

Built-up coal tar pitch membranes are especially suitable for large plaza projects in which dependability and durability are critical. Large projects can justify the additional expense and inconvenience of bitumen-heating kettles. This traditional system is especially suitable for large projects with large, uninterrupted expanses of waterproofed decks without complex contours, elevation changes and other transitions, or penetrations.

On projects complicated by the above-listed factors, built-up membranes become impracticable, their advantages outweighed by their disadvantages. Foremost among these disadvantages is the difficulty of flashing built-up waterproofing systems. Problems with numerous, or complicated flashing problems call for some alternative system — modified bitumen, prefabricated, single-ply sheets, or, in extreme instances, even liquid-applied membranes. In fact, built-up waterproofing membranes and liquid-applied membranes are at opposite ends of the spectrum. For large expanses of uncomplicated waterproofing, where the problem is to provide dependable, durable waterproofing, hot-applied bitumen is among the prime candidates unless, of course, environmental conditions preclude bitumen heating. Where the project features complicated geometric contours and numerous penetrations, a liquid-applied system may be best. (For intermediate situations, prefabricated single-ply sheets probably offer the best compromise.)

Materials

Waterproofing bitumens are the same basic materials used for built-up roof membranes, but restricted to the lower viscosity range. For both roofing and waterproofing, bitumens come in two basic types: coal tar pitch and asphalt.

Coal tar pitch, the superior waterproofing bitumen, is a byproduct of the so-called "destructive distillation" of bituminous coal during the manufacture of coke, which furnishes the carbon alloy for steel. At temperatures well above 2,000°F in coke ovens, the distillation process drives off gases and vapors from the coal, leaving coke as a more or less pure carbon for charging the blast furnace. Cooling and condensation of the evaporated coal gases yields crude tar as one byproduct separated from other compounds in the condensate. Coal tar pitch is one of roughly 200,000 products made from the crude tar.

Petroleum asphalt (differentiated from natural asphalt) is the dense "bottom-of-the-barrel" residue left after petroleum distillation drives off the lighter hydrocarbon compounds used in gasoline, jet fuel and a huge number of other products. The asphalt content of crude petroleum varies from zero to more than half.

For waterproofing, unlike roofing, water repellance is the paramount performance criterion, with nothing else even a close second. In its protected, better insulated locations, waterproofing asphalt can sacrifice other desirable properties to this one overriding requirement. As a consequence, waterproofing asphalt is normally unblown asphalt — i.e. an asphalt not subjected to the blowing process used to produce the harder, less viscous asphalt used for roofing.

Among the liabilities of blown asphalts is deterioration from contact with soil contaminants — notably, hydroxyls. These vulnerable blown asphalts may hydrolyze in the presence of water contaminant chemicals. This corrosive process make the asphalt water-soluble. The surface may erode with the rise and fall of water tables or the flow of underground water. Built-up waterproofing membranes made from these asphalts can suffer severely shortened service lives.

Coal tar pitch owes its superior waterproofing capacity to a physical property known as *cold flow*. Even at moderate ambient temperatures — e.g., around 60°F — coal tar pitch slowly heals cracks formed at lower temperatures when it becomes a viscoelastic solid.

This cold-flow property stems from a chemical peculiarity of coal tar pitch. Although its molecules have very strong intramolecular attractions between linked benzene rings, they have relatively weak intermolecular bonds—i.e., the molecules readily flow over one another in slow response to gravity. This desirable waterproofing property limits coal tar pitch's use in roofing to very low slopes. For waterproofed decks, this limit on slope means little or nothing, since these slabs are only slightly sloped.

Waterproofing, like roofing, when applied on structural slabs, requires a slope to drain. Recommended minimum slope is 1% ($^1/_8$ in./ft.), but settlement, creep, and concrete casting tolerances can reduce this to zero. Therefore, to maintain positive slope, 2% is recommended. The maximum slope depends upon the waterproofing materials — chiefly on bitumen viscosity.

Coal tar pitch's cold-flow property obviously poses problems on vertical surfaces, where gravity exerts perpetual slippage forces in the bitumen adhesive. As a consequence, felts adhered with coal tar pitch in wall waterproofing must be backnailed into wood nailers set in concrete walls, or with concrete or masonry nails. Felts adhered with asphalt also require backnailing on walls more than 8-ft high.

Waterproofing bitumens require high penetration and low softening point, an index of a bitumen's tendency to flow when subjected to rising temperature. Tested via ASTM standards, these properties are indexes of the bitumen's ductility or toughness, important properties for membranes subjected to the dynamic stresses accompanying backfilling and placing of overburden. (See Table 7-1).

Reinforcement stabilizes waterproofing bitumens and allows the membranes to be built-up to the specific quantities required to resist hydrostatic pressure. Reinforcing felts and fabrics come in a broader spec-

Product	ASTM	Softening Point °F
Asphalt	D-449-49	
	Type I Type II Type III	115-145 145-170 180-200
Tar Pitch	D-450	
	Type II	120-140

Table 7-1   Table of recommended softening points for waterproofing bitumens. Type I asphalt and Type II coal tar pitch have self-sealing characteristics.

trum of materials for waterproofing than for roofing. Felts are glass fiber, polyester, or organic. Fabrics are woven from glass fibers, cotton, or jute.

Organic felts contain cellulose fibers — shredded wood and felted papers. Organic felts are impregnated with coal tar pitch or very soft asphalt called "flux". These felts are vulnerable to fungus rot, which weakens and eventually destroys them. Organic felts are not recommended for asphalt built-up membranes.

Fiberglass felts, the predominant felts in both roofing and waterproofing entered the U.S. market in the late 1940s. Long, glass filaments drawn from molten glass stream through tiny orifices made of precious metals. The glass filaments are usually bound with binders — phenol formaldehyde, urea-formaldehyde, or acrylic resin — and coated with a hard-grade, blown asphalt. In the cross-machine (i.e., transverse) direction, glass-fiber felts have tensile strengths of 1½ to 4 times that of organic felts. Unlike organic felts, glass-fiber felts are water resistant, and thus immune to deterioration from fungus rot.

Despite their vulnerability to moisture-caused fungus rot, organic felts are generally superior to glass-fiber felts in coal tar pitch waterproofing membranes, one of the most dependable waterproofing membrane. Glass felts D 2718 (asphalt-coated) and D 4990 (tar-coated) tend to migrate to the bottom of coal tar pitch membranes. This migration destroys the integrity of the built-up membrane, which depends on the retention of alternating layers of bitumen membrane. The advantage of water-resistant glass-fiber felts is outweighed by the loss of strength and cohesiveness caused by the felt migration. For coal tar pitch membranes, specify coal tar pitch-saturated organic felts (per ASTM D 227).

Fabrics of cotton and jute (burlap), coated with asphalt or coal tar were traditionally used to reinforce built-up waterproofing membranes, either alone or in combination with organic felts. Like organic felts, which have been largely replaced with glass felts, cotton and jute have mostly been replaced with woven glass fabrics. Cotton and jute are now mostly used with cold bitumens. Jute, a very coarse fabric, can hold more bituminous material and is thus favored for vertical surfaces, and flashing. Woven glass fabrics are coated with coal tar pitch, asphalt or resin. They possess superior strength, are rot-proof and conform to irregular surfaces. They are used mainly for flashing and reinforcing corners, and also with glass and organic felts as membrane reinforcement.

In summary, except for coal-tar saturated D 227 felts, designers should avoid all other types of organic felts and organic fabrics for waterproofing membranes. For corner reinforcing and flashing, use woven-glass fabric or polyester felts. For asphalt built-up membranes, specify polyester or glass-fiber felts, ASTM D 2178, Type IV or Type VI, available in recently improved versions that are performing well.

Specifications

Specifications for built-up waterproofing membranes range from a minimum of three to a maximum of six plies. Since the 1930s, manufacturers have published tables listing the number of plies recommended for different hydrostatic pressures (measured in ft of water, or head (=62.4 psf/ft). According to some authorities, you should specify an absolute minimum three plies for heads less than 3 ft, and up to six plies for heads of 50 to 100 ft (see Table 7-2). There is, however, no scientific basis for correlating the number of plies with hydrostatic pressure. Three plies of inorganic felt or tar-saturated organic felt are normally satisfactory, but four plies are recommended.

For equal material and construction quality, additional plies obviously increase a waterproofing membrane's water repellance and durability. For the trivial saving of reducing the number of plies, the addition of virtually any incremental risk is probably unjustified. (Saving the cost of onsite inspection is even less justifiable on a life-cycle costing basis, since poor application practice is a major source of waterproofing membrane failure and doubtless poses a greater incremental leakage risk than the reduction of one ply of reinforcing.)

Unlike built-up roof membranes, where shingling of felts is almost universal, built-up waterproofing membranes are usually "phased". In phased construction, the waterproofing contractor applies alternating layers of felt (or fabric) in separate "ply-on-ply" or "one-on-one" patterns instead of overlapping the felts, shingle-style, in a continuous operation that often completes the entire membrane. The separate operations of phased application provide superior waterproofing because they isolate each bitumen layer from the adjacent layer, creating, in effect, a multi-ply series of waterproofing layers (see Fig. 7-1).

Shingled felts, in contrast, can eventually wick moisture from an exposed felt edge diagonally down from the top of the built-up membrane to a base sheet, or, in a totally shingled membrane, through the entire cross section to the substrate. Defective application resulting in a fishmouth or other lap defect can thus open a direct leakage path through

Hydrostatic Pressure Head, feet of water	1-10 ft. (25mm-3m)	11-25 ft. (3.4 - 7.6m)	26-50 ft. (7.9 - 15.2m)
Number of plies	3	4	5

Table 7-2 Minimum number of plies recommended for various ranges of hydrostatic head. (National Roofing Contractors Association.)

"One and One" or "Cap Sheet" Method   **5 Ply Waterproofing – "Shingle" Method**

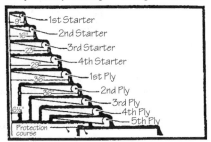

Fig. 7-1 Diagrams of shingled and phased applications. "One and One" provides a continuous film of bitumen and the direction and materials of alternate layers can be changed.

the entire membrane cross section. In a "one-on-one" patterned membrane, a similar surface defect is far less likely to result in leakage.

As a compromise between the shingled and phased application, waterproofing experts have devised a combination of phased and shingled application for membranes containing five (or six) plies. Application of three shingled plies is followed by two (or three) shingled plies. This procedure creates a continuous waterproofing film between the two multi-ply installations, meanwhile giving the applicator the convenience of shingling. Laying the top two plies perpendicular to the lower three plies also produces a membrane with more nearly isotropic strength and strain properties (a particular advantage with organic felts).

Ply-on-ply construction is, however, the norm for built-up waterproofing membranes through the entire membrane cross-section, as it promises better waterproofing quality. This procedure does require greater care in felt-laying operations — making sure that the felt is laid within several seconds after the hot bitumen is deposited. It also requires greater limitation of poor weather conditions — not only with regard to ambient temperature, but more importantly, to wind conditions. Even at relatively high ambient temperature, wind drastically accelerates hot bitumen's cooling rate, at an exponential rate with increases in wind velocity.

Combining different reinforcement materials to exploit their complementary properties offers several benefits in built-up waterproofing membranes. Alternating glass-fiber felts with woven-glass fabric alleviates the threat of interply mopping voids caused by glass-fiber felts "memory" — i.e., its tendency to retain kinks and other irregularities instead of relaxing like woven glass fabric after installation. A coal-tar-pitch membrane reinforced with alternating organic felts and woven glass fabric may be the best of all probable waterproofing worlds.

Vertical Surfaces

As previously indicated, application of built-up membranes to vertical surfaces is much more difficult than application to horizontal substrates. Instead of retaining stable positions after the adhesive bitumen cools, felts can slowly slide down vertical surfaces with the flow of the less viscous waterproofing bitumens — especially coal tar pitch. Both coal tar pitch and asphalt built-up membranes require anchorage, preferably with roofing nails driven to horizontal treated wood nailer strips, but at least with concrete nails into a concrete masonry substrate (see Fig. 7-2).

All built-up membranes are anchored at the tops of foundation walls. This top anchorage may be sufficient for asphalt membranes less than 10 ft. high. Coal tar pitch membranes, however, require backnailing at a minimum vertical spacing of 8 ft. Asphalt membranes require a minimum 10-ft vertical spacing.

In vertical applications the felts are usually laid vertically. They are cut into 6 or 8-ft lengths and either shingled or laid ply-on-ply. Application may proceed full height, for a length of wall. The membrane is then covered with protection board and backfilled. Backfilling each lift eliminates the need to install scaffolds, with the application proceeding from

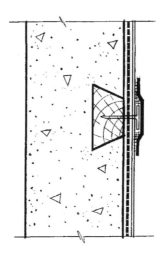

Fig. 7-2   Vertical cross section through foundation wall shows top of membrane and protection board anchored to foundation wall with capped masonry nail, driven into horizontally oriented wood nailer at 12-in. spacing, 2 to 5 in. below top of sheet. A 4-in.-square piece of protection board set in roofing cement shields masonry nail cap.

the bottom up. Because mops cannot carry as much bitumen to vertical surfaces, it is often necessary to apply two moppings to attain specified interply mopping weight. Note that built-up membranes require a cant at reentrant angles. They are also reinforced at interior and exterior corners, both vertical and horizontal (see Fig. 7-3).

All built-up membranes, for both slabs and walls, require priming of substrates to provide a tack surface assuring continuous, dependable adhesion. Priming of parged masonry and concrete surfaces absorbs dust and other contaminants that impair adhesion and create voids that expose the membrane to punctures or progressive disbondment.

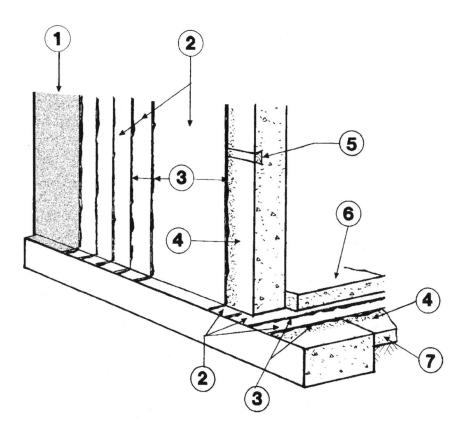

Fig. 7-3   Typical application of plies on foundation wall. (1) Protection board, (2) felt or fabric plies, (3) bitumen, (4) primer, (5) nailer, (6) structural slab, (7) mud mat.

Built-Up Membrane Failure Modes

In their normal subsurface locations, shielded from solar radiation, extreme temperature changes, and wind forces attacking roof membranes, built-up waterproofing membranes are virtually immune to several maladies that afflict built-up roof membranes — notably blistering and ridging. They do, however, share in built-up roof membranes' vulnerability to the following:

- Slippage (on vertical surfaces)
- Rotting of reinforcing felts
- Punctures
- Splitting
- Defective Flashing

Slippage on vertical surfaces is a major problem for built-up waterproofing membranes, especially those made of coal tar pitch. As previously noted, built-up membranes require backnailing anchorage on vertical surfaces. Slippage failures can leave partial areas of foundation wall unprotected as the membrane slowly descends.

Avoiding slippage failures is not difficult. It merely requires backnailing of built-up membranes on vertical surfaces. Horizontal wood nailers should be cast into the exterior concrete wall face at maximum vertical distance of 8 ft for coal tar pitch and 10 ft for asphalt membranes. All membranes require backnailing at the top (see Fig. 7-2).

Backfill settlement is an aggravating factor promoting slippage. To the gravitational slippage force, settlement adds the frictional force of downward-moving soil mass in contact with protection boards. (See expanded discussion of backfill settlement in Chapter 12, "Waterproofing Failures").

Rotting of organic felts is a disappearing problem as their use has drastically declined. Organic fibers are notoriously susceptible to fungus rot promoted by moist conditions.

There is, however, one exception to the general taboo against organic felts. In coal tar pitch membranes under continuous hydrostatic pressure, organic felts may prove better reinforcement than glass fiber felts. Organic felts are superior to their alternatives in segregating the interply moppings of adhesive bitumen into separate waterproofing layers. Their lower tensile strength counts for little in waterproofing membranes, where waterproofing quality is paramount, and perpetual submersion can protect them from the fungus rot that thrives in moist, but not in submerged conditions.

Punctures and abrasions can destroy the waterproofing capacity of built-up membranes if the contractor fails to install protection boards immediately after completion of membrane application. Membranes on vertical surfaces can be damaged by backfill operations, even with protection boards in place if the backfill includes sharp-edge rocks or the bulldozer or grader operator slams a steel blade against the wall. Unprotected membranes on slab-on-ground and structural slabs lacking protection boards can be damaged by reinforcing bar supports, the bars themselves, edges of reinforcement mesh, electrical conduit, pipes, foot traffic, concrete buggies, vibrators, rakes, spades, and other puncture-threatening hazards associated with construction.

Built-up membranes (like other types) are also vulnerable to rupture from hydrostatic pressure exerted against an irregular substrate — e.g., a honeycombed concrete surface. This pressure can exert a combination of shearing and flexural stresses and ultimately rupture the membrane. Materials of greater elasticity — notably modified bitumens, PVC and synthetic rubber — have a great advantage over built-up membranes in resisting such stresses.

Lack of adhesion to the substrate, resulting from moisture, curing agents, and omission of primer (or defective application of primer) can also promote puncture of built-up membranes (as well as other types.)

Splitting is a lesser problem for built-up waterproofing membranes than for built-up roof membranes, because waterproofing membranes are not subjected to the extreme temperature dimensional changes experienced by exposed roof membranes. Splitting in waterproofing membranes is limited to the propagation of tensile stresses from shrinkage cracking of concrete or masonry substrates, or failure to reinforce corners and dynamic construction joints.

Defective flashing, resulting from use of felts instead of more flexible fabrics at external corners, is another common cause of built-up waterproofing membrane failure. The erroneous use of felts creates a problem similar to that created by the failure to apply primer to a substrate. Poor backing for the membrane makes it vulnerable to puncture or other mechanical damage. It may also open a leakage path, where stiff glass fiber felts, in particular, fail to close an overlapped joint.

Alerts

1. Provide minimum $1/8$ in. slope (1%) (preferably $1/4$ in.) in structural deck.

2. Slope deck away from expansion joints and rising walls.

3. Avoid organic felts and asphalt on horizontal surfaces and elsewhere where they will be in constant contact with water.

4. Use fabrics for plane transitions. Glass felts, in particular, cannot be carried around corners.

5. Prefer coal tar pitch to asphalt, especially where hydrostatic pressure is high.

6. Detail cants and bevels at corners.

7. Specify one-on-one, phased application rather than shingling.

8. Even if coal-tar-pitch built-up membrane is permitted by pollution-abating ordinances, beware of specifying this product where toxic odors may emanate from the coal tar pitch after construction is completed.

8

Single-Ply
Waterproofing
Membranes

The new membrane materials discussed in this chapter have evolved largely as solutions to problems with traditional built-up waterproofing membranes. There are two major reasons for the dramatic decline of built-up waterproofing membranes in recent decades. They are labor-intensive, field-fabricated products that require diligent installation. Moreover, their bitumen-heating kettles foul the air with hazardous hydrocarbons increasingly banned by pollutant-abating ordinances. New materials, products of the postwar chemistry marvels that have transformed many other industries, have filled this vacuum left by the decline of built-up membranes. This chapter, accordingly, covers modified bitumens, single-ply elastomeric and thermoplastic sheets. Omitted from this chapter are liquid-applied membranes (LAMs) and bentonite, which is not a membrane. The unique nature of these two materials qualifies them for their own individual chapters (i.e., Chapter 9 and 10).

Polymer-Modified Bitumens

Polymer-modified bitumens can be considered an advanced stage in the evolution of traditional built-up below-grade waterproofing membranes, reducing their three to six-ply, field-fabricated construction to a single sheet, generally 60 mils thick. Compared with built-up membranes, modified bitumens offer much greater flexibility and breaking strain, with comparable toughness and puncture resistance. For conservative building owners who want to exploit the benefits of progress without making a total break with traditional waterproofing technology, modified bitumens offer a comfortable compromise, less radical than the new single-ply elastomeric or thermoplastic sheets. Via its many virtues, modified bitumen waterproofing enjoys skyrocketing popularity.

Like the new single-ply sheet materials, modified bitumens are a triumph of polymer chemistry, popular in both roofing and waterproofing applications. Various polymers — atactic polyproplene (APP), sequenced-butadiene styrene (SBS), styrene ethylene butylene styrene (SEBS), and polyisobutylene — are compounded with asphalt (or in rare instances, coal tar pitch) to make it more viscous, less temperature-sensitive, and more elastic. Asphalt is a viscoelastic solid at low temperatures and a viscous fluid at high temperatures, with radically different properties (e.g., breaking strain, tensile strength, thermal coefficient of expansion/contraction). Modified bitumen has superior properties — up to 150% breaking strain vs. 2% for built-up membranes, plus much higher cold-temperature flexibility. Modified bitumen can thus resist tensile and flexural stresses that would rupture an asphalt (or coal tar pitch) built-up membrane. (See Table 8-1, for modified-bitumen waterproofing performance criteria.)

Modified-bitumen waterproofing membranes are suitable for all three components: structural slabs, slabs-on-ground, and foundation walls. Their uses include all the applications previously dominated by hot-mopped, built-up waterproofing membranes. Modified bitumens combine two big labor-saving advantages in the field: (1) substitution of a single, prefabricated sheet for several felts incorporated into built-up membranes, and (2) *cold application* instead of built-up membranes' hot application, with its labor-intensive hot kettles and air-polluting fumes.

Modified bitumens offer special benefits on vertical surfaces, where the ease of hanging single sheets of factory-controlled thickness eliminates the problem of hot-mopping multiple plies of built-up membrane or brushing, trowelling or squeegeeing two layers of LAM. (See Fig. 8-1).

Contemporary modified bitumen membranes have evolved from a 70-mil sheet introduced roughly 30 years ago by W.R. Grace, under the proprietary name, Bithuthene. Like contemporary modified bitumen products, Grace's Bituthene was a rubberized asphalt, modified by reclaimed rubber and resin modifiers, laminated to a special cross-laminated HDPE film. After Grace's patents had expired, other manufacturers began marketing basically similar products, but with different asphalt modifiers. These self-adhering sheets require substrate *priming*, to complete the chemical curing that assures tight adhesive bond at the membrane-substrate interface. They also require pressure rolling of field seams, to assure tight adhesion at these vulnerable joints (see Fig. 8-2).

The predominant contemporary modified bitumen waterproofing membrane is a self-adhering, 56-mil sheet laminated to a 4-mil HDPE film.

This HDPE film provides multiple benefits:

- increased tensile strength and breaking strain
- resistance to acid soils and organic growth

Property	Test Method (ASTM, except as noted)	Typical Value
Thickness (Mils) (Incl 4 Mil HDPE)		60
Flexibility, 180° bend over 25mm (1 in.) mandrel at -43°C (-45°F)	D 146 or D 1970	Unaffected
Tensile Strength Membrane (PSL)	D 412 Die C Modified	250-320
Elongation, Ultimate Failure of Rubberized Asphalt	D 412 Die C Modified	300%
Crack Cycling at -32°C (-25°F), 100 Cycles	C 836	Unaffected
Lap Adhesion at Minimum Application Temperature	D 1876 Modified	4 to 7 lb/in.
Peel Strength 16/in.	D 903	7.5 to 9
Puncture Resistance Membrane (lbs)	C 154	40
Resistance to Hydrostatic Head (ft)	D 5385	150 to 230
Exposure to Fungi in Soil, 16 weeks	GSA-PBS 07115 16 weeks	Unaffected
Permeance (perms)	E 96 Method B.	.05
Water Absorption (by wt)	D 570	0.1 to 0.25

Table 8-1 Suggested prescriptive and performance criteria for modified-bitumen waterproofing membranes.

Fig. 8-1   Before primer application, the concrete
foundation wall surface requires grinding of fins
created at formwork joints where concrete was
extruded from gaps between plywood panels. Air
holes and other depressions in surface also require repair — i.e., grout fill to create a smooth
substrate for the waterproofing membrane.

- improved resilience, self-healing property, and bondability
- easier joint seaming
- improved resistance to vapor flow
- enhanced crack bridging
- improved bonding adhesion

These self-adhering sheets have a silicone release paper on the modified-bitumen side, designed to prevent sticking. System accessories for
installation include a solvent primer (some in a VOC-compliant formulation), a water-based primer, mastics, trowel-grade sealants generally called
"liquid membranes". (For a step-by-step depiction of membrane applica-

Fig. 8-2   Field-spliced seams over butted membrane joints between self-adhering, modified-bitumen waterproofing sheets must be rolled to compress the contact adhesive and assure tight bond between 6 in. wide splicing tape and membrane sheets at these vulnerable joints. (TC MiraDRI - Top Photo) & (W. R. Meadows, Inc. - Bottom Illustration.)

tion to a foundation wall, see Fig. 8-3, which shows the installation process from priming of the substrate through application of an inside corner strip and mastic application. See also Fig. 8-4, showing application of self-adhering modified bitumen membrane to a mud slab).

Fig. 8-3 Application of a modified-bitumen waterproofing membrane to foundation wall starts with priming of previously repaired concrete substrate (top left); followed by removal of release paper from the membrane (center left); and application of corner strips (bottom left). Workmen then apply the membrane (top right); apply roller pressure to assure tight adhesion at the membrane-concrete interface (center right). Workman seals membrane terminations with rubberized-asphalt mastic (bottom right). (TC MiraDRI).

Fig. 8-4 Application of a self-adhering modified-bitumen membrane to a mud slab creates an ancillary problem — i.e., disposal of the release paper peeled from the unrolled modified-bitumen sheets.

Like every other waterproofing material, however, modified bitumen has some limitations:

- It is unsuitable for blindside application.
- It does not adhere to slabs-on-ground when applied to a mud slab.
- Like most waterproofing sheets, modified bitumen membranes have poor ultraviolet-radiation resistance (and thus should not be exposed to the atmosphere).
- Its application is limited to temperatures of 25°F and higher.

Waterproofing designers should be alerted to the efforts of several manufacturers of modified-bitumen sheets to extend products previously limited to roofing applications into waterproofing. These expanded waterproofing uses are generally limited to plazas, though a few manu-facturers have published specifications for waterproofing of foundations.

Designers should beware of the more rigorous requirements that may disqualify modified-bitumen roofing sheets as waterproofing mem-branes. Excessive water absorption is a major factor disqualifying most APP and SBS-modified bitumen roofing membranes as waterproofing membranes. To qualify as waterproofing membranes, modified bitumen sheets should have a maximum water absorption of 3.2% (by weight) per recently published ASTM standards. Test data indicate that absorption rates for these smooth-surfaced, modified-bitumen roof membranes range from a highly satisfactory 1% or less up to a highly unsatisfactory 10% or higher. Moreover, these tests are conducted under more or less ideal laboratory conditions, on membrane specimens with sealed edges. These lenient laboratory conditions may be satisfactory for testing roof membranes, but not for membranes in a perpetually wet environment. Wicking of water can cause waterproofing membranes to swell and disbond. For this reason, reinforced modified bitumen roof membranes are generally rejected as waterproofing membranes.

Several cold-applied built-up waterproofing membrane systems feature materials that could be classified as modified bitumens. In one such system, a polymer-modified asphalt adhesive can be cold-applied to a polymer-modified sheet reinforced with a glass mat. This system is applied shingle fashion, with one to three plies, depending on hydrostatic pressure. Plies are rolled in, hung, or rolled out on the flat. The adhesive reacts with the polymer-modified sheets and fuses them. After curing, the individual plies are indiscernible — i.e., the membrane becomes an integral, reinforced sheet rather than a multi-ply, built-up laminate. As a major advantage, this system can be applied to damp surfaces.

Another unique, cold-applied system features a multi-laminated sheet, usually 4 x 8 ft in plan, with taped seams, applied to primed surfaces (concrete or parge-coated masonry). It is suitable for both vertical and horizontal surfaces.

Application starts with repair of the concrete surface to provide a smooth substrate for the waterproofing membrane. Workmen then prime the substrate, peel the anti-stick (releasing) sheets, position the membrane, and roll-press them into the primer. Panels can be cut and trimmed with roofers' knives, fitted for tight butt joints. As the final step, workmen prime the splice bands at the butt joints before applying a 6-in.-wide gusset tape with the same roll pressure applied to adhere the membrane panels. The tape-membrane splice tests at a higher parallel shear strength (33 psi) than the membrane-concrete adhesion, according to the manufacturer.

Elastomeric and Thermoplastic Membranes

The principal single-ply sheets used in waterproofing are butyl rubber, 60 to 120 mil thick and specially formulated PVC sheets, 59 to 120 mils thick. Both types differ from their synthetic rubber and PVC counterparts used as roof membranes.

Butyl wins out over EPDM, the most popular synthetic rubber roofing material, chiefly because of its superior water absorption rates: 1%-2% vs. 4% for EPDM (see Table 8-2). Butyl also offers vastly superior vapor permeance, .0025 perms vs. .05 perms for EPDM. The principal advantage of EPDM, its excellent ultraviolet resistance, is largely wasted on below-grade waterproofing sheets.

Physical Requirements for Vulcanized Rubber Sheets		
	I	II
Type	EPDM	Butyl
Thickness, min, in. (mm)	.054, (1.37)	.054, (1.37)
Hardness, durometer A	60±10	60±10
Tensile strength, min psi (MPa)	1300 (9)	1200 (8.3)
Elongation, ultimate min %	300	300
Tensile set max %	10	10
Tear resistance min, lbf/in. (kN/m)	150 (26.2)	150 (26.2)
Brittleness temperature, max °F (°C)	-49 (-45)	-40 (-40)
Heat aging at 240°F		
Tensile strength, min psi (MPa)	1200 (8.3)	900 (6.2)
Elongation ultimate, min %	210	210
Linear dimensional change, max %	±1	±2
Water absorption max, mass %	4	2
Factory seam strength min, psi (MPa)	50 (8.8)	50 (8.8)
Water vapor permeance max, perms mg/pasm^2	.060 (3.5)	.0025 (.14)
Resistance to soil burial (% change max in original value)		
Breaking factory	10	10
Elongation at break	10	10
Puncture resistance lbs (Kg)	70 (32)	95 (43)

Table 8-2 Butyl prescriptive criteria. (American Society for Testing and Materials.)

PVC (polyvinyl chloride) sheets, like butyl, have the essential properties of low absorptance (2%) and low permeance, which makes PVC the only thermoplastic material recommended for waterproofing (see Table 8-3). CSPE (Hypalon) and other plastic roofing sheets are unsuitable for waterproofing because of their high permeability, high water absorption, or both.

PVC waterproofing differs from PVC roofing in both thickness (59 to 120 mils for waterproofing vs. 45 to 60-mil maximum for roof membranes) and also in composition. Additives have been introduced to resist algae and alkalines. UV stabilizers and high-temperature inhibitors have been removed.

Both butyl and PVC offer excellent resistance to bacteria, fungi, and soil chemicals. Butyl, however, can deteriorate in contact with petroleum-based poisoners and oils. Hydrocarbons can similarly promote deterioration of PVC.

Both butyl, as a representative of synthetic rubber materials, and PVC, as a representative of thermoplastics, owe their high tensile strength chiefly to the reinforcing fabric. Tensile properties are also enhanced by the long chain molecules, built-up from monomers (the basic molecular units). Polymerization increases monomeric molecular weights from 30 to 150 range, to so-called macromolecules, 100 to 10,000 times as large.

A major chemical distinction differentiates thermosetting synthetic rubber sheets — e.g., butyl — from thermoplastic polymer sheets — e.g., PVC. Thermosetting materials harden permanently when heated, like an egg. Thermoplastics soften when heated, like butter, and harden when cooled. With thermoplastic materials, thermal cycling can repeatedly change their physical characteristics; viscosity changes accompany temperatures changes.

This contrasting behavior stems from a basic difference in molecular structure. Thermosetting resins start as tiny threads. Heat promotes chemical reactions that cross-link these tiny molecular threads, creating a permanently rigid matrix. This molecularly cross-linked structure makes a thermosetting material more resistant to heat, solvents, general chemical attack, and creep (i.e., plastic elongation under sustained stress). Unlike thermoplastics, elastomers not only elongate, but recover their original shape as well, thus accommodating stress concentrations that can split built-up bituminous membranes. Their breaking strains range upward from 300%, over 100 times that of built-up membranes.

Thermoplastics comprise long, threadlike molecules, so intertwined at room temperature that they are hard to pull apart. When heated, however, they slide past one another, like liquid molecules, and the material will elongate (i.e., creep) under constant stress.

As one tentative general conclusion about thermosetting vs. thermoplastic materials, you might consider thermosetting materials as superior to thermoplastics on a direct material-to-material basis. But ther-

Parameters	ASTM Test Method	Typical Physical Properties
Color	-	orange/grey
Overall thickness mm (inches), min.	D-751	3.00 (.120)
Tensile strength, psi, min.	D-638	1,600 psi
Elongation at break, min.,%	D-638	300 MD 280 CMD
Seam strength, min. % of ten. strength*	D-638	90%
Retention of properties after heat aging	D-3045	-
Tensile strength, min. % of original	D-638	95%
Elongation, min % of original	D-638	95%
Tear resistance (lbf)	D-1004	35
Low temperature bend (-40°F)	D-2136	pass
Linear dimensional change, max., %	D-1204	0.01
Weight change after immersion in water, maximum, %	D-570	2.0
Puncture resistance	FEDERAL TEST METHOD 2065	66.74

*Failure occurs through membrane rupture, not seam failure.

Table 8-3 PVC prescriptive criteria. (Sarnafil, Inc.)

moplastic materials offer superior, easier field joint-sealing processes. Thermosetting synthetic rubbers require use of self-adhering tapes or contact adhesives, which require a wait before the field-seaming process can be completed. Moreover, these field-fabricated seams never attain the tensile strength of the sheet material. PVC seams, in contrast, are as strong as the base material. They are welded with hot air at temperatures above 1,000°F. Butyl and PVC are available in up to 20 ft x 100-ft sheets, thus minimizing field seams.

Though generally less environmentally hazardous than hot kettles for built-up bituminous membranes, solvent-based primers and adhesives for field joint-seaming in butyl membranes may exceed VOC limits.

PVC sheets are normally reinforced with non-woven glass-fiber felts, which increase both tensile strength and puncture resistance. Butyl rubber normally requires no reinforcement.

Application

Both butyl and PVC sheets are suitable for application to all three basic waterproofed components: structural slabs, slabs-on-ground, and foundation walls. Butyl sheets are usually fully adhered both to horizontal and vertical substrates (see Fig. 8-5). They can, however, be loose-laid on framed slabs and, for slabs-on-ground, over mud slabs. PVC sheets can also be fully adhered or loose-laid over framed slabs.

Fig. 8-5 Workmen apply adhesive to butyl sheet waterproofing a concrete foundation wall. (Carlisle Coatings & Waterproofing, Inc.)

Butyl sheets are adhered or loose laid over a "smooth" concrete slab, whereas PVC requires a "floor quality" steel trowel finish for fully adhered. Butyl sheets can be fully adhered by hanging 8-ft to 10-ft strips as backfilling progresses. Alternatively, sheets can be hung for the full height of the foundation by bonding the upper 25% and 18 in. on the sides. This saves on adhesive, but requires better concrete surfaces than loose laid.

On vertical surfaces, there are notable differences in application techniques for the two materials. Butyl sheets are difficult to install on vertical surfaces. With their lack of reinforcement and low elastic modulus (i.e., stress/strain ratio), synthetic rubber sheets tend to stretch when vertically oriented. Reinforced PVC sheets, with their higher elastic modulus, are less vulnerable to this problem. In contrast with butyl sheets, which must be fully adhered to vertical surfaces, the less stretchable PVC sheets are adhered to mechanically fastened thermoplastic discs. This process facilitates installation by dividing it into two more readily performed operations: (1) installing the mechanical anchors, and (2) following with application of the sheets.

Butyl and PVC sheets on vertical surfaces may be oriented either vertically or horizontally, but vertical orientation is preferred.

PVC is usually draped down from the top whereas butyl is applied by rolling into the adhesive from the bottom up. The orientation that results in the fewest seams is preferred.

On framed structural slabs and slabs-on-ground, there is no essential difference between installation practices for butyl and PVC. PVC is laid out and heat welded. Butyl is laid out, relaxed, and seamed with tape. It is preferable, but optional, to use cover tape on seams for 60-mil butyl; it is mandatory for thicker sheets.

Loose-laid waterproofing membranes are often compartmentalized, by adhering the membrane to the slab in an approximately 10-ft grid. This practice localizes leaking — i.e., restricts the distance between the leak source (e.g., a defective lap seam) and its horizontal distance from the leak's appearance (e.g., at a crack in the ceiling surface of a framed slab). The manufacturer's water cutoff mastic is an appropriate adhesive for compartmentalizing, which blocks lateral flow of leakwater from the compartment where it has penetrated the membrane.

Under slabs-on-ground, rubber and plastic membranes can be laid loose on mud slabs, or compacted sand. To shield them from puncturing they must be covered with protection boards. This practice also prevents their adhesion to the concrete slab above. Asphalt-based protection boards cannot be placed directly on PVC membranes. The system requires an isolating layer of polyproplene geotextile and protection layer of HDPE or PVC to prevent damaging contact with hydrocarbons.

Flashing for butyl membranes consists of non-vulcanized EPDM sheets, which conform to their backing and later cure to attain the elastic properties of fully cured (i.e., vulcanized) material.

PVC is flashed with the same membrane sheet material, usually reinforced, except at corners and penetrations, where conformability rather than strength is a prime requirement.

Modified Bitumen Failure Modes

Modified bitumen failures can be categorized as disbonding from the substrate, defective seams and ruptures. Disbonding is the most prevalent (See Fig. 8-6). It results in blistering, slippage, and wrinkling.

Disbonding results from a number of factors, notably:

• Failure to promptly cover the membrane after installation. Self-adhering modified bitumen sheets have a film of HDPE that is an effective vapor retarder. When the sheet is exposed to sunlight for relatively short periods of time the black surface temperatures soar, vaporizing volatiles in the primer. (Applying the primer too thickly or installing the sheet too soon aggravates this situation.) The HDPE prevents the release of the vapors, resulting in blistering and disbonding. This condition is frequently found at brick shelves where masonry erection is often delayed for weeks or months.

Fig. 8-6 Slippage, resulting in total disbonding of self-adhering modified-bitumen waterproofing membrane on foundation wall, is accompanied by delamination of drainage composite.

- Failure to seal the top edge of vertically applied self-adhering sheets at day's end. This permits moisture to flow behind the sheet and disbond the top edge. Dust and dirt from backfilling operations inhibit adhesion. When the next sheet is applied, there is a continuous unadhered strip.
- Failures attributable to incorrect primer application — e.g., failure to reprime if the sheet is not installed the same day; to wait until the primer has dried, with all solvents flashed off; or to use the appropriate grade, consistent with the ambient temperature.
- Failure to fill tie rod holes, bug holes and others flush with the concrete surface.

Defective seams result from two main causes:

- Failure to roll the seams or to exert sufficient pressure promptly after application.
- Failure to cut out fishmouths rather than trying to flatten them.

A third allied problem is the lack of patches over tee joints.

The most common cause of rupture is a failure to reinforce dynamic joints — e.g., where a structural slab bears on a foundation wall.

Alerts

Modified Bitumens

1. Beware of modified bitumen roofing sheets promoted as waterproofing membranes. (Check their water absorption rates, plus their vulnerability to wicking of moisture through their edges).

2. Require inspection of all modified bitumen installations, with special attention to pressure rolling of membrane and field-splicing seams, to assure tight bonding adhesion. (See Fig. 8-7).

3. Require sealing of top edges at end of day's work.

4. Use liquid waterproofing on vertical and horizontal reentrant angles to seal between sheet and substrate.

Butyl and PVC

1. Assure that bonding adhesive is kept off seams.

2. Check PVC seams at beginning of each day and after lunch to verify welder settings (calibration).
3. Verify that substrates are smooth and clean.
4. Walk each seam and check with a pointed tool at end of day's work.
5. Walk seams after flood testing.

Fig. 8-7   Horizontally oriented joints of self-adhering modified-bitumen membrane applied to deep foundation wall should be inspected by QA inspector to assure pressure-rolling of seams. (Waterproofing Systems of New Jersey.)

Chapter

9

Liquid-Applied
Membranes

Liquid-applied membranes (LAMs) are field-fabricated from a variety of liquid components applied to the substrate via rollers, brush, spray, trowel, or squeegee and cured via chemical reaction, exposure to moisture, solvent evaporation or by cooling. They are often applied in two-coat systems (see Fig. 9-1).

The major distinction between LAMs concerns their basic application technique — i.e., *hot-applied* or *cold-applied*. Hot-applied LAMs are generally far superior to cold-applied. They cure faster (almost as soon as they cool); they are usually reinforced (unlike the majority of cold-applied LAMs); and they are roughly three times as thick as cold-applied systems (thereby providing superior puncture resistance, tensile strength, and other desirable properties).

Hot-applied LAMs nonetheless share with cold-applied LAMs the necessity of more rigorous field controls than alternative waterproofing systems. These requirements start with substrate preparation, which demands fastidious care and cleanliness, a challenge to construction workers' practical religion. Weather conditions are critical during application, and the application process itself places further demands on the applicator's abilities. In short, a reliable contractor, backed by a good quality assurance (QA) program is essential to produce a dependable LAM system.

If you put a coating in a can, there is a high probability that someone will open the can and use the contents improperly. That is a durably accurate warning against careless use of LAM materials.

Despite these disadvantages, there are some projects for which their advantages make liquid-applied systems the obvious choice — i.e., when prefabricated-sheet systems can be almost immediately rejected. Their

Fig. 9-1 Notched squeegee applies single-component, moisture-cured tar ure-thane film, one of several methods — also including rolling, brushing, and spray-ing — for installing liquid-applied membranes (LAMs) to concrete substrates.

self-flashing property and their availability in thixotropic grades suitable for vertical surfaces make liquid-applied systems suitable for projects with complex geometric contours; multiple plane transitions; and numerous pipe, duct, and other penetrations. Any one of these complicating factors can disqualify conventional, prefabricated-sheet waterproofing systems from an experienced designer's consideration.

Determining the precise degree of complexity needed to establish the superiority of a liquid-applied membrane devolves into a risk-balanc-ing exercise. But it doesn't take too many changes in a structural slab's elevation, unsymmetrical or irregular flashing contours, or penetrations through slabs and walls to make the flashing details of a prefabricated sheet system less practicable than the extra care required in preparation and application of a liquid-applied membrane.

Historical Background

LAMs were first introduced as waterproofing systems at least as far back as the early 1960s. According to the late Philip Maslow, an expert on construction sealants and waterproofing techniques, pour-grade polysul-fide sealants provided the stimulus to expand this material's use into LAMs. The polysulfide sealant formulation was modified to increase its breaking strain, as a means of preventing shrinkage cracking in a concrete substrate from propagating through the adhered LAM.[1] In the pioneering LAM formulations, liquid polysulfide polymers were blended with coal tar oils.

Several fatal problems soon led to the disappearance of polysulfide systems as LAM waterproofing. Their sensitivity to temperature posed a major obstacle. At high temperatures, they cured too quickly; at low temperatures, too slowly. Their pot life was also limited below a tolerable duration.

Polyurethanes, similarly blended with coal tar oils, solved the problems associated with polysulfide polymers. As usually happens, in construction as in economics, there is no free lunch. Though not *temperature*-sensitive, the polyurethanes were *moisture*-sensitive. This problem was resolved, however, and today's systems include a hot-applied rubberized asphalt system, in use for over a third of a century, according to one manufacturer.

Materials

Liquid-applied waterproofing membranes come in the following types:

- Hot- or cold-applied polymer-modified asphalt
- Single-component coal-tar modified urethane
- Two-component urethane

The above listing *excludes* unreinforced asphalt cutbacks and emulsions that cure via evaporation of water or petroleum solvents. These materials qualify only for *dampproofing*, not *waterproofing* (see Chapter 3, "Dampproofing").

Compared with single-component membranes, two-component membranes offer several notable advantages:

- Fewer weather restrictions on application
- More predictable curing
- Longer shelf life

These advantages stem from the two-component coatings' chemical curing, which makes them independent of site humidity. They can be applied at lower ambient temperatures than single-component coatings and will cure at lower temperatures. Most single-component coatings require exposure to air with limited absolute humidity to assure proper curing.

---

1. Philip Maslow, *Chemical Materials for Construction*, Structure Publishing Co., Farmington, MI, 1974, p. 464

Single-component coatings' curing rates are less predictable than those of two-component coatings. This exposes them to construction damage avoided by two-component systems. Premature installation of protection boards on single-component coatings can retard — or at worst, prevent — complete curing. Incomplete curing impairs waterproofing integrity.

As its one comparative disadvantage, two-component coatings require thorough field mixing to assure complete blending. And though they have longer shelf life than single-component coatings, observance of a two-component coating's shelf-life limit is even more critical than for single-component coatings.

The tradeoffs in construction convenience vs. dependable curing are also exemplified by the few liquid-applied coatings that require jacketed (i.e., double-boiler) kettles on the jobsite for hot application. Polymer-modified asphalt coatings designed for hot application require these more expensive kettles. As a counterbalancing advantage, hot-applied coatings offer almost instantaneous curing.

In contrast, cold-applied LAMs require much longer curing times - in extreme cases up to 72 hours at 75°F (and more at lower ambient temperatures). At a minimum, cold-applied LAMs require overnight (12-hr) curing time at 70°F, 50% RH (longer at lower temperature or lower RH). Two-coat, cold-applied membranes may require 48-hour curing time, to assure evaporation of solvents in the underlying coat. (Pinholing can occur if curing time is inadequate.)

As a consequence of these long, variable curing times required for cold-applied LAMs, hot-applied membranes are much less vulnerable to sudden temperature drops, rain, or premature traffic. This obviously gives hot-applied LAMs a huge advantage over cold-applied.

Pros And Cons

In comparing LAMs in general with competitive types of waterproofing systems, the designer can follow these preliminary design rules:

- Specify LAM on projects with many penetrations
- Specify LAM on projects with complex contoured surfaces and plane changes
- Specify LAM on new construction with cast-in-place structural concrete decks (min. 110-pcf concrete density)
- Favor urethane LAMs where resistance to chemical attack is a major design requirement
- Use LAMs on horizontal surfaces (i.e., plazas, structural slabs, slabs-on-ground) rather than vertical surfaces (where it is difficult to assure adequate and uniform thickness)

Weighing against LAMs are the following negative factors:

- Beware of LAMs on rough, irregular (i.e., non-planar or ripply) surfaces. (For obvious reasons, rough surfaces make it difficult to achieve minimum thickness.) Unless the LAM material is thixotropic and trowelable, two coats are normally required to assure minimum thickness. For mud slabs, which normally have rough, irregular surfaces, hot LAM can be specified, because you can get a roughly 200-mil dry-film thickness, more than three times the minimum 60-mil thickness for cold-applied LAMs.
- For equally obvious reasons, don't specify LAM over lightweight insulating concrete, over precast concrete or prestressed concrete units or concrete fill over these members. Lightweight insulating concrete fills are subject to excessive shrinkage cracks, which can propagate upward into the LAM.
- Beware of LAMs' relatively limited crack-spanning ability.
- Don't specify LAM on concrete decks over non-vented steel forms.

These non-vented decks can blister the LAM with vapor-pressure buildup resulting from excess moisture retention. LAM substrates require a relatively dry substrate.

- Don't specify hot-applied LAM on walls, unless they are parged. (Vertical surfaces make control of uniform thickness difficult.)
- Don't specify cold-applied LAM on masonry walls. (The parging cracks.)
- Beware of LAMs for remedial waterproofing projects, because the substrate may be contaminated with incompatible materials or too coarse for economical application.
- Don't use cold-applied LAMs when ambient temperature may fall below 45°F during application. (Hot-applied LAMs are an exception to this rule.)
- Avoid LAMs where tight construction schedules may force application before the concrete cures, and before the inevitable shrinkage cracking occurs. (Superplasticized or high-early-strength concrete can alleviate this problem, but at a substantial cost increase.)
- Don't specify LAMs in confined spaces where VOC limits or fume toxicity are limiting factors.
- Don't permit LAMs to be used to fill or level surface irregularities.
- Don't use LAMs under a continuous head of water. A compression of 95% maximum dry density per ASTM D 1557 or greater acting on an unsupported membrane can cause it to deform, extrude, or even rupture.

- Because some LAMs emit fumes during the curing stage, which might be toxic to sensitized people, avoid their use on, or even in close proximity to, occupied buildings. Moisture-cured, coal-tar-pitch modified urethane is one LAM that can emit odors. Since LAM is especially popular on waterproofed plazas, where air intakes, ventilators, and adjacent windows may admit fumes into the building, the waterproofing designer must be especially alert to toxic emissions in such applications. Check with the manufacturer to avoid these curing-stage emissions.

General Requirements

Formulated after long experience, the most important prescriptive criteria for cold-applied LAMs set minimum solids content and dry-film thickness (DFT). Minimum solids content is 80% (by weight); minimum thickness (DFT) is 60 mils (double the 30 mil thickness set for LAMs on sprayed polyurethane foam roofs).

Minimum 80% solids content (i.e., residual material remaining permanently in place after initial evaporation of solvents) is required to reduce the probability of pinholing, a major defect that can impair the waterproofing integrity of liquid-applied coatings. As discussed later in this chapter, pinholing is the most prevalent defect in liquid-applied waterproofing membranes.

Minimum coating thickness (60-mil DFT) averts several hazards associated with liquid-applied coatings. Substrate cracking, propagated vertically from a concrete slab or horizontally through a concrete or masonry wall, can produce stress concentrations in thin coatings where irregular substrate reduces cross-sectional thickness (see Fig. 9-2). Thicker membranes are also less susceptible to wrinkling from absorbed moisture, which expands the membrane and disbonds it from its substrate. Thicker membranes also reduce the incidence of pinholing, by reducing the probability of voids extending through the entire membrane cross section.

In selecting a liquid-applied waterproofing coating, the designer should note that uniform coating thickness is easier to achieve on horizontal than on vertical surfaces. (Gravity is a friendly force on slabs, an enemy on walls.) This disparity is accentuated for hot-applied coatings, which are less thixotropic than cold-applied coatings.

General criteria for cold-applied LAMs are listed in *ASTM C 836 High Solids Content Cold Liquid-Applied Elastomeric Waterproofing Membrane for Use with Separate Wearing Course*. These criteria include:

- Hardness
- Weight loss (20% = 80% solids)

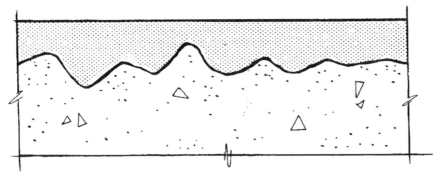

Fig. 9-2   60-mil minimum thickness is required for LAMs to avoid excessively thin cross sections over rough, irregular substrates. Stress concentrations can split the membrane at thinned cross sections, thereby destroying the membrane's waterproofing integrity.

- Low-temperature flexibility
- Low-temperature crack bridging
- Adhesion in peel after water immersion
- Extensibility after heat aging
- Stability

Application

Most LAMs are applied in single coat, to a roughly $^1/_{16}$-in.-thickness, either by roller, trowel, or squeegee. Most, if not all, coatings can be sprayed. Coatings with 100% solids (i.e., those containing no evaporative solvents) require trowel, roller, or squeegee application. As already warned in this chapter's introduction, liquid membrane application requires much greater care and considerably greater skill than built-up, modified bitumen, or prefabricated, single-ply sheet installation.

Two-coat systems, reinforced with woven glass or polyester, are generally hot-applied to a thickness of roughly 200 mils (=0.2 in.) The two coat application obviously reduces the potential for pinholes and thin spots.

Low-solids, two-coat, cold-applied single component reinforced membranes should be avoided. Low-solids LAM on reinforcing may cause pinholing, because the cold-applied liquid tends to flow down between the strands of reinforcing mesh and the reinforcing may inhibit moisture curing. Hot application avoids this problem, its rapid change from liquid to solid promotes a smooth, plane surface over the reinforcing mesh.

Substrate irregularities obviously cause variations in coating-film thickness. Frequent checks with wet-mil gauges are thus required during installation operations to assure maintenance of minimum 60-mil thickness. Coupons should be cut from each square (100 sq ft) of cured membrane and measured for thickness.

Where membranes are found to be below gage, either in film thickness or where cratering is extensive, additional coats are required to provide the *minimum* thickness throughout. Most LAM materials readily bond to themselves when cured, providing the prior coat is clean and dry. Some require a primer.

Concrete substrates for liquid-applied membranes must be rigorously prepared: fully cured, free of adhesion-inhibiting curing agents, sharp fins, and other irregularities.

Most manufacturers require either a steel-trowel finish or wood trowelling plus a lightly broomed hair broom finish. When the surface is cured to the manufacturer's satisfaction, it is swept clean or preferably vacuumed. Cracks and joints should be air-blasted.

Virtually all LAMs require a primer. Primers are water-based where solvent-based primers are not VOC-compliant.

Cracks and joints must be stripped with woven glass strips adhered with liquid-membrane material, or caulked and then stripped. Flashing of liquid-applied systems with a thixotropic version of the membrane liquid is a simple operation. For LAM systems with sheet flashing — neoprene rubber or polymer-modified bitumen — flashing becomes a more complicated problem. (EPDM flashing may prove unsuitable for use with bitumen-based LAMs, because of their exudation of oil.)

Failure Modes

Defects in liquid-applied membranes can be classified as follows:

- Pinholing
- Cratering
- Wrinkling
- Blistering
- Splitting

Pinholing, the most common defect, has several possible causes. A wet, dusty substrate can produce pinholes. Urethane is especially sensitive to moisture, which can set off a carbon-dioxide foaming reaction. Concrete curing compounds on the substrate — sodium silicate or animal fats — can also produce pinholes. In addition to chemical reactions and inadequate substrate preparation, faulty mixing of a two-component coating can entrap air bubbles within the membrane film. These entrapped air bubbles can either reduce film thickness or even extend through the entire membrane cross section.

In addition to air, solvents within the LAM can also cause pinholing. In a poor LAM formulation, the liquid can form into a premature gel state at the surface. Solvent escaping from the bottom of the membrane can then bubble up from the membrane cross section, creating pinholes in the surface gel stratum.

Pinholes are difficult to repair with high-viscosity coatings. The remedial coating bridges the pinhole; the coating dries from top and bottom to form a concave lens cross-sectional shape over the pinhole; and the lens-shaped cross section can break at its thinnest point, thereby recreating the pinhole.

Cratering forms in a manner similar to pinholing. Entrapped air bubbles exposed to solar heat expand and burst, leaving craters in the membrane's top surface. There is another crater-producing mechanism in single-component LAMs. When protection boards are prematurely placed on under-cured, single-component LAMs, entrapped air bubbles form depressions in the film, with consequent drastically reduced thickness.

Both pinholing and cratering can be limited, or even eliminated, by backrolling or the use of a spike roller on lower-viscosity liquids or by scheduling the application for falling temperature — for example, from mid to later afternoon. Weather-sensitive scheduling can thus prevent solar expansion of entrapped air bubbles by assuring falling ambient temperatures and solar-radiation intensity, both of which normally decline in the later afternoon hours. (As another advantage, afternoon scheduling averts the problem of morning condensation on the slab.)

Wrinkling generally represents a continuing degeneration of a membrane already damaged by pinholing. Under low hydrostatic pressure, surface tension will normally be high enough to prevent water passage through a pinholed membrane. Under a hydrostatic head, however, water will readily leak through pinholes. Once it penetrates the membrane, water will migrate along the substrate, at the interface plane between substrate and membrane.

Absorbing water from both sides, under-gage membranes swell and disbond from the substrate. The lengthening membrane buckles under compressive stress induced by adhesive restraint at the substrate. This swelling-disbonding process produces the familiar wrinkled "brain" appearance (see Fig. 9-3).

Wrinkling can also be caused by solvent, which expands the liquid membrane's volume. You can test adhesion of a first coat with a solvent. If it wrinkles, it obviously is not adhered. (The crests of the wrinkle waves indicated a disbonded membrane directly underneath.) If it doesn't wrinkle, it is adhered. This adhesion test provides another advantage for two-coat LAMs; application of a second coat tests the adhesion of the first coat.

Blistering occurs during, or soon after, application, and usually results in cratering, where the blister bursts (see Fig. 9-4). Blisters are formed when moisture migrates up through the concrete after the membrane is partially or fully cured. It thus indicates premature LAM appli-

Fig. 9-3   The wrinkled "brain" pattern of the failed hot-applied, modified-bitumen LAM (top) indicates swelling caused by moisture absorbed from concrete below. (The rectangular ridge pattern was formed by protection boards.)   Surface moisture was evident when membrane was test cut (bottom photo.)

cation, which should be delayed until the concrete has completed most of its curing. LAM application should not be scheduled until at least 28 days after concrete casting, or when tested per ASTM E 1907, with the approval of manufacturer and applicator.

Fig. 9-4 Blisters, and craters indicate poor surface preparation or air entrainment during application. LAM should be applied on dry, dust-free surfaces.

Blistering is a manageable problem if it occurs during application and if it produces craters. It is another story — a horror story — if it occurs after installation of the protection board and overburden.

Splitting in LAMs can occur over unrepaired cracks in the concrete substrate. An unrepaired concrete crack concentrates membrane strain (and consequent stress) as the crack opens or closes in response to temperature, moisture change, or structural deflection. Splits can also occur at substrate cracks that develop after installation of the LAM.

Another common location for splits is at joints between sheet flashing and the LAM membrane. Stress concentrates at these joints because the flashing is less elastic than the LAM and the membrane is often thinner (and consequently weaker) at these locations.

Alerts

General
1. Use these alerts in conjunction with manufacturer's recommendations.
2. Require certification of applicator as a qualified liquid-applied contractor.

3. Consider on-site inspection of application as part of the designer's contract.

Design
1. Consider liquid-applied membrane only after elimination of other membrane types as impracticable.
2. Check with the LAM manufacturer about his product's possible emission of toxic odors in the LAM's curing stage, and avoid such products' use on occupied buildings.

Field
1. Require pre-application approval of substrate preparation and penetration details by manufacturer's representative and inspector.
2. Establish a dependable QA program, preferably with on-site inspection throughout the application process.
3. Require checking of wet-film thickness during application.
4. Require cutting of dry-film-thickness test coupons during application, at rate of one per square.
5. Assure that squeegee notches are clean at the beginning of each day and after the lunch break.

10

Bentonite Waterproofing

Like built-up waterproofing membranes, bentonite is a traditional waterproofing material whose use goes back three-quarters of a century. But unlike the declining popularity of built-up waterproofing, bentonite has gained in popularity. Transmuted by modern polymer chemistry into a protean spectrum of composites, bentonite has become the most versatile waterproofing material, available in the following forms:

- Prefabricated panels (of kraft or biodegradable paper)
- Prefabricated geotextile sheets (filled with bentonite granules) (Fig. 10-1)
- High-density polyethylene HDPE sheets with adhered bentonite compound
- Trowelable mixtures for detailing

Designers should be warned at the outset, however, not to consider bentonite's many formulations as a sort of collective waterproofing panacea.

Bentonite's versatility comes with the liability summed up in the old (updated) maxim about a jack-of-all-trades being master of few. Bentonite is especially good for otherwise intractable problems — notably, blindside waterproofing in deep excavations — for which it has little competition. It is an excellent material for waterproofing vehicular tunnels, subways, and other structures where minor leakage is tolerable. Bentonite has a long history of successfully waterproofed utilitarian spaces in New York City basements. But for specialized, sensitive occupancies that require minimal risk of leaking combined with maximal control of humidity, bentonite is closer to a last than a first resort.

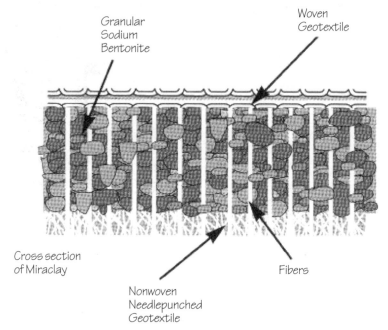

Fig. 10-1 Bentonite panel comprises a core of sodium bentonite (1 psf) within a corrugated biodegradable kraftboard stabilizing filler or, as illustrated above, between two layers of puncture resistant polypropylene fabric needle punched together. The confined bentonite is an impervious gel that bonds to its substrate, providing a permanent, active waterproofing layer, capable of sealing small substrate cracks. (TC MiraDRI.)

Historical Background

The contemporary spectrum of bentonite products evolved from the basic material introduced as a waterproofing material in the mid-1920s. Used only in granular form in those days, bentonite was limited to the sealing of pondliners and compacted-earth dams until the late 1950s, when it was introduced to the building waterproofing market. By the mid-1960s, it was available in panels, sheets, trowelable and sprayed formulations, the precursors of today's versatile panoply of products.

The replacement of traditional forms of bentonite follows the pattern set by metallic oxides' replacement by crystalline coatings and built-up membranes' replacement by self-adhering modified-bitumen sheets. Sprayed and troweled granular bentonite has virtually disappeared from the market, a consequence of the difficulty in applying uniform thickness and a tendency to prehydration (the evils of which are explained later in this chapter). Sprayed mixtures of bentonite and asphalt also proved ineffective (for reasons also explained later).

Bentonite-filled cardboard panels are among the sole survivors from traditional bentonite products. They have been supplemented by bentonite products marketed in rolls, for easier installation, in composite sheets containing bentonite granules either (a) encapsulated in polypropylene geotextile fabrics, or (b) laminated to geomembranes or high-density polyethylene (HDPE) on one side and a water-soluble film on the other. Panels for underslab and blindside waterproofing have also been upgraded by coatings of temporary water-resistant resins that inhibit harmful rehydration from ground water or precipitation prior to concrete placement.

Encapsulated composites are especially appropriate for underside and blindside applications. They contain approximately 1 psf of bentonite granules sandwiched between support fabrics of woven and nonwoven polypropylene geotextiles. In one manufacturer's product, the bentonite is adhered to the fabric. In another proprietary product, the interlocked, needlepunched fabric fixes the bentonite in place.

Polypropylene support fabrics are porous, non-biodegradable, and non-toxic, featuring a weave that mechanically bonds it to its concrete substrate. These fabrics reportedly prevent harmful prehydration from rain or ground water. They also provide sufficient shielding against construction damage to justify elimination of protection courses, according to a manufacturer. Panels are 48 in. square. Sheets are 40 in. wide, in lengths varying from 20 to 45 ft. Thickness varies, depending on application and site conditions.

These large prefabricated bentonite composites, nearly 150 sq ft in area for the largest sheets, greatly facilitate field labor. And this, in turn, vastly improves construction productivity, which thrives in transferring site labor to the factory.

Physical Properties

Bentonite (chemically, sodium montmorillonite) is a granulated smectite clay that derives its waterproofing property from a propensity to swell up to 15 times its dry volume when it absorbs water.[1] In hydrated state, under sufficient hydrostatic pressure bentonite becomes a water-repelling gel that will adhere to many different materials — concrete, stone, wood. In fully hydrated state, bentonite has low vapor permeance. When only *partially* hydrated, however, bentonite gains in vapor permeance. This obviously reduces its efficacy as a vapor retarder, precluding its use for humidity-sensitive occupancies.

These limitations — the need for high hydrostatic pressure to assure impermeability to liquid moisture and low permeance to gaseous moisture — stem from bentonite's physical properties. A complex elec-

---

1. It is more technically correct to refer to the bentonite's hydration rather than its absorption of water, hydration resulting from its solubility in water. Water is the *solvent* — i.e., the dissolving agent — whereas bentonite is the *solute* — i.e., the dissolved material.

trochemical process promotes bentonite's spontaneous swelling in the presence of liquid moisture. As a consequence of repulsive ionic forces created between the microscopic particles (roughly .00005-in. width) by the water molecules, the hydrated bentonite exerts an osmotic or swelling pressure. To perform at peak waterproofing efficiency, the bentonite must be compressed under continuous pressure to three or more times its base (i.e., unhydrated) density, a fraction of its unrestrained swollen volume. This requires a uniform compressive stress at least 40 psf.

These demanding requirements for bentonite's hydration explain the frequent failure of traditional forms of bentonite to provide dependable waterproofing. Sprayed mixtures of bentonite and asphalt proved unsatisfactory. (The asphalt inhibited the hydration process, by reducing the surface contact area between bentonite particles and water molecules). Granular bentonite, sprayed or troweled, eventually proved undependable for the opposite reason: premature hydration of the bentonite before it was properly restrained by hydrostatic pressure.

In practice, its physical properties restrict bentonite's use to projects where continuous hydrostatic pressure seldom falls below some minimum value — say, 30 psf. That requirement eliminates bentonite in situations involving intermittent flooding alternating with dry spells that totally eliminate hydrostatic pressure. Bentonite is also unsuitable where underground streams can flow across its surface or water tables rise and fall. These erosive water movements can cause migration of bentonite granules.

The need to maintain minimum 30-psf hydrostatic pressure is a prime preliminary design criterion for bentonite waterproofing systems. Hydrostatic pressure can be lost under several conditions. Settlement of backfill can reduce hydrostatic pressure by compacting the soil, thereby making it less pervious to intrusion of groundwater from the surrounding area. When the soil is already more or less impervious, hydrostatic pressure can similarly diminish with the passage of time. And when sheets are rehydrated, the hydrating water can leak out into surrounding soil, unless this soil is water-saturated.

For horizontal components waterproofed with bentonite, additional concrete weight is recommended to assure adequate compressive stress. For slabs-on-ground, where waterproofing is located below the slab, a minimum thickness of 6 in. (75 psf weight) is recommended. (Don't specify bentonite for structural slabs where it is located above the slab.)

Soil character imposes further limits on bentonite. Highly salinated soils are especially hazardous. Salt inhibits the swelling of bentonite clay in the presence of liquid moisture. This reduction in swelling jeopardizes bentonite's unique waterproofing property. For projects located in coastal areas, the designer should require analysis of the soil's salinity and verify acceptability with the bentonite manufacturer before specifying his material.

In addition to the problem of contamination, there is a peculiar soil requirement for bentonite panels faced with biodegradable cardboard. These panels require soil bacteria to maintain their waterproofing integrity, for they depend on the cardboard's decay under bacterial attack to expose the bentonite to the liquid moisture required to expand it. If there are insufficient bacteria present in the soil, water can penetrate seams or even infiltrate behind the panels before hydration. Backfilling with sand of high silica content can aggravate this problem, by retaining the bacteria and minerals and preventing their leaching through the soil.

Problems resulting from the biodegradable cardboard's failure to decay occur more frequently with horizontal surfaces — i.e., earth-covered structural slabs — than with vertical surfaces of foundation walls. The problem is, again, prehydration, from the water that has penetrated seams or infiltrated behind the unexpanded panels. There are, however, bentonite panels available with special coatings designed to temporarily inhibit premature hydration. These panels are suitable only for slabs, not for walls. Failures have been traced to misuse of these specially treated panels. Over-coating of the panels, which can cause excessive delay in hydration, can also cause failure.

Bentonite Installation

The replacement of sprayed and troweled granular bentonite by composite bentonite-based sheets and panels has drastically simplified bentonite application techniques. Spraying and troweling require skilled applicators, to assure uniform thickness essential to the bentonite's waterproofing integrity. In contrast, panels for waterproofed slabs-on-ground are simply laid on the substrate and lapped. Panels or sheets are nailed to foundation walls and lagging. On vertical surfaces, sheets are oriented horizontally or vertically. Hydration must be delayed until after backfilling or casting of slabs-on-ground. Tapes can seal joints in panels or sheets if precipitation is predicted. Taped seals are mandatory at the joints left at the end of the day's work.

Bentonite sheets and panels require a solid substrate. For slabs-on-ground, mud slabs are desirable, but not essential, if the subgrade consists of a compacted aggregate or soil base.

Prior to application, the concrete surface must be prepared, with removal of fins and other projections over ½ in., to provide a plane surface for application of the bentonite. Honeycombed spots, rock pockets, indentations, tie-rod holes, form kickouts, and gaps at panel corners must be filled with trowelable bentonite in hydrated gel or mastic formulation. Flashing sheets are not required. Bentonite-filled tubes, hydrated bentonite in hydrated gel, and mastic are applied at penetrations and the bottom of foundation walls (See Fig. 10-2).

There is also a trowelable grade, one-part urethane for sealing cor-

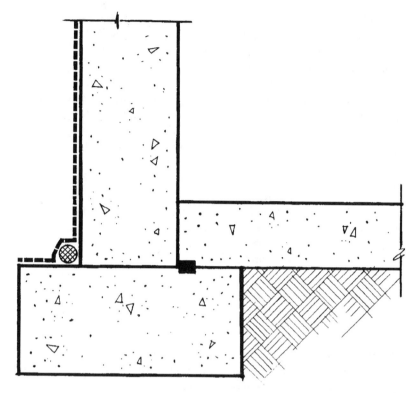

Fig. 10-2 In non-hydrostatic conditions the vulnerable joint between wall footing and foundation wall should be reinforced with a bentonite-filled tube. Note: Waterstops are critical components with bentonite waterproofing.

ners and penetrations in some laminated and encapsulated sheets. This material also flashes drain flanges and seals bentonite at drain cutouts.

Trowelable-grade bentonite has another use, again limited to detail — i.e., filling gaps and joints in soldier piles, lagging, steel sheet piling, earth-formed shotcrete retaining walls, and auger-drilled caisson walls. Irregular surfaces such as shotcrete and caisson walls should be grouted to provide smooth, plane substrates for the bentonite waterproofing. (see Fig. 10-3) A ½-in.-thick plywood facing ("boarding out"), to provide a smoother, more uniform substrate, is optional for sheetpiling, but mandatory for lagging (see Fig. 10-4).

Bentonite panels pose a termination problem at grade. To maintain the required lateral pressure, they should be terminated 6 in. below grade, with a membrane flashing strip — e.g., modified bitumen — or a metal cap flashing over the termination joint. The flashing should extend 8 in. above grade and overlap the bentonite by 6 in. (see Fig. 10-5). Termination bars are the best method of anchoring panels and sheets where they

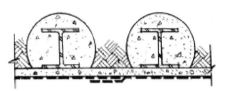

Fig. 10-3   Panels and sheets can be installed on plane shotcrete surfaces (left hand detail), but flexible sheets are more suitable to grouted augered piles (right hand detail).

terminate near the tops of foundation walls.

Backfill must be scheduled to follow panel placement, with separate backfill lifts required after installation of each panel course. Backfill requires compaction to at least 85% proctor density, to within 2 in. of the panels' top edges. If backfill is not placed immediately against the panels, they require temporary protection against rain or snow with plastic film, insulation boards (e.g. extruded polystyrene), or protection boards. Damaged panels must be replaced before completion of backfill operations.

Blindside Bentonite

Bentonite sheets and panels are generally the best materials for blindside applications, notably the following:

- Concrete foundations cast against soldier piles and lagging
- Steel (or wood) sheetpiling
- Concrete caisson retaining walls
- Slurry (or shotcreted rock)
- Diaphragm walls retaining earth

Several techniques for applying these blindside bentonite waterproofing systems are illustrated in Figure 10-6 (caissons), Fig. 10-7 (wood

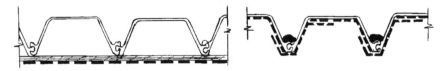

Fig. 10-4   For bentonite panel waterproofing on steel sheet piling, "boarding out" with plywood (left detail) provides a more suitable substrate than direct application. Bentonite sheets, however, may be applied directly to the sheet piling (right detail). For both sheets and panels, the joint at the bottom is critical. Horizontal sheets must be carefully fitted to the steel profile.

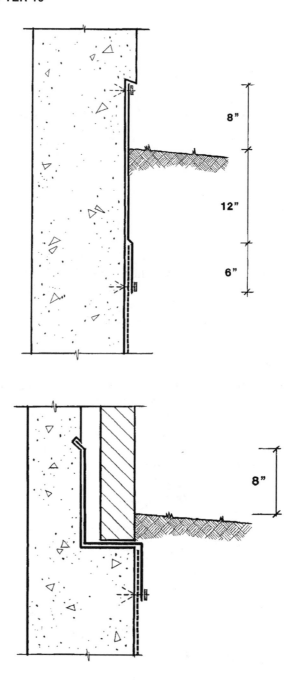

Fig. 10-5   Flashing details above show grade-level termination of bentonite panels with metal flashing carried a minimum 8 in. above grade (top detail) and into a grade-level reglet (bottom detail). Of the two, the left-hand detail is superior. Note, however, that this detail requires level grade around the entire building.

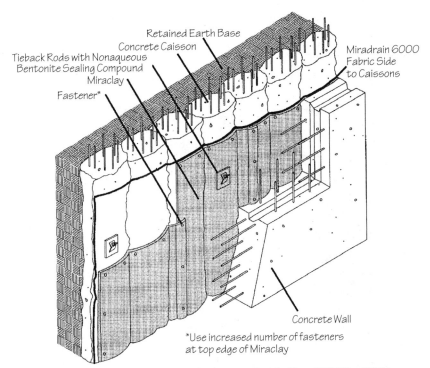

Retained Earth Base
Concrete Caisson
Tieback Rods with Nonaqueous
Bentonite Sealing Compound
Miraclay
Fastener*

Miradrain 6000
Fabric Side
to Caissons

Concrete Wall

*Use increased number of fasteners
at top edge of Miraclay

Fig. 10-6   Bentonite sheets applied on augered piles. (TC MiraDRI.)

lagging), and Fig. 10-8 (shotcreted rock). As their major advantage, these bentonite sheets can be nailed directly to foundation walls or tight lagging. Unlike most positive-side membranes, they seldom require "boarding out" with plywood to provide the plane, smooth substrates required for thin modified bitumens or built-up membranes. They do, however, require blockouts in walls for tieback plates or rakers. The designer must detail these blockouts carefully, leaving the waterproofing contractor no opportunity to substitute a cheaper, possibly defective, detail (see Fig. 10-9).

A detail for the vulnerable footing-wall joint is accompanied by the manufacturer's warning to divert jobsite water, rain, and snow melt away from the excavation (see Fig. 10-10). This warning stems from the necessity of delaying the bentonite's hydration until after the concrete footing and wall are cast.

Assets And Liabilities

Bentonite waterproofing systems offer the following advantages:

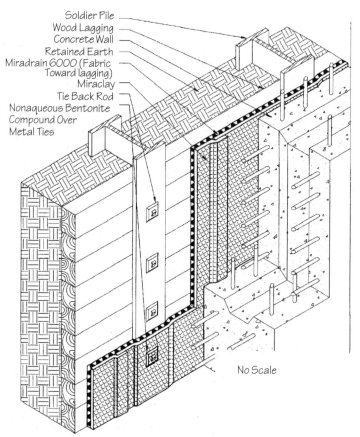

Soldier Pile
Wood Lagging
Concrete Wall
Retained Earth
Miradrain 6000 (Fabric Toward lagging)
Miraclay
Tie Back Rod
Nonaqueous Bentonite Compound Over Metal Ties

No Scale

Fig. 10-7 Prefabricated bentonite panels can be nailed directly to wood lagging substrates as blindside waterproofing. Wood lagging in the illustration above is installed behind the front flange of the pile. It can also be installed in front of the front flange or behind the back flange. These configurations complicate the installation of panels and sheets. Bentonite mastic is trowelled over soldier pile flanges, tie-back plates, she bolts and other fasteners to complete the seal. It is also packed around utility penetrations. Bentonite sheets and panels can accommodate slight irregularities, but large holes and splits and wide joints between the sides and ends of the lagging boards must be patched or boarded out. (TC MiraDRI.)

- Fast and relatively easy installation
- No VOC restrictions
- Safe application at extreme temperatures
- Relatively easy leak detection
- Bridging cracks up to ¼ in.
- Adaptability to complex geometric shapes

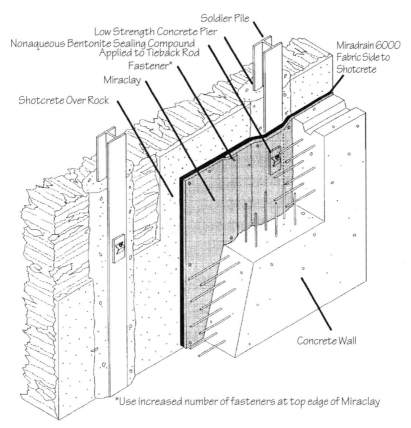

Soldier Pile
Low Strength Concrete Pier
Nonaqueous Bentonite Sealing Compound
Applied to Tieback Rod
Fastener*
Miraclay
Shotcrete Over Rock
Miradrain 6000
Fabric Side to
Shotcrete
Concrete Wall

*Use increased number of fasteners at top edge of Miraclay

Fig. 10-8   On blindside shotcreted rock, composite drain board is first nailed to shotcrete, followed by similarly nailed bentonite panels. Tieback rod anchors are sealed with nonaqueous bentonite compound. (TC MiraDRI.)

Fast and relatively easy installation applies to all bentonite products. Bentonite applications don't require the precise tolerances of membrane applications, where lap seams may require fastidious attention both to dimensions and to technique. Compared with other waterproofing systems, bentonite requires little substrate preparation before application.

The lack of VOC restrictions gives bentonite an obvious advantage over materials subject to such restrictions.

Safe application at extreme temperatures — from -40°F to 130°F — fits bentonite for installation at any otherwise feasible temperature, limited not by the material, but the workers' tolerance for cold and heat.

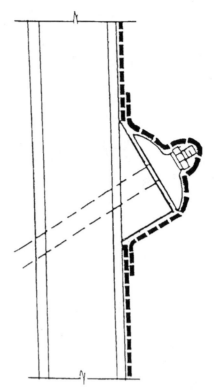

Fig. 10-9   Tie-back rods in concrete foundation walls can be waterproofed as shown above. The flexible bentonite filled fabric panel can be easily molded around irregular projections to maintain a continuous seal.

As a contrasting material, liquid-applied membranes not only require greater care and skill by the field crews installing them; they are also more severely limited by both temperature and humidity for proper curing.

Leak detection is relatively easy with bentonite systems because leaks normally occur near their source.

Bentonite's ability to bridge cracks up to ¼-in. width stems from its propensity to expand many times its original dry volume. This ability is, however, limited to cracks that do not feed conduits for washing bentonite particles through the crack and into interior voids within the concrete. Extra protection against such defects can be applied to construction joints, control joints, wall-foundation joints, and other locations where cracking can be anticipated and thus needs extra protection. Bentonite-based caulking or bentonite tubes that decompose like cardboard panels are required at these vulnerable, crack-prone joints.

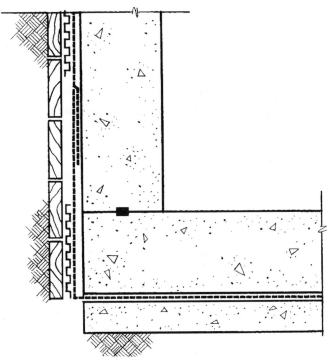

Fig. 10-10 At the vulnerable footing-wall joint, blindside waterproofing of an excavation retained by a soldier piles and wood lagging is waterproofed with composite drainage panels and bentonite panels lapped vertically and horizontally at the wall-slab intersection. Jobsite water, rain, and snow melt must be diverted away from the excavation in the interval between application of the waterproofing and casting of the foundation slab.

Adaptability to complex geometric surfaces derives from the flexibility of bentonite compound sheets and, to a lesser degree, panels, both of which can accommodate some geometric irregularities in the substrate. This advantage is, however, tempered by the vulnerability of bentonite sheet and panel systems at corners, where the need for troweled bentonite mastic caulking demands a level of applicator skill far above that of the sheet installers. (For expanded discussion, see next section, "Bentonite failure modes").

The author reluctantly mentions another bentonite advantage: lower first cost compared with many competing materials. Consistent with the advice reiterated throughout this manual, first-cost economy should be the last factor considered by the designer. Only after he has assured himself that the product satisfies all the project's performance criteria should the designer consider first-cost economy. It can, however, be gratefully accepted as a fortuitous bonus.

Briefly summarized, with some repetition, here are bentonite's liabilities:

- The need for constant, relatively high hydrostatic pressure to maintain the material's waterproofing integrity
- Lack of dependable resistance to vapor migration
- Limited options for future repair or replacement

This last-cited liability springs from the difficulty of removing bentonite. This is especially so for troweled bentonite compounds. Tight adhesion is a virtue for effective waterproofing, but a vice for defective waterproofing requiring replacement.

Because of bentonite's lack of dependable performance as a vapor retarder, prudent designers will avoid bentonite for humidity-sensitive occupancies when there are practicable alternatives. One such alternative, recommended by a PVC membrane manufacturer, would incorporate bentonite as part of a redundant system in which the underground waterproofing would comprise bentonite sheets, encapsulated between polypropylene geotextiles, then covered with PVC membrane. In addition to functioning as a redundant line of waterproofing defense, the PVC membrane would serve as a vapor retarder. Thus the dual bentonite-PVC system would be suitable for humidity-sensitive occupancies, according to the proponent PVC manufacturer.

Bentonite Failure Modes

Though less common than roofing failures, waterproofing failures — including bentonite's — span a wider spectrum of locations. Roofing seldom fails in the membrane field; its major failure locations are at penetrations and terminations. Waterproofing is similarly prone to failure at these locations, but it is also vulnerable at other locations: concrete construction joints, dynamic substrate cracks, and plane changes — especially at interior and exterior corners.

Because they rely heavily on trowel-grade mastics to seal joints, bentonite systems are notoriously vulnerable at these generally failure-prone locations. The man with the trowel at these critical spots becomes the key to the system's integrity, foremost among the cast of usual suspects when failure occurs. As they perform their vital caulking operations, these applicators should sense "the shadow of the boss," in the late consulting engineer Jacob Feld's apt phrase, and even more importantly, the suspicious eyes of the owner's inspector.

Perhaps the most vulnerable, and certainly the most difficult, location to waterproof properly is the joint at the footing-foundation wall intersection. It is extremely difficult to keep the top of the footing free of dirt or mud. (A water jet may be required to clean the surface.) It is also difficult to work in the narrow trench at the bottom of an excavation well below grade, with moisture-sensitive materials lowered from the top of the excavation. Working in this cramped space on his hands and knees, the applicator must place bentonite-filled tubes, with abutting ends, carefully aligned along these joints as a caulking. To say the least, these conditions are not conducive to meticulous application practice. They obviously demand alert attention from the construction superintendent and the owner's inspector.

Slovenly construction practice is, however, only one source of bentonite failure. Some bentonite failures reported to the author are attributable to a flouting of the simplest warnings issued in this chapter. At an Illinois project, the fluctuating watertable elevation adjacent to Lake Michigan caused erosion of bentonite from the rise-fall cycling of groundwater. Bentonite waterproofing of a building on a steep slope in Ohio experienced similar erosion of bentonite waterproofing. Water flowing down the slope deposited bentonite as a gray coating on the ground below. These failures may not have occurred if the designers had observed the most elementary rule in specifying bentonite: Limit its use to locations where hydrostatic pressure is stable, with no running groundwater.

Designer ignorance can cause other types of failure. Bentonite materials are unsuitable for covering expansion joints, for the obvious reason that their movement induces huge strains in materials adhered to them and bentonite lacks the high breaking strain characteristic of elastomers. Instead of covering expansion joints with bentonite, the designer should specify a flexible cover, anchored at perimeters to seal the joint. The cover must be anchored on both sides of the joint, to prevent its separation from the concrete when the joint moves. The cover must also resist hydrostatic pressure normal to the expansion joint plane.

Detailing these joints can be difficult. The chief problem: creating a watertight seal with the bentonite. Neoprene sheet over the tube is probably the best solution. Another type features a prefabricated metal and neoprene assembly. Both types require anchorage on both sides of the joint; they cannot be stripped into the flanking bentonite. Panel covers degrade, HDPE liners and geotextiles are not bondable.

As a final warning on expansion-joint design, designers specifying bentonite must beware that they are on their own. Bentonite producers routinely warn that expansion-joint design is the "responsibility of others."

As a final warning on bentonite failures generally, note that the versatility of bentonite's variegated spectrum of products demands close attention to the special limitations of individual products. Designers sometimes specify the wrong panels for foundation walls despite manufacturer's warnings limiting these products to horizontal applications. These displays of ignorance are usually rewarded with dismal consequences.

Alerts

1. Remember the need for continuous hydrostatic pressure (30-psf minimum) or other means of maintaining compressive stress in a bentonite system.

2. On projects with humidity-sensitive underground occupancies, investigate vapor-permeance properties of a bentonite system with the manufacturer.

3. Specify tubes and bentonite mastic at footing-foundation joint.

4. Protect material from rain and damage.

5. Design a minimum 6-in.-thick slab-on-ground, and verify that slab weight is sufficient to resist bentonite expansion pressure.

6. On projects located in coastal areas, require a soil-salinity analysis before specifying bentonite.

7. Where mud or other sediment has been deposited on top of footings to be waterproofed with bentonite, require removal by water jet to assure intimate contact between concrete and bentonite.

8. Seal expansion joints in bentonite systems with other materials, as bentonite components are unsuitable.

Plaza
Waterproofing

Under the economic pressure of higher land costs and consequent need for more efficient use of building space, waterproofed plazas and roof terraces (sometimes called waterproofed decks) have become more popular over the past four decades. These spaces were traditionally limited to underground storage areas, access tunnels, and parking garages. With the advent of airconditioning, however, these spaces became suitable for computer rooms, offices, and public-assembly rooms, occupancies now routinely located below plazas, planters, and sidewalks.

Waterproofed plaza systems differ greatly from roof systems in their performance criteria. In conventional roof systems, the weather-exposed membrane must resist ultraviolet degradation and extreme temperature variations. A waterproofed plaza membrane experiences far less temperature change and is permanently shielded from ultraviolet radiation. Its primary performance criterion is to resist continuous exposure to moisture. For earth-covered membranes, resistance to vegetation roof penetration and soil contaminants are additional performance criteria. And because a waterproofing membrane may be far less accessible than a roof membrane, its anticipated service life must approximate the service life of the building, not merely the normal 10 to 20 years anticipated for a roof membrane. Reroofing is an inconvenience; rewaterproofing is, by comparison, an economic holocaust. It costs at least 10 times the cost of a roof tearoff to remove up to 8 ft of earth fill with plantings or to jackhammer a concrete topping and haul it away.

Waterproofing on structural slabs over occupied space falls into two basic categories:

- Plazas or terraces, located at or slightly above grade
- Earth-covered structural slabs

Plaza/terrace systems come in two basic sub-categories, in which the differentiating feature is whether the membrane is *accessible* or *inaccessible*. In the accessible sub-category, the system has a removable wearing course — pavers on insulation, pedestals, or sand beds. In the inaccessible sub-category are two further subdivisions: (a) systems with concrete protection slabs, and (b) systems with solid mortar setting beds. Both subdivisions are classified as inaccessible for an obvious reason: they both require demolition — e.g., jackhammering of the concrete protective slab or of solidly grouted pavers — to provide access to the membrane. With its removable pavers on removable insulation, pedestals, or sand beds, accessible systems obviously require no demolition for repair or even replacement of the membrane.

Ruggerio makes a further distinction within the plaza/terrace category. Plazas, or promenades, differ from terraces in the following respects:

- Location at or near grade
- Insulation (almost always)
- Structural capacity for vehicular traffic (e.g., fire engines, snow-removal equipment)[1]

Earth-covered waterproofing systems must satisfy more rigorous performance criteria than plazas in two important respects:

- Chronic exposure to greater hydrostatic pressure
- Exposure to more destructive soil contaminants

The greater hydrostatic pressures experienced by earth-covered slabs result from rainstorms, high ground-water tables in earth fills up to 8 ft high, discharges from parking lots and downspouts, and accumulation of water at the base of curtain walls. Moreover, stronger concentrations of chemical contaminants — fertilizers, soil poisoners, waste-water runoff — can attack earth-covered membranes. In combination with the possibility of root extension from plantings, these and other threats to earth-covered membranes made their design more difficult than plaza design. First-cost economy for earth-covered slabs becomes even less important than for plazas, and durability more important.

The scope of this chapter is limited to these two basic waterproofed deck systems, with the foregoing sub-categories. Omitted are related systems featuring coatings for combination waterproofing/traffic surfaces for parking garages and balconies. The thin, liquid-applied coatings and

1.   Stephen Ruggerio, *Effective Plaza Deck Waterproofing Seminar*, University of Wisconsin, Dec. 16, 1994.

traffic-resistant applications "waterproofing" these systems can resist only minimal hydrostatic pressure. As a consequence, they are unsuitable for use on slabs over enclosed spaces with rigorous water-resistant performance criteria. Also omitted are garage roof decks, defined as uninsulated decks above unheated garages, sports facilities, and grandstands. These decks must withstand pedestrian and vehicular traffic, resist oil and gasoline and de-icing salts. What disqualifies them for consideration in this manual is their vulnerability to occasional leaks.

A waterproofed plaza system with a separate wearing course contains (bottom to top) some or all of the following components (see Fig. 11-1):

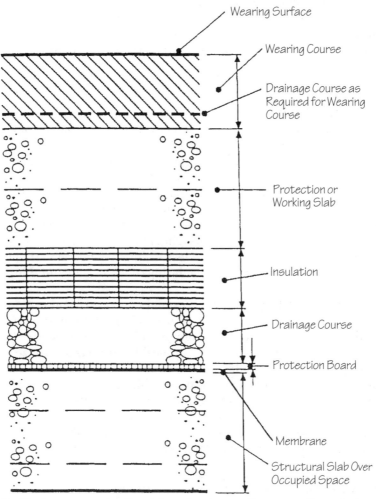

Fig. 11-1 Basic components of membrane waterproofing over a framed structural slab. Insulation and drainage course are often reversed from the above order. (American Society of Testing and Materials.)

- Structural deck
- Membrane
- Protection boards
- Drainage course
- Thermal insulation
- Concrete protection (working) slab
- Flashing
- Wearing surface

An earth-covered system comprises essentially the same components listed above, with exception of the wearing surface, for which it substitutes overburden (see Fig. 11-2).

Designers of waterproofed decks should consult two ASTM standard guides: C 981 for built-up membranes and C 989 for liquid-applied membranes. The following discussion incorporates material from these standards.

Structural Decks

Cast-in-place, monolithic structural concrete slabs make the best substrates for waterproofed deck systems. Their continuity gives them a big advantage over precast concrete, which usually requires a concrete topping (normally 2 in. thick) to provide a smooth, continuous top surface uninterrupted by joints. The rotation of bearing ends of precast structural members can open and close these joints, possibly requiring expansion joints to accommodate movement. Standard-weight concrete (150 pcf) is preferable to lightweight structural concrete (110-pcf minimum density), as it experiences less ultimate deflection attributable to longterm creep. Lightweight insulating concrete is unsuitable as a deck substrate.

Structural design for earth-covered structural framing requires special care. Dead load for these structures often approximates total design load. Heavy, saturated soils weigh up to 120 pcf, constituting a 360-psf dead load for a 3-ft-depth of overburden.[2] Dead loads maximize the effect of longterm creep on deflection, thus requiring a conservative approach to assure retention of adequate slope for drainage. To assure permanent retention of 1% slope in a reinforced concrete slab, its initial slope should normally be at least 2%, and even this may be inadequate. Creep in structural concrete — i.e., increasing deflection under constant, prolonged loading — is inevitable in both reinforced and prestressed concrete. To-

---

2.   Where soil depth exceeds 3 ft or so, barrel vaults sometimes replace flat slabs, for more efficient structural action. Expanded or extruded polystyrene, depending on the requisite compressive strength, is often used as a filler material to lighten dead load, along with vermiculite/perlite/soil mixtures.

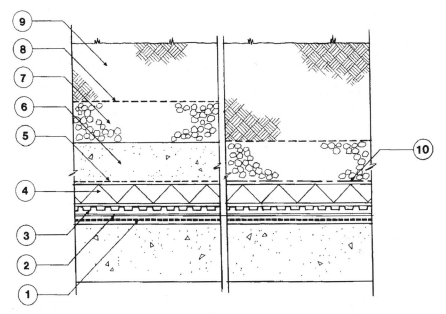

Fig. 11-2   Basic components of membrane waterproofing under earth, (1) waterproofing membrane, (2) protection board, (3) composite drainage, (4) insulation, (5) filter sheet, (6) concrete protection slab (sloped to drain), (7) gravel drainage, (8) filter sheet, (9) soil, (10) polyethylene sheet. Concrete protection slab indicated on the left side is optional. Both the structural and protection slab should be sloped to drain.

tal longterm deflection may equal 3 times instantaneous elastic deflection. Creep is thus an especially significant factor in structural concrete slabs supporting heavy overburden loads, as opposed to plazas, where intermittent live load may constitute 50% or more of total design load. Structural design of plazas focuses more on live loading. As one example of possible plaza live loading, the service weight of a small, two-axle firefighting pumper can exceed 26,000 lb in concentrated wheel loads.

The architect or other waterproofing designer should make sure that the structural engineer is briefed about the need for positive slope for drainage. In some instances, supporting structures have been underdesigned even for load-carrying capacity. Preliminary coordination among waterproofing designer, landscape architect, and structural engineer is essential to assure adequate load capacity and slab slope. When this pre-design coordination has been lacking, landscape architects have occasionally been forced to alter their preferred design to accommodate a faultily designed structure's limited load-carrying capacity.[3]

---

3.   "Technics: Roofs for use," Progressive Architecture, July, 1990, P. 36ff

Membranes

Membranes for waterproofed deck systems include conventional built-up, modified-bitumen sheets, single-ply sheets, and liquid-applied elastomers. As in roof membranes, glass-fiber felts have replaced organic felts in waterproofed deck membranes because of their greater strength and moisture resistance. Glass-fiber felts can be alternated with woven glass fabric, which offers greater flexibility than glass-fiber felts and is more easily molded to corners and other substrate irregularities. Membranes range from a minimum of three to a maximum of five plies, depending on the required degree of waterproofing.

Woven-glass fabric provides a better reinforcement than glass-fiber felts for coal-tar-pitch membranes. The glass fabric, has larger openings than the random fibers in glass felts. Its consequently greater flexibility allows it to maintain its position within the built-up membrane. In coal-tar-pitch membranes, tar-saturated felts are also preferable to the stiffer glass-fiber felts because of their greater stability within the membrane cross section. Alternating tar-saturated organic felts with woven glass produces a superior membrane.

The bitumen of choice is coal tar pitch (ASTM D 450, Type I or II), because of its self-healing property. Even the softest asphalt (ASTM D 449, Type A) can hydrolyze in the presence of water containing the high or low pH chemicals in soil poisoners and fertilizers.

Felt plies can be shingled or phased (i.e., laid in continuous planes). Ply-on-ply construction results in continuous films of interply bitumen. Moisture penetration through a lap thus leads only to the next layer, not through the entire membrane cross section, as in a shingled pattern. Some five-ply membranes have three shingled plies of alternating felts and fabric, crossed with two shingled plies of felt or fabric at right angles. This arrangement produces a strong, highly waterproof BUR membrane.

As in roof construction, however, single-ply elastomers, weldable thermoplastics, and modified-bitumen sheets are rapidly replacing the more labor-intensive built-up membranes. A popular modified-bitumen sheet is a self-adhering single ply, laminated to a polyethylene backing. Called "peel-and-stick," these sheets are applied over a concrete substrate primed with either a solvent or an emulsion-type primer. They must be protected from ultraviolet degradation within a few days of application. (See Chapter 8 for expanded discussion).

Among elastomeric single-ply sheets, butyl rubber has an advantage over EPDM in its much lower moisture absorptivity, a more important property for a waterproofing membrane than EPDM's much greater ultraviolet resistance. PVC sheet, for improved puncture resistance, is another common single-ply waterproofing membrane.

These single-ply elastomeric and thermoplastic sheets are either fully adhered or loose laid. When loose laid, however, they are nonetheless adhered in grid strips, usually 10 ft each way, to form watertight compartments that aid in restricting leakwater migration and facilitating leak detection.

Liquid-applied membranes include hot and cold polymer-modified asphalt, single-component asphalt or coal tar-extended urethane, and two-component urethane elastomer. For proper performance, these membranes must contain minimum 65 percent solids to reduce pinholing. Their resistance to crack propagation from the deck below depends on thickness, normally a minimum 60 mils dry film thickness. (The thicker the membrane, the greater the elongation over the crack.)

Liquid-applied membranes' advantages include localization of leaks (compared with compartmentalization of leaks with loose-laid sheet membranes). Weighing against this advantage, however, is the need for extremely rigorous preparation of the substrate, which must be dry and largely dust-free, with patched cracks. As an additional precaution, the designer should never specify a LAM to fill or level surface irregularities. (The variable thickness of the LAM creates multiple risks, discussed in Chapter 10.)

Moisture is a deadly enemy of liquid-applied membranes. It causes urethane to foam and hot-applied modified bitumen to froth. Single-component liquid-applied coatings are most vulnerable to high humidity. They require exposure to air with minimum absolute humidity for sufficient time to assure full curing. Premature application of protection boards may delay, or even prevent, full curing. In contrast, two-component coatings are relatively unaffected by humidity. They also have these advantages: greater latitude for low-temperature application, long shelf life, and noncuring in the can. Their countervailing disadvantage: carefully controlled field mixing is required to assure complete blending.

Dust is also a problem for liquid-applied coatings. Pinholing can be caused by dust, or by overly rapid application, which can entrain air bubbles in the coating film.

Hot-applied rubberized asphalts, heated in a jacketed kettle, are often reinforced with polyester or woven glass. This process requires two applications, which minimize pinholing and thin spots via a thicker more stable membrane. Since they cure as soon as they cool, these coatings are less vulnerable to rain or sudden temperature drops, which jeopardize the slower-curing cold-applied coatings.

All of these highly elastic, liquid-applied coatings are capable of bridging small cracks. They have low permeability, are easily applied to contoured surfaces, and are generally self-flashing. Their chief liability is their great dependence on rigorous field supervision and application, requisites for uniform thickness and film integrity.

For more detailed discussion of these various waterproofing membranes, refer to Chapter 5, "Positive-side Waterproofing" and Chapters 8 through 10. And remember the general rule of waterproofing design: to avoid use of different, possibly incompatible materials when they require a joint to produce a continuous waterproofing film. When foundation walls also require waterproofing in conjunction with a plaza or earth-covered structural slab, choose the same waterproofing membrane material to facilitate the junction at the slab-wall intersection. (See Fig. 11-3).

In an exception to the general rule against multiple systems, plaza structural slabs have been successfully waterproofed via a combination of liquid membrane applied directly to the concrete substrate and then covered with a loose-laid rubber sheet. In this belt-plus-suspenders approach, the loose-laid rubber sheet serves as the primary line of defense, and the LAM provides a secondary line of defense. By its very nature, a LAM is subject to a large number of small defects, whereas a loose-laid rubber sheet is more liable to a single major rupture — e.g., at a defectively sealed lap seam.

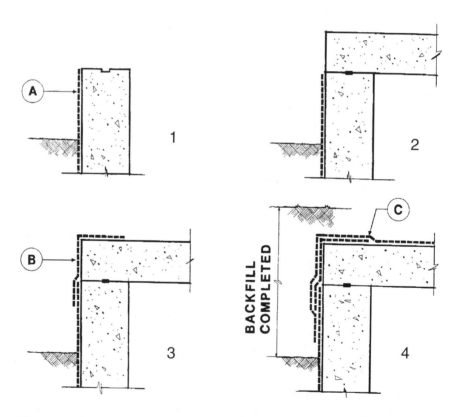

Fig. 11-3 Details illustrating construction sequence, steps 1 through 4, show correct membrane lapping required to assure dependable waterproofing at the vulnerable joint between the foundation wall and the structural slab, a common source of waterproofing problems. If membrane material C is different from B, or B is different from A, impaired adhesion between membranes can promote leakage through the wall-slab construction joint.

Protection Boards

All waterproofing membranes require shielding from construction damage and ultraviolet radiation as soon as practicable after installation and floodtesting. The most common material is an asphalt-core, laminated panel, $^1/_{16}$, $^1/_8$, or $^1/_4$-in.-thick, faced with polyethylene film on one side, to prevent sticking. Though sometimes used instead of protection boards, prefabricated plastic drainage composites are unsuitable, because they are too soft to shield against construction traffic. They are also easily dislodged by wind and traffic before overburden is installed.

Installation of protection boards is mandatory immediately after completion of a horizontal waterproofing membrane and termination of flood testing. Scheduling of these three operations — membrane application, flood testing, and protection-board installation — must proceed in uninterrupted sequence, with no intervening delays exposing the membrane to the multiple hazards of other construction operations. Among these membrane-puncturing hazards are pipe scaffolds, sometimes erected without the required wood planks to distribute the concentrated loads; stockpiled masonry units; reinforcing bars; welding rods; sharp-pointed fasteners; loose aggregate; and other debris scattered randomly over an unshielded membrane. Pipe cutters may be dripping contaminated oil, mortar droppings can fall from masonry construction under way at the perimeter. Any of these hazards can end the membrane's service life in its infancy, before it has had a chance to prove durability. Delayed installation of protective insulation, drainage composite, and even a concrete protection slab is obviously worthless over a membrane already destroyed by careless construction operations. These components merely add the cost of their removal to the total rewaterproofing cost.

Field inspection is critical at this stage of a waterproofing project. At the designer's insistence, the owner should have a qualified representative at the site to assure that protection-board installation takes place immediately after the membrane has passed the flood test. If the membrane fails the flood test, protection-board application obviously must await repair of the membrane and successful passing of a flood retest. Flood testing, membrane repairs, and protection-board installation should also be observed by the manufacturer's representative.

Drainage Design

Drainage of a waterproofed deck system should incorporate all components, from wearing surface down to membrane, according to ASTM C 981.

Plaza drainage should minimize saturation of the wearing course, which might disintegrate from freeze-thaw cycling.

At membrane level, drainage is required to avoid the following:

• Hydrostatic pressure from accumulated drain water

- Freeze-thaw cycling of trapped water
- Reduction of the insulation's thermal resistance

An absolute minimum of 1% slope, and preferably 2%, is recommended to assure positive drainage. (See previous discussion under "Structural Deck" for effect of longterm concrete creep on slope.)

Either a percolating gravel stratum or plastic drainage panels can provide the pervious medium facilitating water flow to drains. In very cold climates, where snow meltwater flows over the membrane, locating the drainage course above the insulation may reduce the probability of condensation below the membrane. But as a countervailing disadvantage, this location may impair drainage, which is promoted by a below-insulation location of the drainage course.

Designers of waterproofed decks should specify multilevel drains, designed to permit differential movement between the strainer at the wearing course and the drain body embedded in the structural slab. A detail allowing relative movement between wearing course and structural slab prevents rupture of the drain body or connected pipes (see Figs. 11-4a, 11-4b, 11-4c & 11-4d).

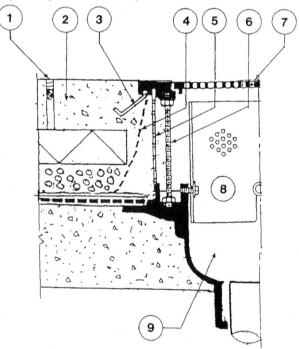

Fig. 11-4a Plaza drain with concrete wearing surface. (1) caulked expansion joint, (2) cast concrete wearing surface, (3) anchor, (4) stainless steel wire mesh, or (5) perforated stainless steel, (6) adjustable threaded rods, (7) cast iron or bronze top rim and grate, (8) removable perforated filter, (9) cast iron deep sump drain with clamping ring.

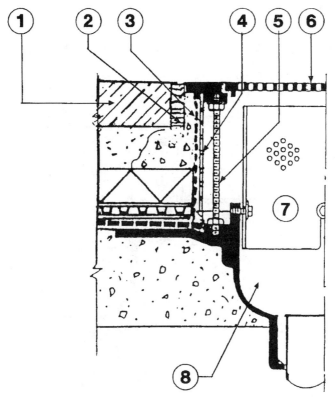

Fig. 11-4b Plaza drain with stone wearing surface. (1) stone wearing surface, (2) caulked expansion joint, (3) filter fabric, (4) perforated stainless steel, (5) adjustable threaded rods, (6) cast iron or bronze top rim and grate, (7) removable perforated filter, (8) cast iron deep sump drain with extended flange for LAM.

At the wearing surface, drainage is accomplished via (a) an open-jointed system that rapidly filters drain water down to the membrane level, or (b) a closed-joint system sloped to surface drains. Open-jointed systems include pavers on pedestals or placed directly on ribbed insulation boards.

Closed-joint systems have either a mortar-setting bed or caulked joints. An intermediate compromise is provided by bricks or stones in a sand bed. This compromise is inferior to an open-jointed system, but superior to a mortar-set system.

Drainage of earth-covered slabs differs from drainage of plaza systems in several respects — notably, in the choice of an internal vs. external drainage plan. Perimeter drainage is the better choice for earth-covered slabs. Plazas, however, are adaptable to either perimeter or internal drainage plans, depending on a balancing of assets and liabilities.

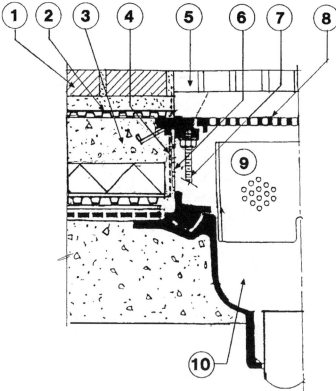

Fig. 11-4c   Plaza drain with brick wearing surface. (1) brick in sand setting bed with sand swept joints, (2) drainage composite, (3) cast concrete protection slab, (4) filter fabric, (5) stone or precast concrete cover with perforations or slots and pedestals at corners, (6) perforated stainless steel, (7) adjustable threaded rods, (8) cast iron or bronze top rim and grate, (9) removable perforated filter, (10) cast iron deep sump drain with clamping ring and optional sediment bucket.

The greatest disadvantage of interior drains for earth-covered slabs concerns the necessity of providing for maintenance, silt and root removal. These maintenance provisions may consist of pipes, basins, and surface cleanouts or telltales. All of these components must remain free from root intrusion and damage from landscaping equipment. Interior drains also introduce drain water into the building, from which it must be discharged into a storm sewer instead of flowing directly into the surrounding soil. As still another disadvantage, drains penetrating the membrane also create a vulnerable flashing posing a significant leak risk. Where there are compelling reasons overriding these disadvantages — e.g., where a large waterproofed earth-covered area cannot be conveniently drained entirely at the perimeter — the designer can use the detail shown in Fig. 11-5.

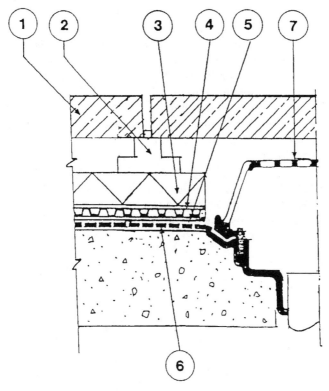

Fig. 11-4d Plaza drain with pedestal supported pavers (1) stone or concrete pavers, (2) pedestals, (3) loose laid insulation, (4) drainage composite, (5) protection board, (6) waterproofing (7) cast iron drain with strainer and optional sediment bucket. Drain may be cast in concrete, welded to a sump or installed in a sleeve and equipped with underdeck clamps.

For waterproofed plaza slabs, the balancing of risks is much less lopsided. There are, of course, the same arguments against interior drains, which introduce leak-prone penetrations in the membrane and possible overloading of the storm sewers. But perimeter drainage has liabilities, too — notably, in subjecting the foundation waterproofing to higher hydrostatic pressure from runoff from the slab perimeter. This runoff may also overload the footing drains, particularly if this water is handled by a sump pump.

Drainage Courses

Specification of a drainage course above the membrane was one of several changes from faulty traditional design practices responsible for numerous plaza waterproofing failures. A drainage course can comprise traditional stone aggregate, normally pea gravel or a drainage composite covered with a synthetic geotextile material. These new geotextiles, made of polypropylene, polyester, or nylon fabrics, can be manufactured to a narrow range of permeabilities. They also serve a secondary function, resisting root intrusion down to membrane level in earth-covered water-proofing systems. They cannot, however, compete with a concrete protection slab as a virtually foolproof shield against root intrusion. (For sizing, stratum thickness, cleanliness requirements, etc., for pea gravel, see Chapter 13, "Specifying Waterproofing".)

Because of their much higher potential for clogging the system with soil particles blocking gravity-impelled flow of water through the water-proofing assembly, earth-covered slabs often require two drainage courses, one above and one below the insulation (see Fig. 11-5).

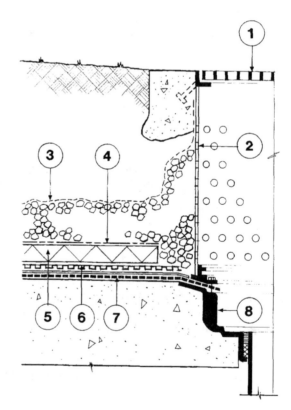

Fig. 11-5 Interior drain for earth-covered structural slab drains at all depths, from concrete collar at surface to membrane level at top surface of structural concrete slab. (1) grating in frame, (2) perforated stainless steel screen extension, (3) filter sheet, (4) polyethylene sheet, (5) insulation, (6) drainage composite, (7) membrane with protection board, (8) drain.

Thermal Insulation

The key question on insulation concerns its location: above or below the membrane? Until the energy crisis of the early 1970s, the key question was whether to specify insulation. But the old practice of simply relying on the aggregate or earth fill to insulate the occupied space is seldom justifiable, unless the space is neither heated nor cooled. Gravel, earth, and coarse sand provide high heat capacity, thus stabilizing heat gains or losses. But their thermal resistances (R values) are very low compared with those of insulating materials of equal thickness.

A third possible location for the insulation, under the deck, has several disadvantages:

- Thermal bridging at walls and hangers
- Subjection of membrane and deck to extreme daily and seasonable temperature cycling
- Possible condensation of upward-migrating water vapor in the insulation
- Fire resistance required

The PMR concept — i.e., insulation located above the membrane — is generally the better design for waterproofed decks, for several reasons. Above a heated interior, even in the coldest winter weather, the above-membrane location should maintain membrane temperature well above the dewpoint. This is a safeguard against condensation dripping down through cracks in the concrete slab. The above-membrane location also interposes the insulation between the potentially heavily trafficked plaza wearing surface and the membrane, thus augmenting the protection board's membrane-shielding function. And because the insulation in a waterproofed deck system normally carries higher traffic loads than a roof system, it already requires high compressive strength, regardless of its location.

The above-membrane location for insulation in waterproofed deck construction limits the material choice to essentially the same as that for a PMR. As a practical matter, that choice is virtually limited to extruded polystyrene board, the only material possessing the two required properties of adequate compressive strength and moisture resistance. Foamglass is the only other material satisfying both the compressive strength and moisture resistance required for below-membrane use. But its vulnerability to freeze-thaw cycling makes it too risky as an above-membrane insulation, unless the climate is mild enough to preclude freeze-thaw cycling.

Even in climates free from freeze-thaw cycling, Foamglas is limited to unfaced blocks rather than boards with two-sided facers. These kraft-paper facers lack the moisture-absorptive resistance of foamglass itself, and this deficiency disqualifies them as suitable insulation for a waterproofing system. Moreover, their brittleness makes them vulnerable to chipping of corners, cracking over irregular substrates, and other field hazards better resisted by the tougher extruded polystyrene.

Extruded polystyrene board should conform to ASTM C 920, Type IV, a closed-cell foam that retains about 80% of its dry thermal resistance in a continuously wet environment. This foam's 60-psi compressive strength is adequate for any plaza or earth-covered design loading. Its roughly 10% permanent deformation under constant compressive stress of this magnitude results in a mere ¼ in. lowering of the wearing surface with 2½-in.-thick insulation. This would normally be insignificant.

For earth-covered slabs, thermal insulation may have still another purpose, in addition to its energy-conserving, membrane-protecting roles. Some landscape architects require insulation under earth fill to prevent trees and plants from leafing during cold winter weather, when heat conducted upward from warm underground spaces can confuse ignorant plantings into a false belief that spring has sprung.

The thermal-insulating benefits of earth-covered slabs depend on several factors — notably, climate, soil type, and soil moisture content. Earth-covered slabs generally provide thermal benefits in summer, chiefly by reducing surface temperatures, which, on dark-colored surfaces can rise far above 100°F when air temperature is 80°F or higher. Where winters are cold and cloudy, in the northern tier of states coast-to-coast across the U.S., there are also significant winter benefits from the insulating and temperature-stabilizing effects of earth cover, with its high heat capacity. But in more southerly, sunny states, winter effects can be negative, as earth cover can reduce surface temperatures and provide little thermal resistance owing to perpetually wet soil. Soil-moisture content is a highly complicating factor. "High" moisture content (i.e., above 20% by weight) can reduce the "dry" thermal resistance (i.e., below 4% moisture) by a factor of 15 in silt and clay. The project mechanical engineer should investigate the thermal effects of earth cover. This investigation may require a study of seasonal variations in soil moisture content.[4]

For expanded discussion of the design factors involved in plaza waterproofing thermal design, see Appendix D in this manual and ASTM Standard Guide C 981, *Standard Guide for Design of Built-up Bituminous Membrane Waterproofing Systems for Building Decks, Section 13, Insulation*. In addition to the design factors briefly discussed in this chapter, ASTM C 981 covers dimensional stability, fungus resistance, vapor permeance, shear stress, fatigue stress, and several other design criteria. ASTM C 981 also explains the problems of below-deck insulation, vapor retarders, and other aspects of plaza waterproofing design.

---

4. Further information can be found in the Proceedings of the Underground Space Conference and Exposition, June 8-10, 1981, Kansas City and others published by Pergamon Press, New York, NY.

Concrete Protection Slabs

A concrete protection slab, minimum 3 in. thick, and normally reinforced with welded wire fabric, is an optional component in waterproofing systems for both plazas and earth-covered slabs. Its chief function in a plaza system is to protect the membrane during subsequent construction. Sometimes called a "working" slab, it provides a hard, stable surface for construction operations. In earth-covered systems it serves a permanent function, shielding the membrane from possible damage from roots that may penetrate the drainage course and protection.

Whether to include or omit a concrete protection slab is a major design decision in a plaza waterproofing system. The designer balances *accessibility* against *reliability*. Accessibility to the membrane, provided by specifying removable components above the membrane, is obviously an enormous advantage, facilitating repair or, in extreme instances, replacement of the waterproofing membrane. But in accordance with the no-free-lunch principle, accessibility normally comes at some sacrifice in reliability. High-density polyethylene and drainage courses with geotextile filters can provide considerable resistance to root intrusion into the membrane. They cannot, however, compete with the virtually impregnable root-intrusion resistance of a concrete protection slab or provide protection from landscape equipment. Is this extra insurance worth the premium cost of the concrete protection slab? Does the reduced risk of failure assured by the concrete protection slab compensate for the higher cost of repair in event of failure? Can the system accommodate the additional 38-psf dead load and the additional 3-in. thickness of the concrete protection slab? The answer to these questions is a business decision that depends upon conditions, surfacing, and sensitivity of the waterproofed occupancy.

Flashing

Like roof systems, waterproofed deck systems require flashing at terminations, penetrations, and expansion joints. In contrast with roof systems, where base flashing installation follows membrane installation, flashing at waterproofed deck terminations must be installed prior to membrane application. In the plaza field, at rising walls and expansion joints, the horizontal leg of base flashing should be installed on a curb at least 1½ in. above the structural slab to direct water flow away from the joint. Material for expansion-joint covers should be elastomeric, supported on neoprene tubes, to prevent distortion from water or earth-fill pressure. A continuous hammock under the tube serves as a vapor retarder and bitumen dam. It can also be sloped to a drain, to provide a secondary means of protection. Some experts recommend installation of a sheet metal gutter under expansion joints over particularly sensitive occupancies.

Internal and exterior corners and similar transitions must be reinforced with at least one membrane ply or liquid-applied fillet. Raising this flashing height above the membrane is good practice, like the similar practice for expansion joints.

Penetrations are flashed like roof penetrations. Individual pipes should be spaced a minimum of 6 in. apart. Avoid ganged pipes in pitch pockets.

Base flashing must extend above the wearing course, preferably 8 in. This is critical if the wearing course is a closed system.

Like flashing in roof systems, flashed penetrations at walls and expansion joints should *always* be at high points, with the drained surfaces sloped away from them. If practicable, penetrations should also be located at high points, but, in any event, never at low points.

Flashing for earth-covered slabs must extend at least 8 in. above the earth at rising walls and parapets, light standards, skylight wells, vent stacks, air shafts, and other slab-penetrating components. Where such extension is impracticable — e.g., where doors open onto paved areas at the same elevation (required for ADA compliance) — a grating-covered gutter is recommended (see Fig. 11-6).

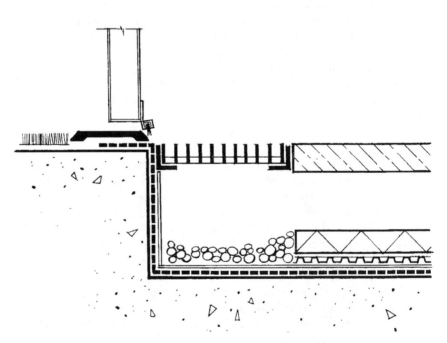

Fig. 11-6 This detail shows a grating-covered gutter at a door opening at the same elevation as a pedestal supported paver-surfaced plaza, it satisfies ADA requirements and prevents wind-driven rain from penetrating under the door or threshold.

Expansion Joints

Where earth-covered slabs, including planters, abut rising walls, an expansion joint is required to accommodate slab deflection that occurs when soil overburden is placed over the waterproofing systems. Slab deflection can exceed 1 in. (see Fig. 11-7). (An alternative expansion joint detail is depicted in Fig. 11-8).

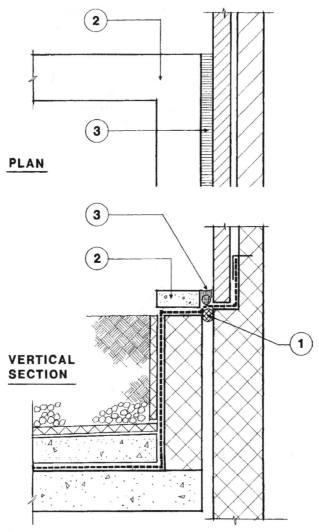

PLAN

**VERTICAL
SECTION**

Fig. 11-7 An alternative method for accommodating deflection of an earth-covered slab is to locate the expansion joint at top of stub wall adjacent to the rising wall, as shown in the detail above. This is the preferred method where parapets intersect the rising wall. (1) membrane tube support with hammock, (2) coping, (3) sealant and backer rod.

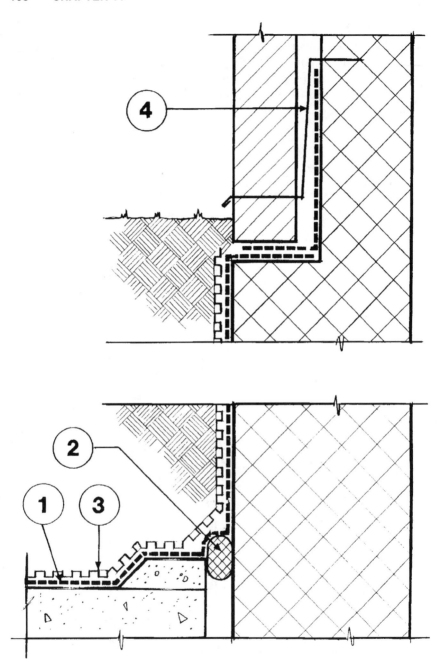

Fig. 11-8 One method of accommodating an earth-covered slab's deflection adjacent to a rising wall is a subsurface expansion joint, as shown in detail above. (1) membrane with protection board, (2) membrane tube support with hammock, (3) drainage composite, (4) flashing.

In addition to perimeter expansion joints, large plazas may require structural expansion joints in the plaza field, generally spaced at 100 to 200 ft. (These joints are usually designed by the structural engineer.) Wearing courses, which are exposed to temperature changes 10 or more times as great as those experienced by the insulated, underlying structure, require a correspondingly greater number of expansion joints extending only through the wearing course section. A wearing course expansion joint must coincide with each structural expansion joint (see Fig. 11-9). At these locations, the expansion joint width at the wearing course must approximate the width of the structural expansion joint. The single exception to this rule is where the wearing course consists of loose-laid units.

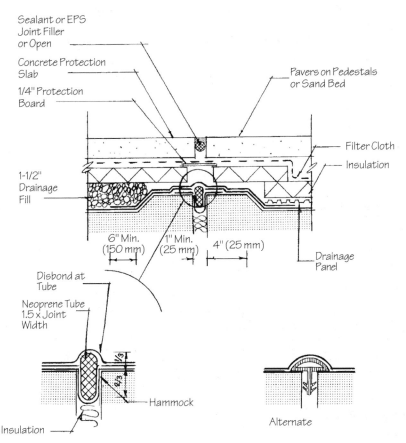

Fig. 11-9   The more closely spaced expansion joints in plaza wearing surfaces must coincide with structural expansion joints, which are carried through the entire cross section. Note higher elevation at the expansion joint. The slab should slope away from the expansion joint line. (American Society of Testing and Materials.)

On earth-covered slabs, the expansion joint need not extend through the entire cross section, as soil can accommodate small joint movements (see Fig. 11-10).

(For more detailed discussion of expansion joints, see Chapter 14, "Detailing Waterproofing.")

Wearing-Surface Design

Wearing surfaces are divided by ASTM C 898 into two basic categories:

- Open-joint systems, drained at the membrane level
- Closed-joint systems, drained at the surface

The membranes of open-joint systems, which resemble PMR roof systems, are rarely subjected to hydrostatic pressures exceeding 5 psf (i.e., a 1 in. depth of water). Closed-joint (i.e., monolithic) wearing surfaces, designed to shed water at the surface, similarly shield the membrane from continuous high hydrostatic pressure.

In heavily trafficked locations, waterproofed plazas must satisfy the following wearing-surface design criteria:

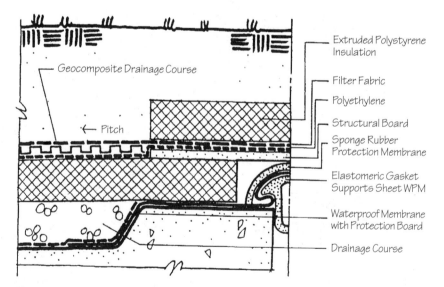

Fig. 11-10   Expansion joint in earth-covered structural slab need not continue through entire cross section, as soil can accommodate small joint deformation. (Adapted from NAVFAC.DM1.4)

- Structural strength to bear traffic loads
- Durability under heavy wear and weathering
- Esthetic appearance (on plazas and roof terraces)
- Heat reflectivity (to avoid summer temperature buildup)

The first two criteria are mandatory; the latter two optional. Cast-in-place or precast concrete, ceramic, or masonry units generally satisfy these requirements. Dark colors — especially black — are normally avoided because of their high heat absorption.

Joints on a roughly 10-ft maximum grid are normally required to accommodate thermal contraction and expansion in surfacing units (see Fig. 11-9). They can experience daily temperature extremes of 80°F and annual extremes of 180°F in the most severe climates. Use of snow-melting equipment (embedded electrical-resistance cables or hot-water pipes) complicates the problem of thermal design of the surfacing. Rapid temperature changes accompanying intermittent operation of the snow-melting system or expansion of corroding embedded pipes can crack surfacing slabs. Heat snow-melting equipment that may be embedded in concrete or over membranes may soften bituminous materials and impair their performance.

Open vs. Closed-Joint Plazas

The basic preliminary decision for surfacing design involves a choice between open and closed joints in the plaza surfacing. If the plaza must carry heavy vehicular live loads — for maintenance, firefighting, and snow-removal equipment — this preliminary design decision may eliminate open-jointed construction, which can seldom carry concentrated wheel loads of 7,000 lb or more. Pedestal-supported pavers are especially vulnerable to such concentrated loads. When open-jointed construction can be considered, however, it offers several advantages (listed later) over the closed-jointed construction dictated by high vehicular loading.

Pavers for open-joint construction are fabricated from two basic materials: precast concrete and natural stone. Precast pavers are hydro-pressed or wet cast in molds into units of square or rectangular shape, ranging from 12 x 24 to 30 in. square, in thicknesses normally ranging from 1¼ to 2½ in., but sometimes as thick as 4 in. These pavers normally weigh 15 to 25 psf. Compressive strength is generally 7,000 psi; maximum water absorption 5%. Precast pavers are available in a wide spectrum of colors and textures. (For detailed data on all types of pavers see Appendix B.)

Natural stone pavers include granite, marble (including travertine), flagging of slate, and high-density limestone. Thicknesses range from 1½ to 4 in., for stones with low flexural strength. Shapes and sizes vary, but rectangular and square shapes are preferred for pedestal-supported natural stones.

Pavers for closed-joint construction cover a wider range than for open-joint construction. In addition to all the precast and natural stones used in open-joint construction, closed-joint pavers include bricks, concrete masonry units, ceramic and quarry tile. Paver bricks should never be facing brick.

Open-jointed surfacing units — precast concrete, tile, or masonry units — can be installed on ribbed insulation that conducts water downward to the waterproofing membrane, where it runs to drains. Fine gravel, clean coarse sand (held on a No. 30 sieve), or no-fines (i.e. porous) concrete can serve as the percolating stratum underlying the open-jointed surfacing units. Loose aggregate can accommodate freeze-thaw cycling of entrapped water, with freezing expansion contained harmlessly within the aggregate interstices.

In a frequently specified and generally superior alternative to loose aggregate percolation, the surfacing units can be installed on pedestals, on insulation, or directly on protection boards, providing faster, less obstructed subsurface drainage. Surfacing soffits can also be grooved, corrugated, or otherwise contoured to create open paths for subsurface drainage.

Filter cloth is not required under open-jointed pavers for two reasons:

(1) It retards drainage (by retaining dirt) although it may reduce clogging in insulation board joints.

(2) Filter-cloth materials, polyester and polypropylene, degrade on exposure to ultraviolet radiation that penetrates the open joints.

This alternative pedestal-supported, open-jointed system has several advantages:

- Adaptability to a dead level wearing surface
- Faster, more efficient drainage, with better surface-dirt removal
- Ventilation drying of subsurfaces areas
- Easier access for maintenance cleaning, and repair of subsurface components.
- Elimination of joint sealants required in closed-joint systems

Offsetting these benefits, open-jointed plaza construction has several liabilities:

- A more complex design/construction problem, at probably higher initial cost.
- Possible hazards for female pedestrians wearing spiked heels (on plazas with wide joints between pavers)
- Rocking of incorrectly set pedestals under pedestrian traffic
- Objectionable reverberations from leather heel impact.

Monolithic (closed-joint) construction changes the waterproofed deck design philosophy, demoting the membrane from the primary to the secondary line of waterproofing defense. The membrane nonetheless is an essential component of the system because the surfacing of waterproofed decks is normally exposed to traffic loads, drastic temperature changes, and freeze-thaw cycling, with expansion of water trapped in cracks, holes, or other imperfections. Insulation is interposed between the membrane and the wearing surface material, with a setting bed for the surfacing units: precast ceramic or masonry tiles or manufactured conglomerates. Surfacing should slope away from adjoining walls and expansion joints to direct water away from them both at and below the surfacing.

For closed-joint construction, there are three methods of paver support: sand beds, mortar beds, and direct bearing on the insulation. Sand beds work best with small pavers because they can accommodate movement of the paver units in the vertical plane with less differential elevation between adjacent units. (Where adjacent units have different elevations adjacent to joints, they may trip pedestrians.)

Sand-setting beds can be installed over a concrete protection slab, but are generally unsatisfactory on rigid insulation. Sand-setting beds should be restricted to narrow thickness to avoid paver settling, rocking, and loosening caused by eccentric loading. Unbalanced compressive stresses in the sand can cause differential displacement in the sand stratum, with consequent tilting of the supported pavers. To avoid these paver disruptions, sand thickness should be limited to 1 in., which is usually adequate to accommodate subgrade variations and a higher substrate elevation at expansion joints.[5] A 1-in. sand bed can be installed over filter cloth on a 3 to 6-in. stratum of coarse aggregate or drainage composite. This practice provides the additional benefit of preventing frost heave in climates subject to freeze/thaw cycling. Sand should be coarse, with single-sized grains — not gap-graded like mortar sand — to promote maximum porosity.

In addition to the previously cited structural advantages, closed-joint construction offers several other advantages:

- Protection of waterproofing membrane from de-icing salts, cigarettes, leaf debris, and dirt in general
- Adaptability to a greater variety of pavers, designs and sizes
- Shielding of insulation and waterproofing from large quantities of water
- Enhancement of pedestrians' sense of solidity
- Damping of cacophonous clatter of high heels striking pedestal-supported pavers

5.   Estenssoror and Perenchino, "Failures of Exterior Plazas," *Construction Specifier*, Jan., 1991, p. 87-92.

One minor disadvantage is that it drains slowly and imposes a hydrostatic pressure on the membrane.

Earth-Covered Slabs and Plaza "Furniture"

Planters, reflecting pools, foundations, and other plaza "furniture" should be installed above the waterproofing membrane. These items are individually waterproofed. Trees should be planted in separate concrete containers to avoid damage to the membrane from root penetration or damage from landscaping shovels when trees must be replaced or replanted (See Fig. 11-11 and Fig. 11-12).

Earth-covered structural slabs can be planted with ground cover, shrubs, and trees. Soil depths, required for different plantings range from 8 in. for grass-growing earth fill to 3 ft or more for earth containing trees. As previously discussed, load-alleviating techniques include fillers — foam blocks and capped hollow tubes — under shallow-rooted plants. Lightweight soils are sometimes specified, but they may provide inadequate ballast for tree roots under windy conditions.

Techniques for maintaining healthy plantings are the province of the landscape architect, beyond the scope of this manual. Guidance on low maintenance, indigenous plant material for plantings is contained in the University of Minnesota's *Earth-Sheltered Residential Design Manual* and similar publications for those waterproofing designers who venture into this aspect of plaza design.

Flood Testing

Flood testing, per ASTM D 5957, is important for waterproofed plazas because a failed waterproofing system is far more destructive and more expensive to correct than a failed roof. If tearoff-replacement of a failed roof system costs $6 psf, its counterpart for a failed waterproofed plaza can cost $60 psf. It is thus advisable to flood-test a waterproofed deck after the membrane and flashing have been installed and before the above-membrane components are installed.

Flood-test with a maximum 4-in. water depth over the entire surface. Plug drains and use permanent or temporary curbs to retain water for 24 hours. Wood dams adhered to the waterproofing membrane can contain the flood test water.

When drains are not connected, make special provisions for pumping and disposal of test water. Cover the membrane with protection boards as soon as possible after drying the membrane surface. (If protection is required prior to flood testing, provide a temporary loose-laid protection layer removed prior to testing.)

ASTM D 5957 sets the following limitations:

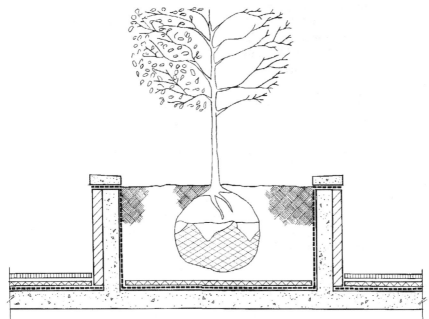

Fig. 11-11 Trees and bushes should never be planted in areas relying on the basic waterproofing membrane under an earth-covered structural-slab, as shown in detail above. They should always be provided with their own separate water-proofed concrete containers. (See Fig. 11-12).

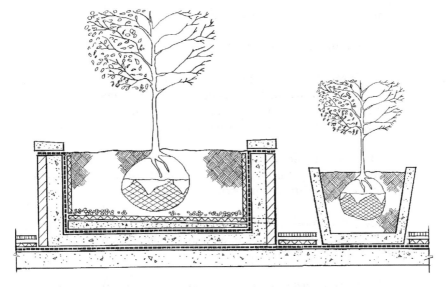

Fig. 11-12 This shows the correct detail providing a separate waterproofed container for a tree planting. Insulation is often installed in the planter to avoid false blooming in winter.

- Slope must not exceed 2%
- Membranes: LAMs, adhered or loose-laid sheets, built-up and modified-bitumens
- Do not test until 24 hours after completion of application (48 hours if waterproofing was installed at ambient temperatures below 50°F).
- Inspect membrane and flashings prior to test and repair any defects.

If leakage is detected during the test, ASTM D 5957 instructs as follows:

- Repair leak-causing defects
- Retest affected area under same conditions as initial test.

See also Chapter 13.

Alerts

Design

1. Provide minimum ⅛-in. slope (preferably ¼-in.) in structural deck.

2. Slope deck away from walls and expansion joints.

3. Specify all-level drains for closed-joint waterproofed deck systems.

4. Over precast concrete decks, provide a 3000-psi concrete topping, minimum 3-in. thick, reinforced with welded wire fabric. Precast concrete units must be securely tied together (to prevent relative movement and consequent cracking of the topping).

5. Coordinate structural design, especially for earth-covered slabs, via a preliminary meeting among waterproofing designer, landscape architect, and structural engineer.

6. Check concrete-deck surface with 10-ft straightedge. Permit maximum "gradual" offset of ¼ in./ft (per *American Concrete Standard 301-72*).

7. Obtain the manufacturer's signed approval confirming the suitability of the product for the project use. Also require manufacturer's certification of the applicator.

8. Require the concrete contractor, not the roofing contractor, to repair defective concrete surface.

9. Maximize single-ply sheet size (to minimize vulnerable field-spliced lap seams).

10. Reinforce substrate joints or cracks.

11. Compartmentalize loose-laid, single-ply systems if not fully adhered.

12. Locate expansion joints at slab high points.

13. Use two-stage drains.

14. Use protection slabs where rising walls, parapets, stairs and trees will be installed over the membrane.

12

Waterproofing Failures

Though less common than roof failures, the perennial leader among building systems as a source of litigation, waterproofing failures are much more serious and expensive to rectify. Reroofing is a great inconvenience, especially when it involves tearoff and total replacement. Waterproofing, however, is a comparative nightmare, often costing 10 times as much as roof replacement. Leakage can make an underground space uninhabitable. Replacement of a failed waterproofing system may entail excavation of tons of earth fill and plantings, or jackhammering of concrete paving surface and its removal, along with drainage courses, protection slabs, and other system elements. Leaking foundation walls are difficult to expose, the deeper the more difficult. Moreover, waterproofing leak sources can be extremely difficult to locate for positive-side (i.e., exterior) waterproofing systems. Leaks through negative-side (i.e., dry-side) systems are easier to detect, and obviously more accessible. But they can require removal of expensive finishes.

Because of these greater difficulties and the horrendous expense of failures, a waterproofing system's anticipated service life should ideally equal the building's service life. Roof systems, on the other hand, like mechanical, electrical, lighting, and other building subsystems, can be rationally designed for 15 or 20 years' service life, with replacement anticipated before the building's useful life is terminated. First-cost economy is thus a minor criterion for waterproofing. It should rank last among the designer's criteria for system selection.

Sources of Waterproofing Failure

Waterproofing failures stem from the following sources:

- Designer error
- Negligent construction practices
- Defective materials

Designer error is probably the chief source of waterproofing failure. It is thus distinguished from roof-system failures, which are chiefly attributable to contractor negligence. Designer error sometimes entails specification of an inappropriate system, through ignorance of its particular limitations and widespread confusion about the proper uses and limitations of various waterproofing systems. This simplest kind of designer error represents a substantial proportion of this source of waterproofing failures.

One explanation of the prevalence of design ignorance as a cause of waterproofing failure stems from the contrasting educational efforts of roofing manufacturers, on one hand, and waterproofing manufacturers, on the other. After suffering along with architects, contractors, and building owners through a quarter century of rampant litigation, roofing manufacturers began providing reference details for a wide spectrum of project conditions. In contrast, most waterproofing manufacturers have lagged in providing this technical guidance, though they have been rectifying this situation in recent years. As a consequence, waterproofing designers have sometimes made disastrous mistakes — e.g., attempting to combine incompatible materials for walls and structural slabs with no satisfactory detail at their intersection.

Why the difference between these two closely related industries? The answer probably lies in their contrasting litigation experiences. Unlike the roofing industry, the waterproofing industry was never buried in an avalanche of costly litigation. This lack of a painful financial goad may explain the waterproofing manufacturers' tardy educational efforts.

The greatest source of designer errors, however, is probably a lack of coordination between the design professionals involved in waterproofing design. Uncoordinated design is more likely to occur on a waterproofing project than on a roofing project. Roof design is normally the sole responsibility of the architect (or a roof consultant retained by the architect or owner.) In waterproofing design, however, responsibility sometimes gets blurred because there are several participants in the design process — soils engineer, structural engineer, and architect. The required coordination sometimes gets lost in the general shuffling of the myriad problems and responsibilities involved in the construction process.

Consider a typical problem waterproofing project. The recommendation for waterproofing originates with the soils (geotechnical) engineer. In addition to its waterproofing recommendation, the soils report incorporates recommendations for foundation design — soil-bearing capacity, depth of footings, seismic forces (if any), etc. Following the soils report's recommendation, the architect and structural engineer jointly decide on the extent of required waterproofing. Plaza waterproofing is designed and detailed by the architect; waterproofing for basement slab-on-ground and foundation wall may be designed by the structural engineer and also by the architect.

This duplication can doom the project. As head of the design team, the architect is responsible for waterproofing design. He accordingly provides details for all waterproofed components — plaza structural slab, foundation walls, and basement slab-on-ground. The engineer, however, may duplicate part of this work — e.g., indicating waterproofing for foundation walls and slab-on-ground with vague notes and lines. The engineer should, of course, refer to the architectural drawings for *all* waterproofing information, providing a unified source of information for the contractor.

Contradictory specifications can pose an even bigger problem - and a more important one, since specifications normally outweigh drawings in a legal sense. The architect's specification may call for membrane waterproofing, whereas the engineer's specification (following engineers' proclivities for these materials) may call for bentonite or negative-side coatings. The architect must always follow through, eliminating such conflicts in contract documents. For when there is a conflict, the contractor may make a choice without checking with the architect - though, of course, he should not do so. Poor communication among design-team members can be as deadly a foe of successful waterproofing projects as technical error.

Technical errors nonetheless account for a large proportion of design-caused waterproofing failures. Defective design is one of the most common sources of waterproofing failure, illustrated in the following examples known to the author:

- In a deep basement, part of the basement slab-on-ground is stabilized by rock anchors designed to resist hydrostatic uplift. The remaining slab-on-ground, not subject to this uplift pressure, is continuously supported on a gravel course with under drains. After completion of the basic design, two sump pits were added: one in the uplift zone, the other in the continuous bearing zone, with one wall of the sump pits in the same plane as the foundation wall. This unusual, if not unique, arrangement required an elaborate detail, but was not brought to the attention of the designer. The contractor's "solution" was a dismal failure; it leaked.
- Defective detailing caused a failure at the expansion joint in a waterproofed structural split slab over an underground gymnasium supporting a plaza. The defective detail, relying on the dubious principle of sliding metal plates, was squeezed into the same plane as the horizontal membrane. It failed at a T joint

and was virtually irreparable. Lesson: Expansion joints should be straight and extend vertically through the entire structural cross section.

Negligent contractor practices account for many waterproofing failures. These negligent practices span the entire spectrum of possible errors. Perhaps the least excusable is omission of protection boards. Puncturing of unprotected membranes over waterproofed slabs is a common source of waterproofing failure. Erection of scaffolding, movement of heavy equipment, or damage from reinforcing bars and general construction debris all threaten a membrane unshielded from such hazards (see Fig. 12-1). Such inexcusable incidents highlight the absolute necessity of inspection by the owner's representative. Practically, if not legally, failure to provide such inspection makes the owner an accessory to the contractor's neglect (see Fig. 12-2).

The biggest villain among contractors involved with waterproofing projects is most likely to be the site contractor responsible for backfilling. Defective backfill materials — rocks, frozen soil, organic matter, and miscellaneous debris — are often dumped into excavations regardless of specifications banning such materials. Some site contractors neither know nor care that a bulldozer blade can be a weapon as well as an earth-

Fig. 12-1 This chaotic scene, depicting an unprotected waterproofing membrane exposed to multiple punctures from reinforcing bars, wood, and nails, plus other construction debris, highlights the necessity of an owner-financed inspector on the site to demand installation of protection boards.

Fig. 12-2   Beer and soda cans thrown into the formwork by irresponsible, care-less workmen are indicated by arrows in the above photograph, just below the joint between the foundation wall and the wall-bearing structural slab. These mislocated cans formed voids at the wall's interior face, not in the exterior face, which formed the substrate for the positive-side waterproofing. They nonethe-less aggravated the leaking discovered at this joint, by reducing wall thickness and creating larger voids than their own volume by obstructing aggregate flow during the concrete-casting operation. A vigilant concrete inspector would readily have spotted these cans. Waterproofing quality depends not only on the quality of the waterproofing subcontractor's work, but also on the quality of the general contractor's work.

moving tool. Inadequate filter-cloth lapping, sufficient to prevent infil-tration of fines, or tearing of filter cloth during backfilling operations can compound these backfilling felonies.

Next in the villains' gallery is the general contractor who presses the waterproofing subcontractor into premature installation of materi-als onto unsuitably prepared, or even unprepared, substrates. The gen-eral contractor obsessively dedicated to the proposition, "Time is money," can be the owner's, and ultimately, his own worst enemy. Good work-manship outranks time-saving in any rational calculation of waterproof-ing project economics. A tiny premium for waterproofing insurance will return a double, or even triple-digit multiple over a penny-saving prema-ture schedule accelerated by a reckless general contractor.

Other negligent practices include contractors' lack of preparation for the inevitable vicissitudes of construction. Under the best of circum-stances, delays resulting from flash storms, snow storms, dewatering equipment failure, or cold-weather sieges freezing concrete surfaces can disrupt a waterproofing project. The contractor must nonetheless be prepared to cope. Installation of wall waterproofing sometimes proceeds so far ahead of backfilling that bad weather can cause long delays in backfilling operations, leaving the waterproofing exposed for weeks. Installation of waterproofing on a basement mud mat while simultaneously excavating an adjacent area is another hazardous, yet not uncommon practice. The excavating operation can ruin the waterproofing application, as dust and dirt are blown and tracked onto the finished waterproofing, or worse yet, onto the waterproofing as it is applied.

Compound Errors

Note, also, that identifying the cause or causes of a waterproofing failure may be more complicated than simply blaming the designer or contractor as solely responsible. Construction culprits often have accessories. In waterproofing construction, as in life generally, a sharply demarcated black-and-white depiction may be less accurate than blurred shades of gray involving two, or more, culprits. The designer, in particular, is likely to be a party to a complicated case involving waterproofing failure. In almost any litigation over a waterproofing failure, the designer's judgment can become an issue, unless the contractor or the materials manufacturer has displayed blatant negligence.

Consider this complex waterproofing failure. Long steel girders, spanning a foundation excavation are dropped into bearing pockets and grouted solid. Solar heat raises the temperature of the exposed girders, and the consequent expansion cracks the foundation wall and its waterproofing. Whom do you blame for this failure? The contractor, for prematurely grouting the girders and failing to anticipate a steep temperature rise? Or do you blame the architect for not alerting the contractor to this hazard or providing for the expansion in his details?

On another project, a structural slab-on-ground is cast over a waterproofed mud mat, and designed to resist hydrostatic uplift pressure. The contractor, however, erroneously deactivates the dewatering system *before* interior shear walls for stairs and elevator shafts are in place to resist the upward movement of the slab. Again, a lack of communication or coordination between designer and contractor produced a failure.

As still another example, a deep foundation wall is cast on a heavily trafficked avenue. The dynamic loads from trucks and buses caused the wall to deflect inward after it had been waterproofed. The vital lateral support of an intermediate structural slab in the deep, two-level basement had not been cast. The wall was later jacked back into proper vertical alignment and the structural slab providing its lateral support was cast. But it was too late for the waterproofing on the foundation wall. It had split from the wall's excessive deflection.

As demonstrated by these examples, the designer must constantly picture the construction process to anticipate the fiendish ways that things can go wrong. On the last-cited project, the problem might have been prevented if the designers and contractor had realized the necessity for temporary lateral support of the foundation.

Foundation Wall Failures

Shifting focus from the underlying sources of waterproofing failure to the failure modes prevalent in specific waterproofed components, we start with foundation failures, which can be attributed to the following:

- Improper backfilling
- Defective joint details
- Concrete wall defects
- Defective flashing at penetrations
- Vapor entrapment

Improper backfilling can cause failure via two mechanisms. The most obvious stems from inclusion of membrane-damaging materials within the backfill — e.g., sharp-edged rocks, tree branches, or roots capable of puncturing protection board and ultimately penetrating the membrane (See Fig. 12-3).

Fig. 12-3 Photo of polystyrene-board application in lieu of protection board. (Waterproofing Systems of New Jersey.)

Backfill settlement, a subtler, yet readily avoidable problem, also results from contractor negligence. Backfill settlement is an aggravating factor promoting slippage. To the perpetual gravitational slippage force, which obviously cannot be avoided, backfill settlement can add the much greater frictional force of sinking soil mass in contact with protection boards, which, in turn, transmit the frictional force to the membrane. Even if the adhered membrane resists this magnified slippage force, the protection boards can be dragged downward, exposing the upper part of the membrane.

Backfill settlement results from negligently supervised backfill operations, dumping backfill into an excavation without proper controls. To avoid harmful settlement, backfill must be placed in small "lifts," maximum 12 in. or so (depending on soil characteristics), mechanically compacted to a density approximating its natural density. Proper backfilling depends upon a competent, responsible contractor — and even more so, upon rigorous field inspection by the owner's representative.

Defective joint details are another major source of waterproofing failures, at tops and bottoms of foundation walls. At the top, where structural slabs support plazas or earth-covered planted sites, the horizontal construction joint where the structural slab bears on the foundation wall creates a plane of potential leakage, especially if not properly reinforced to prevent the joint from opening as the slab deflects or shrinks. The waterproofing membrane should be reinforced at this joint to prevent possible stress concentration and splitting of the membrane at this construction joint (see Fig. 12-4).

At the bottom of foundation walls, a typical (and defective) detail is also vulnerable to leakage. Waterproofing carried across a wall footing at the same elevation as an adjoining mud slab creates a potential leakage path similar to the slab-wall joint described in the preceding paragraph. A vertical, positive-side waterproofing membrane is often extended down from the wall and then horizontally over the wall footing's toe. In the time that inevitably elapses between the application of the mud-slab waterproofing across the footing and the later application of the overlapping wall membrane, the horizontal joint may be soiled by deposits left by excavation or storm water covering the wall footing. This soil residue can destroy adhesion between the underlying and overlapping membranes, leaving a defective horizontal joint vulnerable to leakage.

Failure at this wall-footing joint often occurs with bentonite waterproofing, where the joint is either poorly packed or not packed at all. (For rectification of this problem see Fig. 10-2.) Lack of temporary protection board to protect against foundation formwork installation and stripping also causes failures at wall-footing joints.

Concrete wall defects constitute still another source of founda-

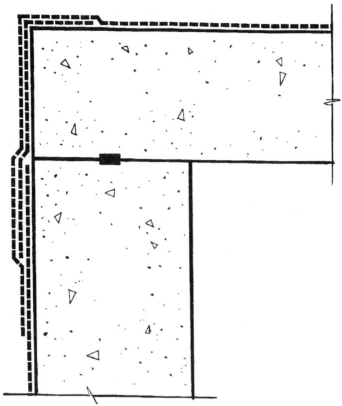

Fig. 12-4   Where structural slabs bear on a foundation wall, it creates a potentially dynamic horizontal joint. Frequently the foundation waterproofing is completed before the slab is cast. The membrane should be reinforced at this joint with a separate strip which may be combined with the corner reinforcing as shown in the above detail.

tion wall problems (see Fig. 12-2). Unlike the surfaces of structural slabs and slabs-on-ground, which must be finished to a more or less continuous plane surface, the vertical surfaces of concrete walls are sometimes pocked with irregular indentations or tie-rod holes, honeycombing voids, rock pockets, formwork kickouts or physically damaged areas. Hydrostatic pressure can produce concentrated shearing and flexural stresses that ultimately rupture a membrane adhered to an irregular concrete surface and admit leak water.

The obvious cause of these concrete wall defects is contractor negligence. The equally obvious preventive precaution is rigorous field inspection of concrete substrates destined to receive waterproofing, *before* its installation. Irregular concrete surfaces should be patched or repaired before membrane application is allowed to proceed. (See chapter 13, "Specifications" for details on wall repair procedures.)

Defective flashing at penetrations for pipes and conduit sometimes occurs because of the designer's failure to require minimum spacing at least 6 in. between adjacent penetrations.

To eliminate these problems, locate penetrations high enough to avoid interference with water stops and reinforcing bar splices. As a safe minimum dimension, penetrations should be located at least 12 in. above the top of the slab.

Vapor entrapment springs from an error in which the designer specifies membranes on *both* sides of a foundation wall. Entrapment of water vapor, given no chance to vent in either direction, can spawn a crop of blisters at the substrate-membrane interface, at consequent peril to the membrane's waterproofing integrity. This design error displays an elementary ignorance of the simplest principles of gas behavior; yet it occasionally occurs.

Plaza Slab Failures

Plaza structural slabs can fail in at least as many ways as foundation walls. Lack of proper drainage has historically been a major source of plaza failures. In past years, failures at wearing surfaces were common. These failures are attributable to inadequate, single-level drainage designed to remove water from the surface, but not at the membrane below. The designer sometimes specified drains with weepholes at the membrane level, an effort that indicated the proper attempt to provide two-level drainage. But these weepholes often got clogged with bitumen moppings or cement leached from the pavers' setting bed. Drain water dammed in ever-widening areas around the clogged drains promoted efflorescence and consequent popping of tiles (from expansion of the grout). This ponded water also promoted mold and vegetable growth in paver joints.

Omission of a drainage course above the membrane was another erroneous traditional practice, responsible for many plaza waterproofing failures. Earth-covered slabs often require two drainage courses, one above and one below the insulation, to avoid drain clogging. Avoidance of these problems requires close attention to the discussion in Chapter 11, "Plaza Waterproofing," and Chapter 14, "Detailing Waterproofing."

Paralleling the omission of protection boards on foundation walls, the contractor's failure to install protection boards immediately after completion of membrane installation and flood testing is another major cause of plaza waterproofing failure. The membrane-puncturing hazards of reckless backfilling operations threatening a foundation wall's waterproofing integrity have their counterparts on horizontal surfaces. Among these hazards are welding rods; reinforcing bars; sharp-edged fasteners; loose aggregate; carelessly stockpiled masonry units; and pipe scaffolds, sometimes erected without wood plank supports to distribute concentrated loads (see Fig. 12-1).

Inadequate slope, designed to provide a minimum 1% *after* dead-load creep and maximum elastic deflection, is another source of plaza waterproofing failure. Plaza junctures with walls and expansion joints are common leakprone locations, usually resulting from the designer's failure to locate these flashings at high points, with the slab sloped away from them. Lack of slope at a closed-joint wearing surface is another aspect of improper slope that can result in plaza waterproofing failure.

Defective expansion joints are a common location for plaza waterproofing failures even without inadequate design for slope. Design of these joints in conformance with the principles promulgated in Chapter 14 is essential. Expansion joints in horizontal surfaces are especially liable to leak.

Membrane defects are another obvious source of plaza waterproofing failures. Pinholing and cratering in the single-component, tar-modified urethane coating depicted in Fig. 12-5 are a major problem with liquid-applied membranes (LAMs). (See Chapter 9 for a detailed discussion of LAM defects, plus Chapters 7 and 8 for other types of membrane defects.)

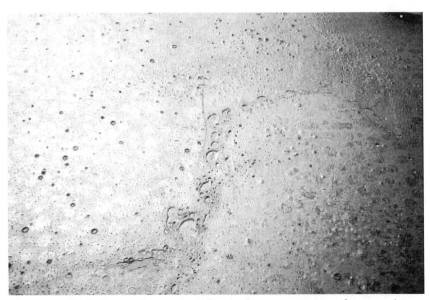

Fig. 12-5 Pinholing and cratering of a single-component urethane, moisture-cured LAM plaza are probably attributable to excessive substrate moisture, which can set off a carbon-dioxide-foaming reaction. Incorporation of air bubbles and some concrete-curing compounds can also produce pinholes, a major hazard of LAMs, discussed in detail in Chapter 9.

Slabs-On-Ground

Like the failure of other waterproofing components, the failure of a slab-on-ground can cause big problems for an owner — e.g., the destruction of an expensive hardwood floor. Slabs-on-ground waterproofing failures resemble roof failures in their most hazardous locations — i.e., at terminations of the slab and penetrations through them. The most common location for leakage through a slab-on-ground is at the joint between the slab and its peripheral basement wall. Other failure-prone locations include interior columns, pits, and pipe penetrations. Far less frequently, slabs-on-ground fail when structurally underdesigned for hydrostatic uplift pressure.

In general, the solution for the common problems of slabs-on-ground is proper detailing at the termination or penetration.

One common leak-prone location occurs where pits or shafts with one wall common to the foundation extend below the slab-on-ground slab. The complex geometry and sequencing of pours frequently creates discontinuities in the waterproofing membrane at changes in plane. Careful detailing requires not only multiple sections, but an isometric that depicts the transitions in three dimensions.

A second, similar leak-prone situation occurs where tunnels or higher basements penetrate foundations with lower slabs-on-ground. The transitions between slabs-on-ground at elevations higher than the bottom of the foundation require careful study to avoid future leaks. To provide a practical, leak-free waterproofing system, the designer must consider normal construction sequence, allowing for adequate concrete curing time and for erection and stripping of formwork.

The designer should also minimize pipe and drain penetrations, frequent leak sites in waterproofed slabs-on-ground. Pipes should penetrate foundations, and drainage should be accomplished via pits with horizontal pipes. Where penetrations are unavoidable — e.g., at interior columns and rock anchors — waterproofing should be indicated in great detail.

Leak Detection

Confronted with a waterproofing failure, the designer's obvious first step is to determine the source of the leak. Anticipating future leakage is much more difficult with positive-side waterproofing, invisible from the occupied space, than with negative-side waterproofing, which is visible from the interior. Though stains or blistering and peeling paint may sometimes presage leakage in positive-side waterproofing, failure is normally discovered only after leakage occurs. Negative-side waterproofing, on the other hand, often gives warning of impending leakage when cracks form in the cementitious/crystalline coatings.

The normal first step in leak detection is to determine the source of the leakwater. The second step is to determine the leak location, or locations, via correlations with design and events.

The investigation starts with a review of the leak history. If the leaking intensifies soon after rainfall, that fact points to surface runoff as the leakwater source. On virtually all structural plaza (or earth-covered) slabs, the leakwater originates with surface runoff. Common locations for such leaks are dynamic construction joints between foundation walls and structural slabs. (These joints sometimes lack the reinforcement required for extra membrane protection.) Rising walls and conduits are also common leak sites. Conduits are the more common of these two sites, and, fortunately, the easier to repair.

Constantly flowing leakwater uncorrelated with rainfall indicates a more difficult problem, with a greater variety of possible sources than rainfall-correlated leakage. Leakwater bubbling up between the foundation wall and basement slab-on-ground can result from a combination of surface water and a rising groundwater level. If the source is a change in direction of an underground stream or discharge from a downspout or ruptured catch basin, sealing the joint may merely shift the leak location to a weaker spot in the wall or slab.

Investigators' Checklist

Continuous leakage may result from a leaking sanitary sewer line. To verify this hypothesis, check infiltrating leakwater for coliform count. Where the sanitary sewer also carries storm-water runoff, flash storms can cause overflow that raises the water table. Again, check for coliform count to detect the presence of sewage.

At densely developed urban sites, where most of the ground is paved, surface runoff is seldom a significant factor in waterproofing leaks. The only exceptions to this general rule are cultivated areas and other unusual modifications of the typically paved urban landscape.

Leakage resulting from storm-water overflow alone, with no contribution from sanitary sewage, can indicate a larger variety of possible sources, notably:

- Sheet metal roof leaders improperly connected to cast iron or tile piping systems.
- Broken connections to gutters and leaders, causing concentrated overflow at foundations.
- Clogged drainage systems (from root intrusion into subsurface drains, infiltration of fines clogging the percolating aggregate stratum, or clogged areaway drains)
- Flashing failures at conduits in pools or planters
- Expansion-joint rupture in plazas and connections of pedestrian tunnels to foundations
- Failure of inadequately compacted cement cants, under increased hydrostatic pressure
- Disintegration of bituminous, butyl, and PVC membranes from leaking underground oil storage tanks.

In addition to the above itemized sources, there are more complicated causes for continuous leakage. An adjacent excavation can initiate a chain of leak-promoting events. If the adjacent well points or excavation goes deeper than the leaking space, it can lower the water table, causing differential foundation settlement. This, in turn, can induce leak-admitting tensile cracks in the foundation concrete.

Defective plaza drains are another source of excess water eventually leaking into the occupied space. Drains may be negligently designed, lacking the two-level drainage feature required for closed-joint plaza construction. If plaza surface gratings are solidly connected to the drains, with no provision for differential movement, the connection can rupture in a shearing failure, allowing excess water to overflow and eventually find its way into the occupied space.

Inspection: The Sine Qua Non

Here, in this chapter on failures, is a good place to stress again the need for quality assurance (QA) — i.e., owner-financed measures to assure installation per specification. Inspection is obviously the indispensable core of a good QA program. The most pennywise, dollar-foolish decisions in the construction industry entail the curtailing, or even elimination, of inspection. This folly springs from a faith in guarantees or litigation as a means of rectifying construction errors. It ignores the glaringly obvious benefits of inspection. You can prevent some of the most common and outrageously obvious causes of waterproofing failure — e.g., the flouting of backfill requirements by the site subcontractor — merely by putting a qualified, full-time inspector on the site.

Inspection, preferably by an independent agency financed by the owner, should be formalized. Lawrence suggests the following submissions:

- Daily reports with photos showing progress of the work
- Location and scope of work, dated and noted on drawings
- Copies of daily weather reports
- Material inventory (to assure installation at the specified rate)

This documentation can serve a dual purpose. It not only reduces the probability of negligent installation practices, which can culminate in a failed project; it also arms the designer and owner with powerful ammunition against the contractor if a failed project winds up in litigation. If the inspector has recorded violation of the specifications, together with warnings to the contractor, these records can be decisive in the courts or at arbitration hearings, where written documentation normally outweighs oral testimony by a huge margin.

13

Specifications

Like roof-system specifications, waterproofing specifications have presented a challenge of exponentially increasing complexity over the past several decades. Since the introduction of liquid-applied membranes (LAMs) back in the 1960s, traditional built-up bituminous membranes, bentonite, and cementitious coatings have been augmented by a proliferating array of materials — modified bitumens, synthetic rubber and plastic sheets, plus additional polyester liquid-applied formulations, laminated bentonite sheets, and other innovations — all confronting the designer with a bewildering range of choices.

System selection is easier for waterproofing than for roof systems in only one way. Because of the normally catastrophic financial costs of a waterproofing failure, the specifier should virtually ignore first cost. Any first-cost economy that adds even a slight incremental risk of failure is not worth considering on the vast majority of below-grade waterproofing projects. Reconstruction may require removal of tons of overburden and backfill, plus removal and replacement of the waterproofing system itself. And if reconstruction is impracticable, costly repair measures, featuring negative-side waterproofing injections with hydrophilic materials, may not provide a totally satisfactory remedy.

Perhaps the most common flaw in waterproofing specifications involves the verbatim copying of a manufacturer's specification. Use of a manufacturer's specification indicates the specifier's diffidence. A knowledgeable specifier will always have a distinctive focus on some aspect of a waterproofing project requiring some unusual provision. These unique aspects of a project will inevitably be overlooked or de-emphasized through use of a manufacturer's unaltered or unamended specification. *Adapting* a manufacturer's specification is acceptable practice; *copying* a manufacturer's specification is not.

In addition to this general criticism, the practice of copying a manufacturer's specification has two specific drawbacks:

- It may eliminate competition (by introducing unique, proprietary requirements)
- It complicates the processing of requests for acceptable substitutions.

Division Of Responsibility

The typical waterproofing project involves at least four principals — architect/engineer (A/E), manufacturer, general contractor, and waterproofing contractor. There is frequently a fifth, the construction manager (CM). Waterproofing requires a virtually unique degree of coordination among these principals, because it is almost always installed in stages. Scheduling these stages and assuring that the parties involved meet their obligations in timely fashion are critical.

In assigning responsibility, the specifier should follow these guidelines:

1. The A/E bears ultimate responsibility for selecting an appropriate waterproofing system, based on soil reports and other factors discussed in other chapters. He must verify the system's suitability with the manufacturer, define the scope of work, and provide details for all conditions.

2. The manufacturer of the waterproofing materials (or system) bears responsibility for providing the proper grade of materials — e.g., those that are temperature-dependent or salt-water resistant. The manufacturer is also responsible for checking soil reports to assure that his products will not be damaged by soil contaminants. The manufacturer must also assist in the preparation of shop drawings.

3. Bearing the greatest range of responsibilities, the general contractor must do the following:

- Schedule the installation of building components on which waterproofing is applied, the waterproofing itself, and backfill operations
- Verify the conformance of backfill aggregate with specified size limits and proper compaction.
- Maintain a water-free excavation
- Assure that the concrete contractor follows specifications on surface preparation, concrete curing, and form-release agents
- Restrict traffic over slab waterproofing by plumbing, electrical, and other trades
- Assure the provision of temporary protection of waterproofing at pipe scaffolds or masonry installations when walls are erected above the waterproofing membrane.

The general contractor's control of scheduling is vital in coordinating the work among the various contractors. Scheduling of waterproofing installation is dependent on the scheduling of backfill operations, as the backfill often serves as a platform for installing waterproofing on foundations.

4. The waterproofing contractor is responsible for installing the work in accordance with the manufacturer's instruction and the contract documents. He is also responsible for examining the waterproofing substrates (concrete or masonry) and assuring himself of their suitable texture, soundness, and dryness.

The waterproofing contractor applying cementitious coatings must coordinate his work with the concrete contractor to assure application of his material while the concrete is still green.

5. The CM must exercise caution in applying the criteria for Value Engineering (i.e., achieving a dependable waterproofing system at least cost). As indicated throughout this manual, first cost is the last consideration in selecting a waterproofing system.

Specifying Unfamiliar Products

Because of the potentially catastrophic cost of a waterproofing system's failure, specifiers should approach their task with an extremely conservative attitude. Consider new and unfamiliar products guilty until proven innocent.

A waterproofing failure involves far more than tearoff-replacement of the failed system; it can involve removal of tons of overburden and horrendous disruption. And, as previously indicated, the alternative of negative-side remedial work may prove ineffective as well as costly.

In pursuing this conservative design policy, the specifier can easily avoid selecting an untested or a new system from a manufacturer with little experience in waterproofing. A more difficult problem arises when a well established manufacturer modifies a product with a good track record or markets a new product under an old name or one from a company he has purchased. If the manufacturer is foreign, the situation becomes even worse. In any event, the prime manufacturer becomes a third party to the construction contract. This complication naturally muddies the legal waters, which are murky at best in the U.S. legal system, making it more difficult to fix responsibility in litigation.

To avoid these complications, the specifier should require the manufacturer's assurance that the product has not been deleteriously modified. At the least, the specifier should request from the manufacturer an exact description of the product modification, an explanation of its purpose, and comparative test results.

If, for some unforeseen circumstance, it becomes necessary for the specifier to consider a new or drastically modified product, he should investigate as follows:

1. Obtain from the manufacturer a list of projects on which the product has been previously used, including the owner, architect/engineer, and waterproofing contractor. By interviewing these principals, you can ascertain whether the conditions on their projects are similar to your project's.

2. Ask the manufacturer's representative about conditions in which the product is not recommended, about the failures as well as its successes. (This advice is not so naive as it might appear. Perhaps the manufacturer will not candidly inform you about the product's shortcomings or failures. But later, in possible litigation involving the product's failure, the architect/engineer may be questioned in cross-examination as to whether there was at least an attempt to get this information. An admission that there was not cannot help but weaken the designer's case.)

3. Notify the manufacturer in writing how you intend to use the product.

4. Request relevant technical data from the manufacturer. (If it cannot be supplied, you have, ipso facto, an excellent reason for not specifying the product.)

5. Insofar as practicable, investigate the manufacturer's past performance, seeking answers to such questions as these:

    a. Does the manufacturer warrant the product's performance?
    b. What is the company's past record for manufacturing and marketing reliable waterproofing?
    c. Has the manufacturer produced previous waterproofing products?
    d. Does the manufacturer require applicators to prove competence via licensing or approval programs?
    e. Has the applicator successfully installed similar products?

Before specifying a new product, the architect should inform the client (preferably in writing) about possible risks, as well as the advantages of using the new product. If the client is unwilling to accept these risks, specify a more conventional material.

For owners who find comfort in roofing warranties and specifiers who routinely seek protection by requiring long-term warranties from the manufacturer and contractor, it may come as a surprise that warranties for waterproofing rarely include removal and reinstallation of overburden. The primary exceptions are for waterproofing on plazas surfaced with pavers on pedestals.

Overburden can range from an easily removable foot of earth or brick pavers in sand beds to 4-in.-thick travertine paving in a setting bed on a 3-in.-thick protection slab. Or more costly still, 10 ft of backfill against a foundation. Costs for overburden removal and replacement can easily exceed 100 times the cost of repairing defective waterproofing and can involve a multitude of trades. For this reason, manufacturers who offer warranties either exclude overburden removal from their warranty, limit the warranty to the cost of replacing defective material only, or are silent regarding overburden.

Before writing warranty requirements, the specifier should inform himself about the limitations imposed by the manufacturer. Designers should alert owners that waterproofing warranties do not offer the protection often included in roofing warranties.

Organizing The Waterproofing Specification

Specifications for waterproofing fall under Division 7 in the CSI (Construction Specifications Institute) MASTERFORMAT. Bituminous, bentonite, plastic, rubber, cementitious and all other materials below-grade waterproofing systems are grouped under sections numbered in the 07100 series.

Many specifiers use the following Section headings:

Section 07105 - Built-up Bituminous Waterproofing (either hot or cold)
Section 07111 - EPDM (or Butyl or PVC) Waterproofing
Section 07115 - Self-Adhering Waterproofing
Section 07120 - Fluid-Applied (Liquid-Applied) Waterproofing
Section 07130 - Bentonite Waterproofing (Panels and laminated)
Section 07145 - Cementitious Waterproofing
Section 07160 - Dampproofing

Plastic sheets used for dampproofing under slabs-on-ground are usually specified under Concrete - 03300. Admixtures for integrally waterproofed concrete are also specified in this Section.

Insulation, drainage composites and protection materials are included in waterproofing sections.

MasterSpec and CSI Monographs publish sections on waterproofing for some systems. However, the specifier should be aware that the technology of most of the current systems is constantly changing. Referring to the manufacturer's current specification, or better yet, to an interview with a technical representative is always the wisest choice of action.

In addition to Division 7, which deals with the waterproofing system per se, several other divisions are also involved in specifying waterproofing:

- Division 1 (Pre-installation meeting)
- Division 2 (Backfill)
- Division 3 (General Requirements)

Division 1

Section 01200. A pre-installation meeting is as necessary for waterproofing as for roofing. At this meeting, require the following attendees: architect/engineer; inspector; general contractor; subcontractors for waterproofing, concrete-casting, backfill, formwork, excavating; foremen for all contractors and subcontractors, plus representatives of manufacturers of materials to be incorporated into the work. If trees are to be installed over waterproofing the landscaper's presence is desirable to review methods of staking.

This pre-installation meeting should be scheduled prior to excavation. It should cover the following subjects:

- Width of the foundation excavation, to allow adequate space for installation of positive-side waterproofing (see Fig. 13-1).
- Sequencing of concrete casting for footing and slab-on-ground, structural slab, and backfill operation
- Waterproofing contractor's review of required concrete finish and surface moisture requirements

A second meeting should be scheduled after casting of the concrete. Its purpose is to allow concrete and waterproofing contractors to inspect sub-

Fig. 13-1 Narrow working space between excavation and foundation wall makes installation of insulation boards on self-adhering modified-bitumen waterproofing membrane a much more difficult job. Setting minimum requirements to avoid cramped working space should be a major topic at the pre-installation meeting.

strate surfaces, to assure their suitability for waterproofing application.

A third, follow-up meeting may be required to re-inspect the substrates after remedial work on the substrate surfaces has been completed.

Division 2

Because the satisfactory performance of a waterproofing system often depends on prompt and proper backfilling, specify the following in the appropriate Division 2 sections:

- Require backfilling as soon as possible after positive-side waterproofing is installed and covered with associated materials.
- Limit backfill lifts to a maximum 12-in. height.
- Require compaction of backfill against bentonite panels to 85-90% maximum density per ASTM D 1557, *Test Method for Laboratory Compaction Characteristics of Soil Using Modified Effort.* Backfill over bentonite-filled tubes must be hand-placed.
- Require dewatering of areas to receive bentonite and membranes above the toe of the mud mat or the top of the footing to assure that surfaces are sufficiently dry for application of the waterproofing system.
- Specify single-graded aggregate, not less than ¾-in. size, as granular base under slab-on-ground and porous backfill.
- Specify filter fabric and porous backfill and subsurface drains.

Division 3

Because the success of a membrane system often depends on proper substrate preparation, specify the following in the appropriate Division 3 sections:

- Surfaces to be waterproofed
- Scheduling of concrete pours (to assure adequate curing time)
- Curing materials that will not inhibit the bond of adhered membranes
- Reference ASTM D 5295, *Preparation of Concrete Surfaces for Adhered (Bonded) Membrane Waterproofing Systems* for preparation of concrete surfaces.
- Require the concrete contractor to exercise care when casting concrete on previously waterproofed surfaces.
- Specify the finish (float, steel trowel) required for the selected waterproofing system. Note that some adhered waterproofing systems require extension of the membrane over the footing and down the toe. These surfaces, which are not usually finished, should be noted in the specifications.
- When pour stops are used on slabs-on-ground, warn the contractor not to puncture the vapor retarder or the underlying

waterproofing and to notify the waterproofing contractor if the waterproofing is punctured.

* Specify cement cants and chamfered corners if required.
* Specify waterstops in this section. (See Appendix C.)

Division 7
Part 1 - General

* Reference appropriate sections in Divisions 2 and 3.
* Under Submittals, require shop drawings for membranes and bentonite. Drawings should indicate all conditions, transitions, and penetrations. Include such items as number of plies, required cants, nailers, and flashing materials. Require product data submission, including installation instructions. If sheet membranes on plazas are compartmentalized, require submission of as-built drawings indicating exact locations of each divider.
* Require submission of Material Safety Data Sheets (MSDS) and stipulate that they be kept on the site.
* Require the waterproofing manufacturer to review soils reports and to state in writing that the soil chemicals will have no adverse effects on the waterproofing.
* For Quality Assurance on all except hot-applied built-up membranes, require manufacturer to certify that the product or system has been manufactured and marketed in the United States for at least 10 years and that the formulation has remained consistent during that time.
* Require the manufacturer's certification of the applicator.
* Require applicator to test for dryness using a method provided by the manufacturer in writing for ascertaining the acceptable dryness of the substrate.
* Require an inspector retained by the owner for full-time supervision of the installation.
* Delivery, Storage, and Handling: Include limitations on shelf life of materials and temperature limitations for stored materials. Require flat storage of plastic and rubber rolls, storage of unboxed bituminous rolls on end. All materials — including membrane, bentonite, and negative-side waterproofing products — must be kept dry.
* Require temporary protection of waterproofing if other trades will execute work over it or when masonry installation on waterproofed brick shelves will be delayed.
* Specify ambient temperature limitations during application. Ban waterproofing application in rain, imminent rain, high winds, or other conditions specified by the manufacturer.
* Sequencing/Scheduling must be specified, for example, when

foundations are waterproofed in vertical stages with intermediate backfilling or when walls are erected on plaza waterproofing prior to surfacing.

Part 2 - Products

- Membranes: Specify ASTM D 449, Type 1 for asphalt; D 450, Type I for coal tar pitch; D 2178, Type IV for glass felts; and D 1668 for woven glass. Use ASTM D 1668, Type II, woven-glass fabric or ASTM D 227 tar-saturated organic felts with coal tar pitch rather than glass felts. Cotton (ASTM D 173), Burlap (ASTM D 1327), and asphalt organic felt (ASTM D 226) are not recommended.
- Specify ASTM C 836 for liquid-applied membranes

Elastomeric sheets: Only one manufacturer is currently (1998) marketing a butyl sheet for waterproofing. The system is for a loose-laid and fully adhered installation. Only one manufacturer is currently (1998) marketing a reinforced, cast PVC sheet for waterproofing. The system is for mechanically attached on foundations, loose-laid or fully adhered on horizontal installations.

Neoprene is no longer marketed for waterproofing. Only one manufacturer markets a CPE sheet.

- Specify ASTM C 578 Type VII extruded polystyrene with minimum 60-psi compressive strength for rigid insulation on framed slabs under a wearing course. Specify Type I expanded polystyrene (0.90 pcf) as a protection layer on vertical surfaces or Type VI extruded polystyrene to insulate below-grade foundation walls.
- Require special winter-grade adhesives and primers for installation below 40°F.
- Specify thixotropic grades of liquid-applied membranes for flashing vertical surfaces or use elastomeric sheets.
- Specify accessories, including: protection board, drainage panels, termination bars, fasteners, filter cloth under concrete protection slabs, closed-cell neoprene tubes or proprietary tubes to support membrane at expansion joints. (Prefabricated expansion joints are not advisable unless they are designed or protected from deforming under surcharge loads.)
- Specify treated wood for cast-in nailers.

Part 3 - Execution

- Surface conditions

For membranes that must be applied to "dry" surfaces, specify testing method. Acceptable moisture level should be determined by the membrane manufacturer, with testing performed by the applicator.

ASTM Standard E 1907, *Standard Practices for Determining Moisture-Related Acceptability of Concrete Floors to Receive Moisture-Sensitive Finishes*, lists several test methods, including:

1. Presence of condensation under a plastic sheet 24 hours after it is taped to the slab
2. Conductance moisture meters
3. Laboratory test to determine relative humidity of a sample
4. Proprietary methods that measure water vapor transmission through slab.

Use two or more methods to cross check results and make tests in each 1,000 sq ft of slab.

Still the most tried-and-true test is to adhere a patch of the membrane and try to pull it up.

Surface Preparation

General: Require installation of flashing and reinforcing prior to membrane application.

Adhered systems: Remove all contaminants, dust, dirt, and laitance on surfaces designed for adhered systems. Reinforce corners and construction joints on substrates receiving self-adhering membranes. Remove curing agents that may limit adhesion. Sodium silicate, animal-fat-based agents and others require special removal techniques. Fill honeycombs, rock pockets, indentations, and tie holes with patching cement.

On all types of adhered sheet membranes, require repair (i.e., cut-out and patching) of fishmouths and wrinkles. Self-adhering sheets and glass felts have "memory" and cannot be pressed flat.

Require priming of surfaces to receive bituminous and modified-bitumen membranes. If prefabricated, self-adhering membranes are not installed on the same day, require repriming.

Bentonite: Remove mud and other contaminants on surfaces designed for bentonite waterproofing. Ground water or heavy rains in the excavation will sometimes flood the top of footings and leave a residue of mud when the water recedes. Require water-jet removal of mud and other materials that would inhibit contact between the bentonite and concrete. Fill honeycombs, rock pockets, indentations, and tie holes with bentonite gel. Patch voids in lagging that are larger than ½ in.

Require troweling of bentonite gel on joints and penetrations. Use bentonite-filled tubes at foundation wall-footing joints where panels terminate. Lap panels and sheets. Replace or repair damaged panels. Protect system from water until slabs are cast and backfill is in place.

Liquid-applied membranes: On concrete surfaces receiving liquid-applied waterproofing, "detail" cracks of width equal to or greater than membrane thickness by applying a strip of fabric over the crack.

Some urethane LAMs may require priming with a solvent-thinned coating of the same material.

Negative-side waterproofing: Acid etch or sandblast surfaces designed for crystalline or cementitious negative-side coatings if they are applied after concrete has cured. Require drypacking at joints. Require mechanical compaction of materials at slab/foundation joint.

Application

General

- Require immediate installation of protection boards if other trades will perform work over it or when masonry installation on waterproofed brick shelves will be delayed.
- Specify the type of finish (float, steel trowel) required for the specific waterproofing system selected.
- Where reinforcing bars penetrate the membrane — e.g., for column dowels at interior spread footings or for rock anchors — seal sheet membranes by finger-cutting the sheets around the bars and sealing them to the bars with the system's liquid or mastic component (see Fig. 13-2). (Liquid-applied membranes are self-flashing.) Do not wrap bars with membrane. (It cannot be sealed to the bars' deformed surfaces.)

Built-up membranes

- Require a visible thermometer and thermostatic controls on all kettles, set to manufacturer's recommended limits. Require rejection of bitumen heated above the specified maximum and reheating of bitumen too viscous for mopping.
- When EVT is provided by the supplier, require hot bitumen temperature at application within ± 25°F of EVT.
- In cold weather, require double or insulated lines and insulated bitumen carriers. (Also store felts in a warm enclosure.)
- Check for continuous, uniform interply hot moppings, with no contact between adhered felts, with average interply mopping-weight tolerance = ± 15 %.
- Require manual brooming or squeegee following 6-ft maximum distance behind unrolling felt.

Fig. 13-2 Where reinforcing bars penetrate a waterproofing membrane (self-adhering on the project depicted above), require the sealing of these penetrations with the system's liquid or mastic flashing component.

- Require immediate repair of felt-laying defects: fishmouths, blisters, ridges, splits.
- Terminate day's work with complete glaze-coated seal stripping.
- Require backnailing on walls. Use woven-glass fabrics for flashing and corner reinforcing.

Liquid-applied membranes
- Specify application on structural slabs to conform with ASTM C 898.
- Require two coats, with thickness and tolerances as percent or in mils, not in liquid content per unit area.
- Require delay in installation of protection boards on one-component, liquid-applied waterproofing until membrane has fully cured.
- Specify unvulcanized neoprene or polyester reinforcing for flashing.

Self-adhering sheets
- Require applicator to roll sheets and double roll seams after application.
- Require mastic on all edges at day's end.

- Require liquid membrane on tee joints.
- Require prompt application of protection course.

Rubber and plastic sheets
- Require that applicator provide for relaxation of sheets before installation.
- Do not permit bonding adhesive on field seams. Require applicator to use a steel roller to compress sheet and seams after membrane installation.
- Require cover strips on tee joints and preferably on all joints.

Field Quality Control

Flood testing
- Require flood testing of horizontal waterproofing on framed slabs, per ASTM D 5957 *Flood Testing Horizontal Waterproofing Installations.* Water should be sprayed first at perimeters, to check proper flow to drains and to detect ponding.

Specify damming method, if not that prescribed in ASTM D 5957. Dams can be constructed from sand or water-filled fire hoses, planks assembled in an "L" shape, or foamed insulation boards covered with PVC, EPDM or polyethylene sealed to the membrane and weighed with sand bags. Require cushioning of dams to prevent damage to membrane from sharp edges. This is important where a sheet carried over the top of a wood barrier is subjected to an increasing combination of shear and tensile stress from the wood barrier's sharp edge as the weight of flood-test water increases.

Require continuous supervision below the test area until it is drained. Flood-test water should generally be ponded to a maximum 4-in. depth over horizontal membranes and held for 48 hours. After the water has been drained, inspect all seams of sheet-applied panels to check for water entrapment in these seams. Test cuts or moisture-meter probes can also be used if the membrane's watertight integrity is suspect. Preferably drain water into internal drains, not over or into finished surfaces.

General
- Prohibit testing if freezing temperatures can occur.
- Do not permit fire hoses or power equipment to direct stream across laps.
- Make area off limits until membrane is protected .
- Require manufacturer to observe flood testing and to supervise repairs, if required.
- Require waterproofing contractor (or preferably inspector) to

submit at the end of each day:
a. report of work done with location and scope noted on a drawing
b. photographs
c. weather report

Liquid-applied membranes

- Require test cuts and wet-mil thickness check for each square (100 sq ft)
- Require contractor to maintain an inventory to assure that materials are installed at the specified rate.

Single-ply membranes

- Require test cuts across the seams
- Require seam probes

14

Detailing
Waterproofing[1]

Many problems concerning the detailing of waterproofing start with the designer's failure to understand the meaning of the word, "detail". As one of its dictionary listings, "detail" is defined as "treatment of a subject in individual or minute parts." The careless designer who shirks this responsibility to literally detail his project is asking for trouble, and in today's litigious society, he is likely to get it.

In detailing waterproofing, the designer's first decision concerns this question: Should waterproofing go on the structural drawings, the architectural drawings, or both? The third option is obviously the worst. It maximizes the probability of conflicts, since every modification made on one set of drawings must be copied on the other. The author recommends that the architectural drawings show the extent of waterproofing, plus details, with a reference note on the structural drawings.

The architectural drawings should show not only the waterproofing, but also the mud mat, drainage medium, vapor retarder, footing drains, insulation and plaza wearing surface. The structural drawings should show cementitious cants or fillets at reentrant angles and chamfered external corners and other special conditions associated with the concrete work. Failure to include these items on the structural drawings can spawn controversies on the site and possible extra charges.

It is even more important for plumbing or site drawings to show the footing drains in plan (including drainage from leaders) and connections to site utilities. Failure to do so can create jurisdictional disputes, and worse.

---

1. Details in Figs. 14-3, 14-4, 14-6 and 14-7 are taken from ASTM D 5898 for which the author of this manual was the principal author.

Omission of this critical information from the plumbing or site drawings can result in omission of its directives from the project. And the designer may find himself bearing the blame.

The extent of the waterproofing must be clearly indicated. Skimpy specifications that simply require waterproofing of foundations, or drawing notes indicating "waterproofing", with an arrow pointing to the foundation, are inviting claims for extras. Does the membrane stop on the footing, continue across it, or extend down the toe? Does it stop at the top of the foundation, return over the brick shelf or under the coping? Is negative-side waterproofing carried into blockouts for intermediate slabs? Where does it terminate at intersecting shear walls? Does it cover the top of equipment curbs?

To answer such questions, indicate the extent of waterproofing on small-size sections on all subsurface building components. It is often better to use a heavy dashed line to avoid confusing the waterproofing with the outline of the waterproofed component — foundation wall, footing, slab-on-ground, etc.

Draw sections at minimum scale of ¾ in. = 1 ft, details at minimum 1½ in. = 1 ft, and preferably 3 in. = 1 ft at penetrations, drains, dynamic joints, and changes in plane — e.g., internal and external corners. For membrane waterproofing, indicate the arrangement of plies and reinforcing on large-scale drawings. In general, all components should be drawn, with one notable exception. It will simplify the drawing if protection boards are noted rather than indicated, wherever there is a membrane.

Dampproofing and vapor retarders should be distinguished from waterproofing, and one another, if they all exist on the same building. Variations in dashed lines such as long and short dashes, dash-dot, etc., will avoid confusion when, for example, a foundation waterproofing membrane and under-slab vapor retarder are combined in the same detail.

The applicator, in concert with the manufacturer, should submit shop drawings to insure that all details are included, but this does not relieve the designer from his responsibility to provide detail drawings. Beware of applicators that simply submit cuts from the manufacturer's catalogue without customizing them to suit unique project conditions. Also, assure that all conditions are indicated, including critical details of plane transitions and penetrations. One of the most critical is the flashing of a plaza waterproofing system at window walls that finish flush, or almost flush, with the wearing surface. Other critical, and often overlooked details, are sealing of conduits and piping in fountains and planters and the transition of expansion joints at plane changes.

Sequencing

Design professionals are treading on dangerous ground when they involve themselves in sequencing. Sequencing skates close to responsibility for means and methods, a province expressly off limits to architects and engineers in their Owner/Professional Agreements.

Failure to understand sequencing can, however, often mean the difference between waterproofing success and failure. Designers must recognize the normal sequencing of construction. Foundation walls may be cast before or after slab-on-ground. Wall-bearing structural slabs, however, can be cast only after their supporting walls are cast. Waterproofing is applied to individual components and frequently follows this sequence. Constructing underground building components in a suitable sequence can greatly improve the chances for a successful waterproofing installation, as demonstrated in the three following examples:

1. A slab-on-ground and the foundation are to be waterproofed. If the slab is cast before the foundation, the membrane waterproofing installation is simplified. In the less desirable sequence, a footing is cast and waterproofing is installed over it. It is finger cut around the projecting reinforcing bars and extended from toe to toe of the footing. Formwork is erected on the membrane and the foundation wall is cast. Rebars are bent inward for embedment in the slab, yet to be cast. The mud mat follows and is covered with waterproofing. The waterproofing must be bonded to the membrane previously installed on the inboard side of the footing after the formwork has been stripped. After the mud mat is cast, the membrane must be joined to the previously installed membrane on the footing. This unduly complicates the waterproofing installation, as illustrated in Fig. 14-1.

2. Compare this footing-cast-first sequence described above with a different sequence, in which the mud mat is cast first (see Fig. 14-1). Foundation and slab reinforcing bars are installed above the membrane, eliminating the tedious and leak-promoting finger cutting of the membrane around the bars. Formwork is not anchored through the membrane on the inboard side, This procedure obviously minimizes damage to the membrane.

3. An understanding of sequencing is also important where plaza waterproofing is installed before adjacent rising walls or exterior finish materials. Brick on shelves, door sills, and parapet cladding may be applied long after the membrane. Wearing courses may be applied after cladding. Wall flashing details should provide a continuous, watertight transition between counterflashing and membrane base flashing. The vertical transition of the membrane should be installed and terminated with a stub wall upon which the rising wall is erected. Adequate protection must be provided (see Figs. 14-3 and 14-4).

An orchestra pit, depressed below the auditorium slab, also re-

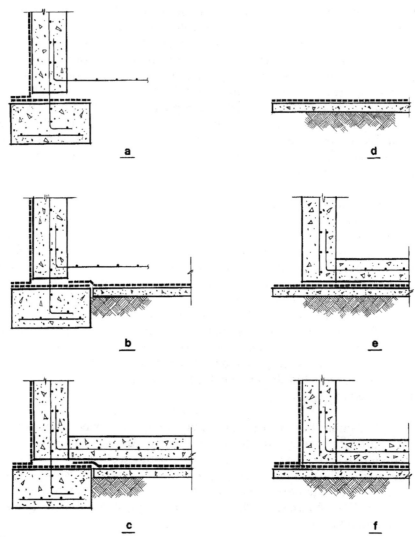

Fig. 14-1 The construction sequence depicted in the left-hand column above complicates membrane installation and reduces the chances of a successful project. When the wall footing and wall are cast before the adjacent mud slab and slab-on-ground, the membrane must be finger cut around projecting reinforcing dowels, and the wall formwork erected on the membrane (a). Reinforcing bars are then bent inward, for embedment in the slab. Casting of the mud slab and installation of waterproofing follow. Slab waterproofing is bonded to the previously installed membrane on the inboard side of the wall footing (b). Finally, the slab-on-ground is cast (c).

In the right-hand column of details, an improved sequence starts with mud-slab casting and membrane installation (d). The slab is a cast next (e), and finally, the foundation wall, followed by installation of a positive-side membrane lapped over the extended mud-slab membrane (f). This sequence facilitates membrane installation and increases the odds on a successful project.

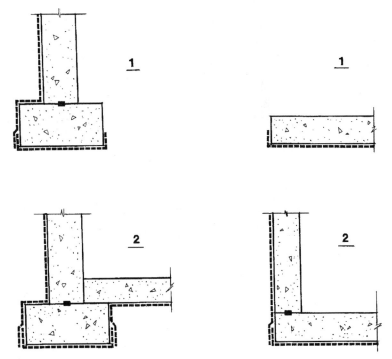

Fig. 14-2   In hydrostatic conditions bentonite waterproofing differs from membrane waterproofing in its location _under_ the wall footing. Bentonite cannot be located between the footing top and the wall because it expands in the presence of moisture. Note that waterstops are critical components with bentonite. The above illustrates the sequence for installing bentonite on the footing on the left and the tunnel on the right.

quires membrane waterproofing. Rather than erect formwork around the pit walls and apply blind-side waterproofing, the components are cast in the sequence illustrated in Fig. 14-5.

Note that in all examples the mud slab is extended at least 12 in. beyond the foundation or toe of a footing to permit tie-in with the vertical waterproofing membrane. Membrane waterproofing can be safely carried through structural components — foundations and interior columns — providing continuity to the membrane. (Because of its propensity to expand and contract, bentonite is never carried through, but installed under the footing.) The membrane is finger cut around the reinforcing and sealed to it with the system liquid or mastic component. Membranes should never be carried up the reinforcing bars; the bars' deformations prevent uniform bonding. Protection board is always in-

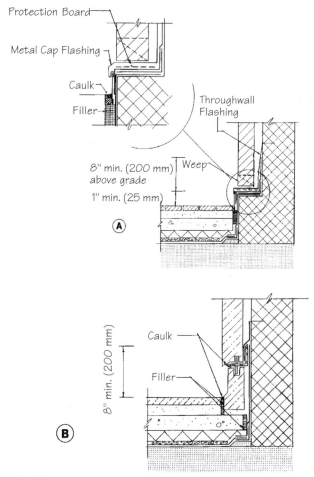

Fig. 14-3 Plaza waterproofing termination at (a) brick-faced wall, and (b) stone-faced wall are shown in the details above. (American Society for Testing and Materials).

stalled over the membrane, even where it is carried under the foundation wall. The board can be stripped before the wall is cast and left in place on the extended mud mat until the wall waterproofing is applied. Thus the protection board reduces damage to the membrane when formwork is installed.

Reinforcement Of Membrane Systems

Most systems require reinforcing at transitions — e.g., internal

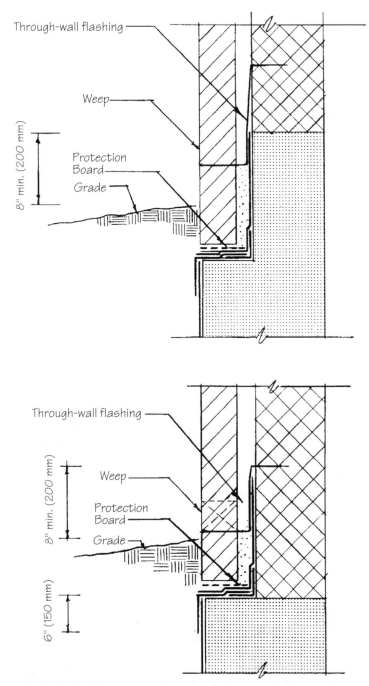

Through-wall flashing

Weep

8" min. (200 mm)

Protection
Board
Grade

Through-wall flashing

8" min. (200 mm)

Weep

Protection
Board

Grade

6" (150 mm)

Fig. 14-4 Top detail shows wall waterproofing termination at foundation wall with brick shelf. Bottom detail shows counterpart termination at foundation wall. (American Society for Testing and Materials).

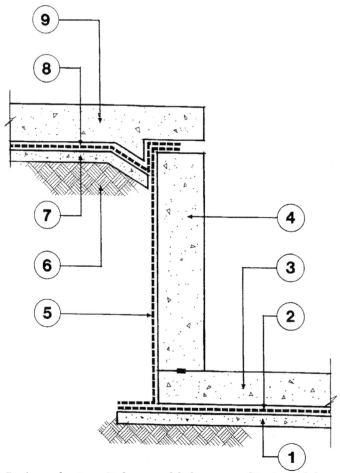

Fig. 14-5 An orchestra pit depressed below an auditorium slab-on-ground also subject to hydrostatic uplift pressure can be waterproofed with a positive-side membrane instead of the less desirable negative-side coating and eliminate blindside waterproofing if the construction sequence follows the nine indicated steps. Proper compaction of the backfill, following Step 6, is the key to the success of this procedure.

and external corners, concrete construction joints (see Fig. 14-6). Reinforcement is also required where reinforcing bars, pipes, and conduits penetrate the membrane.

Reinforcement is usually installed before the membrane, but in some instances may be applied over it later. Refer to the membrane manufacturer's details.

Multi-ply membranes usually require multiple reinforcement plies,

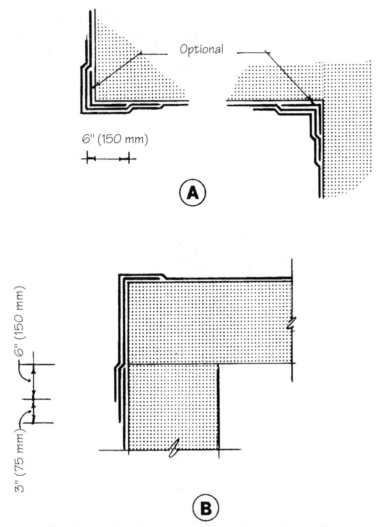

Fig. 14-6 Reinforcing details are shown in (a) for exterior and interior corners and (b) foundation wall-structural slab joint.

whereas single-ply systems generally require only one. Additional plies are required where substrate joints may be dynamic (i.e., subject to relative movement between adjacent structural components.)

When additional plies are used as reinforcement they should extend at least 6 in. beyond the corner or penetration and each succeeding reinforcement ply should extend at least 3 in. beyond the previous ply.

Penetrations

Penetrations in subsurface structures, usually pipes and conduits, can be cast into the concrete or built into the masonry. The more common, and preferable, method is to install them in sleeves (see Fig. 14-7). Conduits are often ganged in boxed sleeves. On plazas, single conduits — e.g., those feeding light fixtures — are cast into the structural slab.

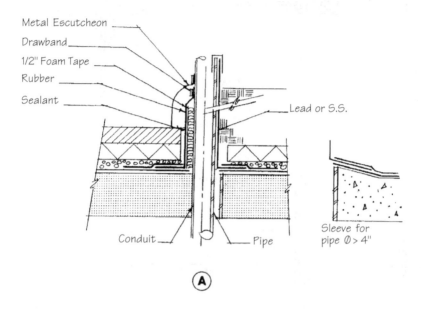

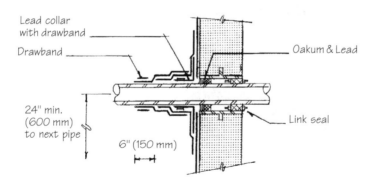

Fig. 14-7 Top detail (a) shows conduit or pipe penetration of plaza or earth-covered structural slab. Bottom detail (b) shows pipe penetration of foundation wall. (American Society for Testing and Materials.)

Sleeves are generally preferable to cast-in-place pipes and conduit for two reasons:

- They permit independent movement of the pipes, thus averting the risk of fracture or distortion caused by movement in the structure.
- They simplify the work of different trades, by reducing the coordination required among them.

Inadequate space between penetrating pipes and conduits prevents the dispersion of aggregate in the concrete mix, creating honeycombed passages vulnerable to leakage. Careful coordination among the architectural, structural, mechanical, and electrical designers is required to assure adequate spacing and consequently solid concrete between pipes and conduits. Pipes and pipe sleeves should never be spaced closer than 6 in. to allow the installation of flashing without overlap.

Penetrations through single-ply, built-up, and liquid-applied membranes are flashed with strips of suitable bituminous or rubber membrane and special adhesive. Two or three successive applications of flashing are wrapped around the pipe, extending 2 to 3 in. beyond each other. A lead collar helps to absorb differential movement between the pipe and structure. A stainless-steel drawband secures the collar. In bentonite systems, penetrations are packed with trowelled-on bentonite.

Conduits, like pipes, should be spaced at least 6 in. apart. Unfortunately, the space allotted in buildings is rarely sufficient to provide for such generous conduit spacing, and they are frequently ganged. Where feeder and cable sleeves are nestled in a blockout in the wall they should be of sufficient diameter to provide not less than 1 in. between the sleeve wall and the conduit or cable. Concrete is packed in the blockout around the sleeves to secure them in place. The membrane must lap the joint between the wall and the blockout at least 2 in. A sheet metal form is fitted over the membrane and around the penetrations 1 in. from the face of the wall. It is then filled with a seal of pourable-grade, two-component urethane or the mastic component of bentonite systems.

Flashing at penetrations in sleeves must accommodate differential movement between the slab and the pipe conduit. The space between the outer portion of the pipe and the sleeve is filled with oakum or a precompressed open-cell sealant. The inner space is sealed with a "Link-Seal"[2] forced tightly against the pipe with bolts. Large diameter pipes may require expansion joints.

Link-Seals are also effective where other flashings may fail due to heat, movement, or chemical attack. The Link-Seals are relatively easy to replace.

---

2. "Link-Seal" is manufactured by Thunderline Link-Seal, Livonia, MI

The casing for a hydraulically powered elevator presents a special problem in pipe penetration (see Fig. 14-8). The top is cast into the concrete, and where the pipe is below ground-water level, it is temporarily filled with water to hold it in place.

The waterproofing membrane is flashed up the pipe to the top and concrete cast around it. A mortar plug with a chemical-conversion additive can be provided as a secondary seal at the top. If the elevator pit is waterproofed with negative-side cementitious or chemical-conversion coatings, the plug at the top becomes the primary seal and must be made deeper and wider.

Termination Of Positive-Side Waterproofing

Membrane waterproofing that terminates at footings should be sealed at the footing with mastic or a liquid-applied sealant furnished by

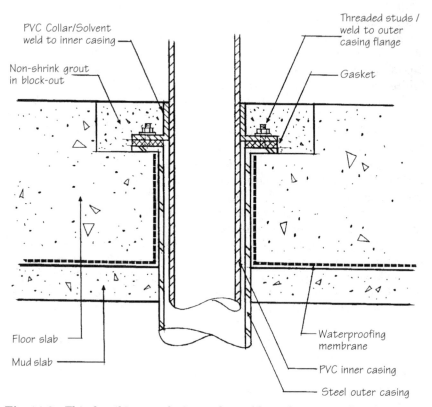

Fig. 14-8 This detail is one solution to the problem of waterproofing the casing for a hydraulically powered elevator penetrating the slab-on-ground of the elevator pit. (Mitchell-Giurgola.)

the manufacturer. It is not necessary to extend the waterproofing over the footing and down to the footing bottom. The footing face is normally irregular, dirty, wet, and probably partially under water, thus precluding the possibility of a bond.

Bentonite panels require bentonite-filled tubes. When the bottom of the slab-on-ground is 8 in. or more above the top of the footing, the membrane is carried to the bottom of the foundation wall. When the slab rests on the footing, the membrane joint is reinforced, the membrane extended to the toe of the footing and sealed.

Membrane waterproofing of all types — built-up, self-adhering single-ply and liquid-applied — should terminate at least 8 in. above grade. Many waterproofing manufacturers show below-grade terminations in a reglet, sealed with mastic, or secured with a termination bar. These details are contrary to good practice, characterized by Anderson as "irresponsible marketing by the product manufacturer". Even when the membrane is turned into a reglet or a cap flashing is installed in a reglet, water can migrate behind the membrane through cracks in the wall above the reglet.

Waterproofing should be carried over a brick shelf or continued up the wall as indicated in Figures 14-3 and 14-4. Above grade, the waterproofing membrane must be protected from damage and UV radiation by cement parging, parge-covered insulation boards, noncorrosive metal or masonry. When the facade is carried below grade, it should be of water and stain-resistant materials such as granite, low absorption stones, SW-grade brick, precast concrete or cement plaster. Keep in mind that the period between the completion of the waterproofing and the installation of the facade may be longer than the membrane's ability to tolerate UV radiation. Permanent or temporary protection should be noted on the drawings.

Expansion Joints

Detailing expansion joints in below-grade construction is one of the designers' most challenging problems. Expansion joints — more accurately called movement joints — are located between structurally independent building segments. Expansion-joint movement is reversible, and these cyclical movements can continue throughout the building's service life. Expansion joints are thus distinguished from control or construction joints, where movement, generally from the concrete's initial settlement and drying shrinkage, consists predominantly of contraction, with consequent widening of the joint.

Although there are over 20 different stresses that can cause movement, the most common for below-grade structures are from temperature changes, settlement, flotation and seismic forces. Other stresses, such as those produced by creep, will usually be accommodated by joints designed for the foregoing stresses. Where movement from moisture changes can be significant in above-ground structures, below ground the moisture content differentials in the soil are relatively small. Moreover, the moisture content of concrete protected by membrane waterproofing is virtually constant.

Thermally induced movement is generally linear where framing materials and systems do not change. Thermally induced movement will be greater in structural slabs supporting plazas than in building components below grade where temperature differentials are small. But it can be significant in structures that are exposed for long periods of time before backfilling.

Differential movement can be expected from settlement, flotation and seismic forces as well as changes in framing, interior environment, relative stiffness and similar conditions. The design to accommodate movement from seismic forces below ground is generally similar to that above ground. Movement from settlement and flotation will be a function of the soil and watertable characteristics, and their magnitudes should be determined by the structural and geotechnical engineers. Settlement is generally non-reversible, but flotation can vary with the ground water level rise and fall. This can be significant where, for example, a lightweight tunnel joins a building foundation in tidal areas.

Properly designed expansion joints permit independent movement of the building elements in three dimensions on each side of the joint. Their size and location should be determined by the structural engineer. Where slopes are integral with structural slabs, expansion joints should be located at the high points.

Joints designed for reversible movement will experience their maximum during and shortly after construction when backfilling is completed and prior to actuating the HVAC systems, which will minimize thermal movement by maintaining a narrow range of temperature and humidity conditions. Initial significant non-reversible movement can be expected when earth-covered slabs are backfilled, heavy plaza wearing courses are installed, dewatering systems are deactivated and foundations are loaded with the superstructure.

Designers must recognize an expansion joint as a clear path between interior and exterior, not to be used indiscriminately. Expansion joints are usually required where below-grade pedestrian and utility tunnels enter basements and where subsurface additions are constructed. Joints are also required in large plazas and where plazas adjoin rising walls.

An expansion joint should be designed as a straight joint with parallel sides normal to the plane of the slab and foundation. It should be covered with a flexible sheet that can absorb movement without dependence on its elastic properties. Early joints were fabricated from folded copper, but they often failed from fatigue and work hardening. Today's joint covers are usually neoprene or silicone, looped over a rubber tube or proprietary support. A factory-fabricated unit with an elastomeric sheet bonded to metal flanges is also used.

Designers should avoid one notoriously defective type of expansion joint, featuring a sealant-filled joint shielded by an elastomeric strip. If the joint is truly dynamic, the width required for a sealant with ±25% movement capability can exceed 2 in. Moreover, if the sealant fails, it is inaccessible for repair. With liquid-applied and self-adhering waterproofing systems, the resistance to stress is dependent on the shear strength between the membrane and the joint cover.

Though not subject to the wide range of thermally induced movement in the building superstructure, expansion joint covers on subsurface structures nonetheless experience cyclical bending stress, subjecting them to flexural failure. The more likely failure mode is ruptures of end seams at joints and plane transitions. Joint covers must be adequately supported to prevent distortion from water and earth pressure.

Expansion-joint covers should be designed to maintain continuity at all changes in plane. For example, a tunnel intersecting a cellar may have an expansion joint on all four sides. The intersections between horizontal and vertical joints should be drawn in isometric.

Expansion joints in horizontal surfaces should be raised up on cant strips not less than 1½ in. Cement cants are preferred over treated wood for two reasons: (1) they don't require mechanical fasteners, and (2) they assure compatibility between slab and membrane (see Fig. 11-9). If the joint does leak, the elevated cant will limit the quality of water entering the building. It will also relieve some of the pressure on the expansion-joint cover. The elastomeric cover supports should be designed to accommodate flexure. The support should be inserted in the joint and designed to resist earth and water pressure. Supports should be round, solid, closed-cell sponge neoprene rods, 25% to 33% larger than the joint width when installed. Tubes should conform to ASTM D 1752 Type 1 (or D 1056) with a 30-pcf lb. density. Solid rods are preferred to hollow tubes because tubes may serve as a conduit if the joint cover leaks. This would increase the difficulty of leak detection and location.

On horizontal surfaces of suspended slabs round (non-proprietary) supports should be installed on continuous neoprene or butyl hammocks to provide a vapor retarder and bitumen stop. The bitumen stop is mandatory when the membrane contains coal tar pitch or coal-tar-modified urethane. Fiberglass insulation may be installed in the joint to reduce heat loss, but it may keep the temperature of the vapor retarder below the dewpoint and cause condensation.

Proprietary rubber semicircular or quarter-circular units with tubes and bayonet extensions may be used in lieu of a rod to support the expansion joint cover (see Fig. 14-9). This detail eliminates a hammock and provides a more uniform surface to support the joint cover. Propo-

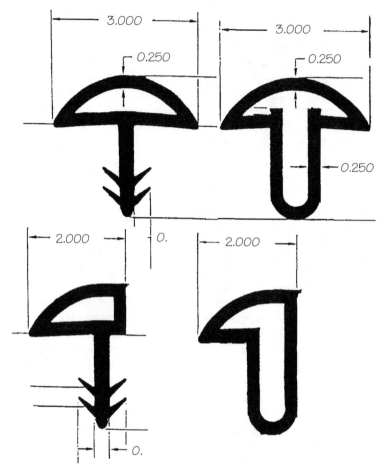

Fig. 14-9   Prefabricated Expansion Joint cover supports. (D.S. Brown).

nents claim that a hammock makes leak detection and identification more difficult. This author nonetheless favors the hammock, because it provides redundancy (see Fig. 14-10). To be effective, it must be discharged to a floor drain or wet sink. Alternatively, the drain line may be equipped with leak-detection instruments to alert maintenance personnel that the expansion joint cover has failed.

Some authorities (Parise) recommend installation of a sheet-metal gutter under the expansion joint. Others (Ruggiero and Rutila) believe this encourages occupants and maintenance workers to overlook the problem. If the hammock/rod is omitted in favor of the proprietary joint cover support, the designer should consider using a sheet metal gutter under the joint to reduce the potential for catastrophic leaking (see Fig.

Fig. 14-10   The intersection between a rising wall and a plaza structural slab has a proprietary quarter-circle expansion joint with hammock and one ply of butyl sheet.

14-11).

When gutters are installed, they should be designed with a 1% slope to drain and a V-shaped bottom to promote water flow and scouring. A piping system to an open drain is required. The top should be at least 4 in. below the slab to permit flushing and maintenance. The slab soffit should be provided with drips on either side of the joint to prevent lateral migration of water.

Expansion joints in plaza wearing courses must be closer together than those in the structural slab. Structural expansion joints should generally be spaced between 100 and 200 ft., whereas joints in the wearing course should be spaced approximately 20 ft. each way.

Joints in the wearing course should always coincide with those in the structural slab (see Fig. 11-9). At these locations the joint width in the wearing course should approximate the joint width in the structural slab unless the wearing course is constructed of loose laid units such as pavers on pedestals or bricks in a sand bed.

Calculating Expansion Joint Width

As with many above-grade buildings, differential, rather than cumulative movement controls the location and size of the expansion joint in below-grade structures. For buildings above grade, exposed to the

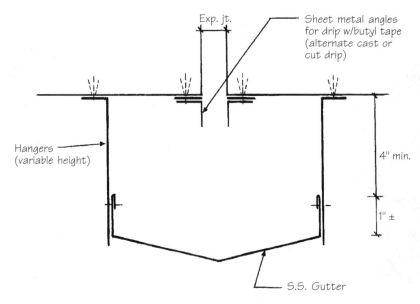

Fig. 14-11   Ceiling gutter, detailed above, should be sloped 1% to drain, with V-shaped bottom to promote flow and scouring. The slab soffit should have drips on both sides of the joint to prevent lateral migration of water. Hangers should extend a minimum 4 in. below the slab soffit to facilitate flushing and maintenance.

elements and the full range of ambient temperatures, expansion-joint widths for thermally induced cumulative movement can be calculated by using the formula: joint width ε x T x L, where ε is the coefficient of thermal expansion, T is the temperature differential and L is the length of the element. Although this formula is applicable to expansion joints in plazas, it is inappropriate for joints in below-grade structures, where temperature differentials are not the dominant force that produces movement at "expansion" joints.

In below-grade structures, differential movement from settlement, flotation and seismic forces often take precedence over thermally induced cumulative movement. Temperature differentials are only significant during construction, before backfilling and prior to insulating structural slabs under plazas.

The width of expansion joints in below-grade structures should be calculated by the geotechnical engineer (for settlement and flotation) and by the structural engineer for seismic movement.

Generally, expansion joints in concrete structures should never be less than 1 in. when installed at the highest ambient temperature to which it will be exposed and may exceed 3 in. in high seismic areas or where tidal-influenced groundwater levels fluctuate. Two-stage seals on the outer and inner faces are strongly recommended for all joints except those in plazas where a single-stage joint is usually satisfactory. The outer part of the joint is formed by an elastomeric membrane carried over a flexible, bulb-shaped support. The inner part of the joint should be filled with a pre-compressed expanding open-cell foam saturated with modified asphalt (See Fig. 14-12). Where joints exceed 3-in. and will be exposed to high hydrostatic pressure, consideration should be given to covers used on bridge expansion joints.

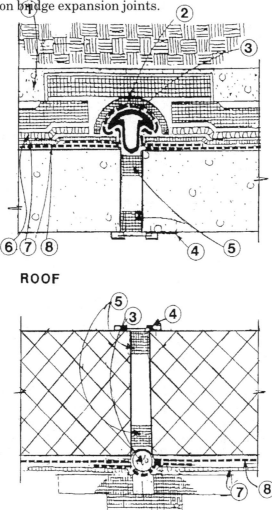

ROOF

WALL

Fig. 14-12 Expansion joints in tunnel walls and roof. 1) protection slab, 2) sponge rubber cushion, 3) flashing support, 4) expansion joint cover, 5) precompressed gasket, 6) drainage composite, 7) protection board, 8) mebrane. (Note: Elevated cant omitted on roof section for submerged joints.)

Planters, Bench And Equipment Supports

Waterproofing membranes on horizontal surfaces should be carried under the planters and supports without interruption. Such items should be installed on the concrete protection slab. Waterproofing of planters should be independent of the slab waterproofing. (Fig. 11-12).

Drains

Two-stage or two-level drains, sometimes called "all-level," are mandatory for structural plaza slabs. The upper drain must be isolated from the lower drain to permit differential movement. (Wearing courses on plaza decks move independently of the structural slab.) To prevent damage to the drainage system or flashing rupture from this movement, drains should be installed in the structural slab with gratings in the wearing course isolated from the drain body (see Figs. 11-4a, 11-4b and 11-4c).

Do not use a drain unit with drainage at the membrane level provided by weepholes. (Weepholes have a tendency to clog from crystallized soluble salts in the concrete or from coal tar pitch.)

Lead reinforcing is recommended for membranes where pipes or drains are installed in sleeves, but is unnecessary where they are cast into the wall or slab. Because of their rigidity and durability, cast-iron drains, cast into the slab with flanges flush with, or slightly below, the slab surface perform better than aluminum, plastic, or sheet metal drains.

A minimum of one additional ply of membrane should be installed at drains. Drain-strainer frames should not be designed to support wearing courses. Lead, if used, should be carried into the drain bowl. Built-up and single-ply membranes and reinforcing should lap drain flanges 4 in. and be secured with clamping rings. LAMs are applied over drains with extended flanges. Clamping rings are not used. Specify sediment buckets where wearing surfaces are water-permeable and where debris is expected.

Root intrusion is a common cause of clogged drains in earth-covered suspended slabs. Access for essential periodic maintenance can be provided by a perforated pipe and cleanout plug at the surface or a clay or concrete pipe manhole fed by subsurface perforated pipes installed in a drainage medium. The top is buried below the surface and identified with a telltale.

Detailing Alerts

1. Put waterproofing details, plus extent of waterproofing, mud mats, drainage media, footing drains, and all other aspects of waterproofing on architectural drawings.

2. Check structural drawings for inclusion of cementitious cants

and other concrete details required for the waterproofing.

3. Draw sections at minimum scale of ¾ in. = 1 ft, details at minimum 1½ in. = 1 ft, and penetrations, drains, plane changes, etc., preferably at 3 in. = 1 ft.

4. Use distinguishing indicators — e.g., alternating long and short dashes, alternating dots and dashes — for dampproofing vs. waterproofing, to avoid confusion when both appear in the same detail.

5. Make sure that plumbing (or site) drawings show footing drains in plan and connections to site utilities.

Glossary of
Waterproofing Terms

Admixture: A material other than water, aggregates, hydraulic cement, and fiber reinforcement, used as an ingredient of concrete or mortar, and added to the batch immediately before or during its mixing.

Asphalt: A dark brown to black cementitious material whose predominating constituents are bitumens that occur in nature or are obtained in petroleum processing.

Asphalt felt: An asphalt-saturated felt.

ASTM: American Society for Testing and Materials.

Backfill: Soil or gravel placed adjacent to a foundation after excavation for an underground structure.

Backnailing: Nailing along the top edge of vertically applied waterproofing sheets or felts.

Bentonite (sodium montmorillonite): A granulated smectite clay that swells 5 to 6 times its original volume in the presence of moisture.

Bitumen: (1) A class of amorphous, black or dark-colored, (solid, semi-solid, or viscous) cementitious substances, natural or manufactured, composed principally of high-molecular-weight hydrocarbons, soluble in carbon disulfide, and found in asphalts, tars, pitches, and asphaltines. (2) A generic term used to denote any material composed principally of bitumen. (3) In the waterproofing industry there are two basic bitumens: asphalt and coal tar pitch. Before application they are either (a) heated to a liquid state, (b) dissolved in a solvent, or (c) emulsified.

Bituminous emulsion: A suspension of minute globules of bituminous material in water or in an aqueous solution.

Blindside waterproofing: Waterproofing applied to the surface of foundation formwork facing the excavation, resulting in its final location on the outside (i.e. "blindside") of the foundation wall.

Boarding Out: The practice of applying a plywood facer to lagging or sheetpiling to provide a smooth, plane substrate for waterproofing application.

Bond breaker: A thin sheet installed in a joint or seam that divorces facing materials.

Bug holes: Small regular or irregular cavities, usually not exceeding $1/2$ to $5/8$ in. in diameter, resulting from entrapment of air bubbles in the surface of formed concrete during placement and consolidation.

Cant: A triangular beveled strip placed or formed in an inside corner to modify the 90° angle to two 45° angles.

Capillarity: The movement of a liquid in the interstices of soil or other porous material due to surface tension, to an elevation above the general ground-water level.

Capillary break: A membrane extended across the top of a wall footing to prevent capillary rise of water in the foundation wall.

Chamfer: Either a beveled edge or corner formed in concrete work by means of a chamfer strip.

Chamfer strip: Either a triangular or curved insert placed in an inside form corner to produce either a rounded or flat chamfer or to form a dummy joint. (also called fillet, and skew back.)

Chemical grout: Polyurethane-based hydrophilic liquids which react with water and change into an elastomeric solid.

Chimney drains: Vertical strips of drainage materials, such as prefabricated drainage composites or porous fill, spaced along the foundation. Usually found on blindside waterproofing where outlets are provided at the bottom to underslab drainage systems. Fig. G-1

Coal tar felt: A felt saturated with refined coal tar.

Coal tar pitch: A dark brown to black, solid cementitious material obtained as residue in the partial evaporation or distillation of coal tar.

Cold joint: A plane of weakness in concrete caused by an interruption or delay in the casting operation, permitting the first batch to start setting before the next batch is added, resulting in a lack of bond between the batches.

Fig. G-1   Chimney Drain. (TC Mira DRI.)

Construction joint: In concrete construction, a formed or assembled joint between two adjacent casting operations ("pours," "lifts," or "placements").

Contraction joint: (Also called control joint).   Formed, sawed, or tooled groove in a concrete structure to create a weakened plane and regulate the location of cracking resulting from the dimensional change of different parts of the structure. (See also isolation joint.)

Control joint: See Contraction joint. Control joints are recessed, with V or U-shaped cross sections detailed to shade cracks and thus minimize their aesthetic impairment.

Curing: (1) The process through which concrete hardens (via hydration of cement by the mixing of water); (2) the process through which liquid-applied coatings harden into solid, elastomeric membranes.

Curing compound: A liquid applied as a coating to the surface of newly cast concrete to retard the loss of mixing water, thus promoting hydration of the cement. Pigmented curing compounds are also designed to reflect surface heat, which prematurely dries the concrete and impairs the cement hydration process.

Cut-back: Solvent-thinned bitumen used in cold-process waterproofing and dampproofing adhesives, flashing cements, and coatings.

Dampproofing: Treatment of a surface or structure to resist the passage of water vapor and water in the absence of hydrostatic pressure.

Deadman: Concrete mass outside an excavation anchoring tie-backs against lateral earth pressure.

Deck: The structural surface to which the waterproofing system (including insulation) is applied.

Drainage composites: Also prefabricated drainage composites (PDC): three- dimensional plastic sheets or fused plastic filaments formed to provide multidirectional flow with one or both sides covered with a geotextile.

Drainage course (percolation layer): A layer of washed gravel or manufactured drainage medium that allows water to filter through to the drain.

Drainage fill: (1) Base course of granular material placed between floor slab and sub-grade to impede capillary rise of moisture. (2) Granular material placed on suspended slabs below grade or on plaza decks to promote drainage.

Dry (n.): A material that contains no more water than it contains at its equilibrium moisture content.

Emulsion: A dispersion of fine particles or globules of a liquid in a liquid. Asphalt emulsions consist of asphalt globules, an emulsifying agent such as bentonite clay, and water.

EPDM: A synthetic elastomer based on ethylene, propylene, and a small amount of a nonconjugated diene to provide sites for vulcanization. EPDM features excellent heat, ozone, and weathering resistance and low-temperature flexibility.

Equilibrium moisture content: (1) Moisture content of a material stabilized at a given temperature and relative humidity, expressed as percent moisture by weight. (2) The typical moisture content of a material in a particular geographical location.

EVT (Equiviscous temperature): The temperature (±25°F) (±1°C) at which the viscosity of a bitumen is appropriate for application. Viscosity units are generally expressed in centipoise or centistokes.

Expansion Joint: A formed or assembled joint designed to allow independent movement between adjacent building segments or components without stress transfer.

Fabric: A woven cloth of organic or inorganic filaments, threads, or yarns.

Felt: A flexible sheet manufactured by the interlocking of fibers through a combination of mechanical work, moisture, and heat, without spinning, weaving, or knitting. Waterproofing felts are manufactured from vegetable fibers (organic felts), glass fibers (glass-fiber felts), or polyester fibers (synthetic-fiber mats).

Fin: A narrow linear projection on a formed concrete surface, resulting from mortar flowing into gaps in the formwork. Fig. G-2

Finger cut: Slitting a preformed membrane, felt or fabric to fit around rebars.

Finished wearing surface: See Wearing surface.

Fishmouth: In built-up and single-ply membranes, a defective, half-conical opening at a wrinkled edge, resulting from a failure to adhere a sheet or felt to its substrate.

Flashing: The system used to seal membrane edges at walls, expansion joints, drains, gravel stops, and other places where the membrane is interrupted or terminated. Base flashing covers the edges of the membrane. Cap flashing or counterflashing shields the upper edges of the base flashing.

Fig. G-2   Lagging on soldier piles. (Robert A.M. Stern, Architects.)

Float finish: A rough concrete surface texture obtained by finishing with a wood or carpet float.

Fluid-applied elastomer: An elastomeric material, fluid at ambient temperature, that dries or cures after application to form a continuous membrane. Such systems normally do not incorporate reinforcement.

Footing: A continuous slab cast under a foundation wall, designed to transmit the wall's compressive load to the underlying foundation soil. Also used under isolated columns.

Footing drain: A pipe drain either porous or perforated located on the inside or outside (or both) of a footing to draw down the surrounding groundwater to relieve hydrostatic pressure.

Form kick-out: A bulge in the foundation where concrete formwork has been displaced laterally.

Form oil: Oil applied to the interior surfaces of forms to facilitate release from the concrete when the forms are removed. (See also Bond breaker and Release agent.)

Foundation: The concrete or masonry support designed as a wall or column footing, pier, caisson, or pile cap transmitting superstructure loads to soil or rock.

Geotextile: polypropylene, polyester or nylon fabrics either woven or non-woven (spun-bonded) manufactured to provide a narrow range of permeability.

Glass felt: Glass fibers bonded into a sheet with resin and suitable for impregnation in the manufacture of bituminous waterproofing, roofing membranes, and shingles.

Grade beam: A below-grade concrete beam spanning between piles or pile caps or between exterior column footings and functioning as a continuous support for the foundation.

Green Roof: A subsurface framed deck covered with earth and vegetation.

Groundwater level (also Watertable):   The elevation in the soil where water is at atmospheric pressure.

Gunite: A proprietary term for shotcrete.

HDPE: High Density Polyethylene: A chemically inert material with fair resistance to sunlight.

Honeycomb: Voids left in concrete due to failure of the mortar to effectively fill the spaces between coarse aggregate particles.

Honeycombing: A defect in concrete construction, characterized by voids where the concrete should be a continuous solid. Honeycombing usually indicates either the casting of a concrete mix of improper slump or a failure to vibrate the concrete mix properly during the casting operation.

Hydrostatic pressure: Pressure exerted by stationary liquid water, in all directions, against adjacent surfaces. Hydrostatic pressure is directly proportional to the depth of water; it equals the product of the water's density (62.5 pcf or 1001.25kg/m^3) x its depth (in feet or meters), yielding a figure in psf or kg/m^2.

Integral waterproofing: A system that relies on additives, such as stearates or superplasticizers, rather than a membrane or coating to waterproof concrete.

Invert: The inside elevation of the bottom of a pipe.

Intermittent water pressure: Variable hydrostatic pressure occurring where the groundwater table is within capillary reach of the foundation.

Lagging: Wood planks spanning horizontally between soldier piles, transmitting lateral earth pressure to the soldier-pile flanges, against which the lagging planks are wedged. Fig. G-2.

Laitance: A weak layer of cement and aggregate fines on a concrete surface.

Liquid-applied membrane (LAM): (see Fluid-applied elastomer).

Loose-laid membrane: An unadhered, single-ply membrane anchored to the substrate only at the edges and penetrations.

Membrane: A flexible or semiflexible waterproofing whose primary function is to prevent the passage of liquid moisture.

Mud mat: (1) A surfacing layer suitable for the application of membrane waterproofing installed on a prepared subgrade; (2) an area of fill compacted to no less than 95% of the maximum dry density of the fill.

Mud slab: An unreinforced concrete slab of 2-in. (50 mm) minimum thickness serving as the substrate for membrane waterproofing for a slab-on-ground or wall footing.

Nailer: A strip of wood or other fitting attached to or set in concrete, to facilitate nailed connections.

Negative-side waterproofing: A waterproofing system in which the source of the hydrostatic pressure and the water-resisting element are on opposite sides of the structural component.

Parging: A thin coat of mortar applied to rough masonry walls to create a smooth surface.

One-on-one: The installation of a multiple-ply membrane in which one ply is installed over the other instead of shingling. It produces a membrane with a continuous film of interply bitumen.

Pea gravel: Screened gravel, with a majority of particles passing a 9.5 mm ($^3/_8$ in.) sieve, but retained on a 4.75 mm (No. 4) sieve.

Perched watertable: A water table elevated above the normal, free-water elevation by impervious, unsaturated soils separating local bodies of water at different elevations.

Percolation layer (Drainage course): A layer of washed gravel or manufactured drainage media that allows water to filter through to the drain.

Permeability: (1) The capacity of a porous medium to conduct or transmit fluids. (2) The rate of flow of a fluid (liquid or gas) moving through a barrier in a unit time, unit area, and unit pressure gradient not normalized for but directly related to thickness. (3) The product of vapor permeance and thickness (for thin films, ASTM E 96; for those over $^1/_8$ in., ASTM C 355). Usually reported in perm inches or grain/ (h.ft^2 . in. Hg) per in. of thickness.

Permeance: The rate of water vapor transmission per unit area at a steady state through a membrane or assembly, expressed in ng/(Pa.s.m^2) [grain/(ft^2 h .in.Hg)].

pH: (1) The negative log of the hydrogen-ion concentration, a measure of acidity and alkalinity. (2) A measure of the relative acidity or alkalinity for water. A pH of 7.0 indicates a neutral condition. A greater pH indicates alkalinity, and a lower pH, acidity. A one-unit change in pH indicates a tenfold change in acidity and alkalinity.

Pinhole: A tiny hole in a liquid-applied waterproofing membrane.

Plasticizer: A material, often solvent-like, incorporated in a plastic sheet to increase its workability, flexibility, or extensibility. The most important use of plasticizers is in PVC membranes, where the particular plasticizer dictates the PVC's use.

Polyethylene: A thermoplastic, high-molecular-weight organic compound used in sheet form, as a vapor retarder. (See HDPE)

Ply: A layer of felt or fabric in a waterproofing membrane; a four-ply membrane should have at least four plies of felt or fabric at any vertical cross section cut through the membrane.

Positive-side waterproofing: A waterproofing system in which the water-resisting element and the source of the hydrostatic pressure are on the same side of the structural component.

Pressure slab: A cast-in-place, reinforced concrete floor slab structurally designed to resist uplift from hydrostatic pressure.

Prime coat: (1) A coating applied to a surface to enhance the bond between the substrate and subsequent coats or sheets. (2) The first liquid coat applied in a multiple-coat system.

Primer: A compatible coating designed to enhance adhesion.

Primer (bituminous):   A thin liquid bitumen applied to a surface to improve the adhesion of heavier applications of bitumen and to absorb dust.

Protection board: see Protection course

Protection course: Semi-rigid sheet material placed on the waterproofing membrane to protect it against damage during subsequent construction and to provide a protective barrier against compressive and shearing forces induced by materials placed on or above it.

Puncture resistance: An index of a material's or system's ability to withstand the pressure of a sharp object without penetration.

PVC (polyvinyl chloride):   A synthetic thermoplastic polymer prepared from vinyl chloride. PVC can be compounded into flexible and rigid forms through the use of plasticizers, stabilizers, filler, and other modifiers; rigid forms used in pipes; flexible forms used in manufacture of sheets for single ply roofing and waterproofing membranes.

Raker: A diagonal brace supporting a soldier pile against lateral earth pressure. (Rakers have been generally replaced by tie-backs, which do not clutter an excavation.) Fig. G-3.

Reglet: A continuous groove or slot in a wall, designed to receive other components — e.g., flashing gaskets, or anchors; a continuous prefabricated metal or plastic device containing a groove, slot or recess which can be cast into (as a form) or mounted onto a building component surface.

Reinforcing: Generally, one or more strips of membrane, felts or fabrics, installed at corners and over construction joints.

Release agent: Material used to prevent bonding of concrete to a surface. (See also Bond breaker and Form oil.)

Rock anchor: Reinforcing bars grouted into sockets drilled into foundation rock and extended into foundation slabs — e.g. isolated column footings to resist upward hydrostatic pressure.

Fig. G-3   Rakers.

Rock pocket: A defect in concrete construction, a severe form of honeycombing, in which large aggregate are exposed in voids formed in cast-in-place concrete foundation walls, as a result of segregation and failure to vibrate the concrete to assure homogeneous distribution of cement, fines, and aggregate forming a continuous cross section through the wall. (See also Honeycombing)

Rupture: A membrane tear resulting from tensile stress.

Scrim: Woven open fabric, usually made from glass or polyester fibers, used to reinforce PVC waterproofing sheets.

Sheathing: The material forming the contact face of forms; also called lagging or sheeting.

Sheet pile or Sheet piling: concrete or wood planks, often splined, or roll-formed interlocking steel sections driven vertically to support the sides of an excavation.

Shotcrete: Mortar or concrete pneumatically projected at high velocity onto a surface.

Slab-on-ground: An unframed (i.e. non-structural), cast-in-place concrete slab, supported by continuous bearing stress on the foundation soil, whose top surface is partly or wholly below the adjoining grade. (Also called slab-on-grade)

Slurry: A viscous, liquid mixture of water and suspended clay or cement particles.

Slurry trench: A trench whose sides are retained by the lateral hydrostatic pressure of a slurry pumped in as the excavation proceeds.

Slurry wall: A foundation wall constructed via use of a slurry trench. When excavation of the slurry trench is completed, concrete is deposited via the tremie process, with the concrete mix displacing the slurry from the bottom and ultimately filling the entire slurry trench with the permanent foundation wall.

Soldier beams: Steel H section piles, usually driven at equal spacing along a building line and designed either as vertical cantilevers or as horizontally supported structural members resisting lateral earth pressure around an open excavation. Supports may be rods and anchors used as tiebacks or diagonal rolled steel sections. (called "soldier beams" because of their resemblance to a line of soldiers at attention.)

Soldier piles: A more technically accurate, but lesser used field term for soldier beams.

Split: A membrane rupture resulting from tensile-stress failure.

Structural slab: (1) A cast-in-place concrete deck over an occupied space spanning between beams, bearing walls, or other supports; (2) reinforced, cast-in-place concrete slab with foundation soil used as a bottom form, but designed to resist bending from upward hydrostatic pressure.

Substrate: The surface upon which films, treatments, adhesives, sealants, membranes, and coatings are applied.

Suspended slab: (See Structural slab, definition (1)

Tanking: Waterproofing both the foundation and slab-on-ground and joining them.

Telltale: A stake or other surface marker indicating an underground drain or cleanout.

Thixotropy: The property of gels of becoming fluid when disturbed, often used to describe the quality of "non-sag" materials.

Tiebacks: (1) Rods or cables anchored into rock or concrete deadmen outside an open excavation providing temporary restraint for wales, eliminating rakers or cross-bracing struts, thus freeing the excavated space from obstacles to construction equipment; (2) A rod fastened to a deadman, a rigid foundation, or either a rock or soil anchor to prevent lateral movement of formwork, sheet pile walls, retaining walls, bulkheads, etc. Fig. G-4.

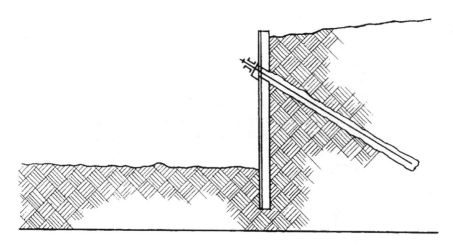

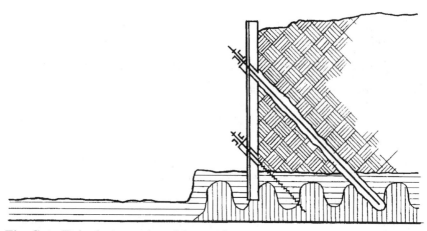

Fig. G-4   Tiebacks in earth and into rock.

Tie-off: The transitional seal used to terminate a waterproofing application at the top or bottom of flashing or by forming a watertight seal with the substrate, membrane or waterproofing systems.

Traffic surface: A surface exposed to traffic, either pedestrian or vehicular, (also called Finished wearing surface.)

Vapor pressure: Pressure exerted by a vapor in equilibrium with its solid or liquid form.

Vapor retarder: A material that retards the flow of water vapor. (Sometimes called a Vapor barrier)

VOC: Volatile organic content: solvents that when released into the atmosphere participate in the formation of reactive pollutants, particularly ozone, which contribute to smog, cause respiratory problems and damage crop yields. Maximum levels are established by the EPA and local regulatory bodies. Officially: Compounds of carbon, excluding carbon monoxide, carbon dioxide, carbonic acid, metallic carbides or carbonates, ammonium carbonate, methane, 1,1,1,-trichlor ethane, methyl chloride and trichlorotrifluoroethane, which may be emitted to the atmosphere during the application of and/or subsequent drying or curing of coatings.

Wale (Waler):   A horizontal structural member that resists lateral soil pressure around an excavation during construction, before the permanent foundation wall is constructed.

Waterproofing: Treatment of a surface or structure to prevent the passage of water under hydrostatic pressure.

Waterstop: A preformed material placed between concrete pours to prevent passage of water through the joint.

Watertable: The elevation in the soil where water is at atmospheric pressure. (Also called Groundwater level)

Water-vapor transmission (WVT):   Water-vapor flow normal to two parallel surfaces of a material, through a unit area, in a unit of time under the conditions of a specified test such as ASTM E 96. Customary units are grains/(h. ft^2).

Wearing surface: A surface exposed to traffic, either pedestrian or vehicular. (Also called Finished wearing surface)

Well points: Small-diameter wells, driven or jetted into soil surrounding an excavation and connected to a header pipe as part of a well-point system designed to drain water from an excavation. Well points thus lower the water table and relieve a building's foundation walls of hydrostatic pressure.

TABLE A-1   SI Conversion Factors

To convert from	To	Multiply by
°F	°C	0.556 (°F−32)
°C	°F	1.8 (°C+32)
mm	in.	0.03937
in.	mm	25.400
g/m²	lb/square (100 ft²)	0.0205
lb/square (100 ft²)	g/m²	48.83
pcf (lb/ft³)	kg/m³	16.02
kg/m³	pcf	0.0624
psf (lb/ft²)	kg/m²	4.882
kg/m²	psf	0.205
psi (lbf/in.²)	kPa	6.895
kPa	psi	0.1450
lbf/in.	kN/m	0.1751
kN/m	lbf/in.	5.710
Perm (vapor permeance) [grain/(ft² · h · in.Hg)]	ng/(m² · s · Pa)	57.45
R [°F/(Btuh · ft²)]	R [K/(W · m²)]	0.176
R [K/(W · m²)]	R [°F/(Btuh · ft²)]	5.678
U [Btuh/(ft² · °F)]	U [W/(m² · K)]	5.678
U [W/(m² · K)]	U [Btuh/(ft² · °F)]	0.176
grain	g	0.0648
Btu	J	1055
gal/square (100 ft²)	L/m²	0.408

Key to abbreviations:

°F = degrees Fahrenheit
°C = degrees Celsius
K = kelvin (= °C + 273.15)
Btuh = Btu per h
lbf = pound · force
N = newton (= 0.2248 lbf)
kN = kilonewton = 10^3 N
m = meter

mm = millimeter
g = gram
kg = kilogram (= 10^3 g)
ng = nanogram (= 10^{-6} kg = 10^{-9} g)
Pa = pascal (= N/m²)
kPa = 10^3 Pa
W = watt (= 3.414 Btuh)

B

Plaza Surfacing

Plazas are surfaced with cast-in-place concrete, natural stone, tile or masonry units installed either in a setting bed or on pedestals with open joints. They differ from pavers used for ballast in PMR (or IRMA) systems in that they are intended for pedestrian and light vehicular traffic and are not installed directly on the membrane or on the insulation above it.[1]

Open-jointed pavers are made from three materials:

- Precast concrete
- Natural stone
- Prefabricated wood decking

Precast concrete is hydro-pressed or wet-cast in molds, in units weighing 15 to 25 psf, in square or rectangular shapes ranging from 12 x 14 in. to 30-in. square. Thickness generally ranges from 1¼ to 2½ in., but

---

1. Concrete pavers for ballasting PMR systems or installed dry on a roof membrane are produced by concrete masonry-unit manufacturers on block-making equipment. Weighing approximately 12 psf, these pavers are square or rectangular, varying from a minimum 6 x 12 to a maximum 12 x 18 in. Thickness ranges from 1½ to 2⅝ in. Most have square edges, but units are also made with beveled edges and interlocks for greater wind-uplift resistance. Faces are available in a variety of textures and a limited range of colors. Backs are flat, corrugated and grooved. Larger units have lugs cast in the corners and center to promote insulation drying. These units have absorption rates in the 10% range and compressive strengths of 2,600 to 3,000 psi. Weight loss after 100 cycles of freeze/thaw testing per ASTM C 1262 should not exceed 1%.

These units are not recommended for a wearing surface subject to normal pedestrian or light vehicular traffic. There is one exception: interlocking concrete-masonry pavers conforming to ASTM C 936, which may be used when set in a sand bed.

sometimes up to 4-in. Faces are available in varied textures and a wide range of colors, exposed aggregates and simulated tile. Backs are usually flat, sometimes with lugs cast in at corners and centers. Maximum allowable water absorption is 5%. Compressive strength is around 7,000 psi. Weight loss after 100 freeze/thaw cycles per ASTM C 1262 test should not exceed 1%. There are no ASTM standards for these units.

Natural stones with water-absorption rates less than 1% include granite (per ASTM C 615); marble, including travertine (per ASTM C 503), and flagging of slate (per ASTM C 629); bluestone and other fine-grained quartz-based stone (per ASTM C 616). Also included among natural-stone paving materials is high-density limestone with maximum water absorption of 3% (per ASTM C 568). For these stones of lesser flexural strength, thickness range from 1½ to 4 in. Sizes and shapes vary, but rectangular and square predominate for pedestal installations. Faces are available in a wide range of textures including thermal (for granite), natural cleft for flagging, sandblasted and smooth. Backs are usually gaged (smooth or honed).

Prefabricated wood decking units are shop-fabricated from a variety of wood species. Certain species, — e.g., teak, redwood and cedar — are inherently weather resistant; others usually require pressure-preservative treatments. Panels are assembled from boards set flat or on edge with open or tight joints. These are screwed to frames or bolted together.

Units should be heavy enough to resist blow-off. Dimensional stability and code requirements for fire resistance are other considerations.

Pavers for closed-joint construction include these materials:

- Precast concrete
- Natural stones (listed above)
- Bricks
- Concrete masonry units
- Tile (ceramic and quarry)

Ceramic tile in locations subject to freezing should have maximum water absorption of 3% per ASTM C 373, plus classification as *resistant* per ASTM C 1026 test. All units should have a minimum coefficient of friction (wet and dry) of 0.6 per ASTM C 1028. Bricks should be brick pavers per ASTM C 902, never facing or common bricks.

Precast units, bricks and stones are laid dry, on pedestals or in sand or mortar beds. Bricks may also be installed in bituminous setting beds. Pedestals create a level surface, whereas sand or mortar beds often follow the contour of the suspended slab below. A typical setting bed is 1:3 to 1:6 Portland cement and sand mixed to a damp consistency, and tamped. The back of the Paving unit or the top of the setting bed is gauged with cement and water. The unit is then laid dry with a tight joint and tamped. The joints are either caulked or the same mix is swept dry into the joints and the excess cleaned with a light spray of water.

Prefabricated rubber and plastic pedestals are manufactured in a variety of designs They provide a level surface over undulating substrates. Heights are adjusted via stacking, interlocking, and shimming, or rotation of male and female threaded units. Some units require stabilizing with mortar-filled cores. Short pedestals can be installed on stacked squares of insulation or small pavers. This technique does, however, create problems when dismantling is required for maintenance or repair. All units contain tab spacers to create uniform joints and shims to adjust pavers individually.

Pedestals are often installed atop the insulation layer, but may be installed on the membrane, provided protection board or several layers of single-ply sheets are interposed between the pedestal and the membrane. Installing the pedestals on the membrane avoids the need to accommodate compressive creep inherent in all plastic foams. But it complicates the insulation installation and creates thermal bridges.

In addition to the pavers noted above, paving brick, quarry tile, and ceramic tile set in mortar beds are also used for wearing surfaces.

Sand-setting beds can be installed over a concrete protection slab or filter cloth on rigid insulation. Brick pavers in sand-setting beds are more successful than mortar setting beds, according to Clayford T. Grimm. Eccentric loading over small areas can cause high stresses in thicker sand beds that promote settling, rocking, and loosening, according to Estensorro and Perenchino. They recommend sand beds of ½ to 1-in. thickness, with an absolute maximum of 3 in. A 1-in. thickness is often inadequate to accommodate subgrade variations and to allow for raising the level of the substrate at expansion joints. To solve this problem a 1-in. sand bed can be installed over filter cloth on 3- to 6-in. strata of coarse gravel or a drainage composite. This provides the additional benefit of preventing frost heaving in areas subject to subfreezing temperatures. Sand should be coarse and single size, gap-graded, not like mortar sand, for maximum porosity.

Slate and other flagstones not exceeding 18 x 18 in. can also be set in this fashion. Larger units should be installed on tamped damp mortar beds of low cement/sand ratios, such as 1:3 and 1:6.

In climates subject to freezing, mortar beds for small stones and tile should contain acrylic additives to prevent freeze/thaw deterioration.

Mortar setting beds over insulation should be installed over a filter sheet and reinforced with hexagonal mesh.

Sand setting beds provide sub-surface drainage, but mortar setting beds must be installed over porous fill or drainage composites.

For construction details and specifications for ceramic and quarry tile refer to the Tile Council of America *Ceramic Tile: The Installation Handbook*, 1997, Roof Deck Membrane F103-94.

Appendix

C

Waterstops

Waterstops are required in both horizontal and vertical "cold" joints — i.e., construction and expansion joints — subject to hydrostatic pressure. They are embedded in the concrete, spanning across the joint to form a barrier to the passage of liquid water. With negative-side waterproofing, waterstops are a primary part of the system; with positive-side and bentonite systems, they provide a secondary line of protection.

The original waterstops were simple metal bars spanning across the joint, with one side greased to break the bond with the concrete and prevent stress concentrations in the waterstop metal at the joint. Despite the greasing precaution, these simple waterstops proved inadequate for moving joints. They were replaced with thin copper sheets, bent to form flanged Vees. These, too, proved inadequate. Cyclical movement work-hardened the metal and promoted fatigue failure. As a consequence, some 30 years ago, rubber dumbbells began replacing copper waterstops. But this material also compiled a dismal record, leaking when water migrated around the ends or when the ends pulled free of the concrete.

Contemporary waterstops are formed from PVC or rubber derivatives in a variety of shapes, including serrated U and V shapes, labyrinth, center bulb, and ribbed dumbbell. (See Fig. C-1). Center bulb types are used for expansion joints in walls. Where these become the sole water barrier, they must be designed for resistance to hydrostatic pressure and water migration around the ends. For design parameters, consult the Corps of Engineers, *Waterstops and other Joint Materials,* EM1110-2-2102 and CRDC-C-572-74.

U-shaped center bulbs with ribbed flanges have increased the flexibility and reduced the infiltration of water around the flanges. They have not, however overcome the greatest weakness of bulb-type waterstops

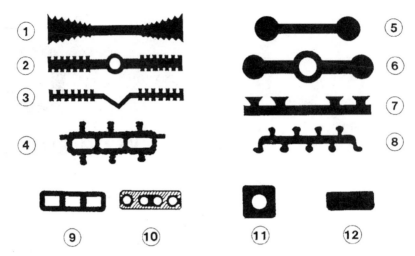

Fig. C-1 Basic types of waterstops, (1) serrated; (2) serrated dumbbell; (3) serrated "V"; (4) cellular; (5) dumbbell; (6) center bulb dumbbell; (7) on-grade; (8) labyrinth; (9) modified; (10) chloroprene; (11 & 12) butyl/bentonite.

— i.e., the difficulty of achieving a perfect weld at end joints and corners.

Units are tied to reinforcing and spliced by site-welding. Great care is required to insure proper positioning and to preserve the integrity of the splices. This care must continue during concrete casting operations, to insure encasement in solid, void-free concrete and to prevent displacement by the concrete mix.

Partly because of the difficulty in assuring this required degree of care, other types of waterstops are gradually replacing the dumbbell and tube-type PVC waterstops. These new types are composed of butyl rubber, bentonite-impregnated butyl, and proprietary plastics, used in static joints.

Formed as square or rectangular rods, they are easier to bend and splice than the intricately profiled shapes they replace. Installation is equally simple; units are nailed to the concrete or to the forms, a practice that eliminates form-splitting. The bentonite/butyl compositions have a further advantage in permitting installation on damp substrates. However, these hydrophilic-type joints have not enjoyed as long a history of satisfactory use as the PVC waterstops. Moreover, there is some concern about the longevity of the bentonite when the waterstop is under a continuous high hydrostatic head.

Reinjectable waterstops are also used in special circumstances. They consist of a network of perforated tubes cast in the concrete. Hydrophilic resins or fine cement pastes are pressure-injected through the tubes and react with water to swell and create a water-impermeable joint. Reinjection stops leaks, if they occur.

D

Thermal Insulation

Thermal insulation design for underground spaces differs markedly from superstructure design in the high heat capacity of the concrete walls and slabs, which store and release heat energy more slowly than the normally thin, light components in roofs and curtain walls. (Steel roof decks have no thermal insulating value and virtually no heat capacity.) High heat capacity is especially beneficial when the occupied space has a cooling load, which is drastically reduced by heavy materials of high heat capacity. It is of less value in cold climates subject to prolonged spells of subfreezing temperatures, which produce high inside-outside temperature differentials persisting for intervals measured in weeks or even months. Under these conditions, thermal insulation is necessary to conserve energy and promote comfort.

For the three underground components, thermal-insulating requirements follow this order: structural plaza slabs, basement walls, and basement slabs-on-ground. A plaza waterproofing assembly has essentially the same exposure to extreme air temperatures as the building superstructure, because its top surface is exposed to the atmosphere. Basement walls have substantially less exposure, because ground temperatures are substantially moderated by a combination of the insulating value, and perhaps more important, the heat capacity of the soil. Even when exposed to extended subzero temperatures in northern areas of the United States, the soil remains above freezing temperature 4 to 5 ft below the ground elevation. Basement slabs-on-ground experience even less temperature variation than basement walls, because of their greater distance from the atmospheric source of temperature variations.

Readers seeking more information on this subject can consult the "Heating Load" chapter of the ASHRAE *Handbook, Fundamentals.* Also,

Chapter 5 of the University of Minnesota, *Building Foundation Handbook*, and Sections 14 and 18 of NAVFAC DM-1.4 *Earth Sheltered Buildings*. The mechanical engineer should set the insulation requirements for all underground, as well as superstructure, components.

Plaza Slab Illustrative Example

Since plaza structural slabs require the greatest amount of insulation, the following example is shown merely for illustrative purposes. To cope with thermal insulation problems, the designer must know the basic indexes of conductive heat transmission:

1. Thermal conductivity k = heat (Btu) transferred per hour through a 1-in.-thick, 1-ft^2 area of homogeneous material per °F temperature difference from surface to surface. The unit for k is Btu/(h . ft^2 °F . in.)
2. Conductance $C = k$/thickness is the corresponding unit for a material of given thickness. (The unit for C is Btu/(h . ft^2 . °F). For a 2-in.-thick plank of material whose $k = 0.20$, $C = 0.10$.
3. Thermal resistance $R = 1/C$ indicates a material's resistance to conductive heat flow. (For a material with $C = 0.20$, $R = 5.0$.) The unit for R is °F . h . ft^2/Btu. That is, for a 5°F temperature difference surface-to-surface, 1 Btu/h flows through a 1-ft^2 specimen.
4. Overall coefficient of transmission U is a unit like k and C, measured in Btu transmitted per hour (Btu/h) through 1 ft^2 of construction per °F from air on one side to air on the other. It relates to the several component materials in a wall or roof. U is calculated from the following formula:

$$U = \frac{1}{\Sigma R}$$

where ΣR = sum of the thermal resistances of the components, plus the resistances of the inside and outside air films. (Designers using SI units can convert to U, in watts transmitted through 1 m^2 per °C by multiplying U in British units by 5.678.)

To calculate the insulation's required thermal resistance R, the designer usually starts with a target U factor set by the mechanical engineer. For the other components, the designer merely tabulates the resistances R for all the materials, including inside and outside air films. Data for conductances of various materials are available from the *ASHRAE Handbook and Product Directory*. If not available in general tables, data for proprietary insulating materials should be furnished by manufacturers.

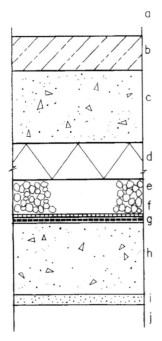

Thermal Resistance (R) tabulation

a, Outside air film	0.25 Heat flow up
b, Paver	0.60
c, Concrete protection slab	0.36
d, Polystyrene insulation	R_i
e, Drainage course	0.20
f, Protection board	0.20
g, Membrane	0.10
h, Structural concrete slab	0.72
i, Plaster ceiling	0.32
j, Inside air film	0.61

$$\Sigma R = 3.36 + R_i$$

Cross Section thru Plaza Waterproofing Construction

Fig. D-1   For the plaza waterproofing assembly shown above, the various R values (i.e thermal resistance units) are approximations from ASHRAE data. To determine the required thickness of extruded polystyrene to yield a maximum U factor = .06 you can use the formula:

$$R_i = \tfrac{1}{.06} - 3.36 = 13.31$$

Assume that the dry R value of extruded polystyrene is 90% of its 6.25/in. dry value (to allow for 10% moisture-reduction). The required thickness is then 13.31/ 5.62 = 2.36 in. Use 2½ in. thickness.

Abstracts of ASTM Standards Relating to Waterproofing

The following ASTM Standards apply to materials and practices commonly found in waterproofing specifications. The abstracts have not been authorized by ASTM, and they may not be complete or current. The specifier should review the standard prior to referencing it in the project manual.

C 578 Standard Specification for Preformed, Block-Type Cellular Polystyrene Thermal Insulation. Covers the types, physical properties and dimensions of cellular polystyrene insulation boards, both those formed by expansion of polystyrene resin beads or granules in a closed mold (also called EPS) or by the expansion of polystyrene base resin in an extrusion process (also called extruded polystyrene). Eleven types are listed with densities ranging from .70 to 3.00 pcf and compressive strengths ranging from 5 to 100 psi. The most commonly used types for waterproofing listed with their density (pcf) and compressive strength (psi) are: VI (1.60 pcf, 40 psi) and VII (2.20 pcf (60 psi). First published in 1965.

C 755 Standard Practice for Selection of Vapor Retarders for Thermal Insulation. Outlines factors to be considered, describes design principles and procedures for vapor retarder selection, and defines water vapor transmission values appropriate for established criteria. Although intended for vapor retarders in connection with thermal insulation, the standard is useful for its discussion of vapor retarder materials. First published in 1973.

C 836 Standard Specification for High Solids Content, Cold

Liquid-Applied Elastomeric Waterproofing Membrane for Use with Separate Wearing Course. Describes required properties and test methods for a cold, liquid-applied, elastomeric-type membrane, one or two-component, for waterproofing building decks subject to hydrostatic pressure in building areas to be occupied by personnel, vehicles, or equipment. This specification applies only to a membrane system above which a separate wearing or traffic course will be applied. Physical requirements include hardness, weight loss, low-temperature flexibility and crack bridging, film thickness on vertical surface, adhesion-in-peel after water immersion, and extensibility after heat aging. First published in 1976.

C 898 Standard Guide for Use of High Solids Content, Cold Liquid-Applied Elastomeric Waterproofing Membrane with Separate Wearing Course. Describes the use of a high-solids content, cold liquid-applied elastomeric waterproofing membrane in a waterproofing system subject to hydrostatic pressure for building decks over occupied space where the membrane is covered with a separate wearing course. Contains design considerations for substrates, membranes, protection course, drainage systems, and wearing courses. First published in 1978.

C 981 Standard Guide for Design of Built-Up Bituminous Membrane Waterproofing Systems for Building Decks. Describes the design and installation of bituminous membrane waterproofing systems for plaza deck and promenade construction over occupied spaces of buildings where covered by a separate wearing course. Contains design considerations for substrates, membrane components, protection board, drainage, insulation, protection, and wearing courses. An excellent primer on plaza design. First published in 1983.

C 1127 Standard Guide for Use of High-Solids-Content, Liquid-Applied Elastomeric Waterproofing Membrane with and Integral Wearing Surface. Describes the design and installation of cold-applied elastomeric waterproofing membrane systems that have an integral wearing surface. The system consists of a reinforced concrete substrate coated with a primer, base and top coats and embedded aggregate. The standard contains installation details. First published in 1989.

D 41 Standard Specification for Primer for Use with Asphalt in Dampproofing and Waterproofing. Defines the minimum requirements for asphaltic primer use with asphalt in waterproofing below or above ground level and applied to concrete and masonry surfaces. First published in 1917.

D 173 Standard Specification for Woven Cotton Fabrics Saturated With Bituminous Substances for Use in Waterproofing.

Defines the minimum requirements for bituminized cotton fabric composed of woven cotton cloth waterproofed with either asphalt or coal-tar pitch. First published in 1923.

D 226 Standard Specification for Asphalt-Saturated Roofing Felt for Use in Waterproofing and in Constructing Built-Up Roofs. Defines the minimum requirements for two types of asphalt-saturated, but not coated, felts: No. 15 and No. 30. Felts may be perforated or non-perforated. First published in 1925.

D 227 Standard Specification for Coal-Tar Saturated Roofing Felts for Use in Waterproofing and in Constructing Built-Up Roofs. Defines the minimum requirements for coal-tar-saturated organic felts for use with coal-tar pitch. First published in 1925.

D 420 Standard Guide to Site Characterization for Engineering, Design and Construction Purposes. Refers to ASTM methods by which soil, rock, and ground water conditions may be determined. First published in 1965.

D 449 Standard Specification for Asphalt Used in Dampproofing and Waterproofing. Defines three types of asphalt suitable for use as a plying or mopping cement in the construction of a membrane waterproofing system. Type I is a soft adhesive "self-healing" asphalt that flows easily under the mop and is suitable for use below ground level under uniformly moderate temperature conditions. Type II is somewhat less susceptible with good adhesive and "self-healing" properties for use above ground level where not exposed to temperatures exceeding 125°F. Type III is less susceptible to temperature than Type II with good adhesive properties for use above ground level where exposed on vertical surfaces in direct sunlight or at temperatures above 125°F. First published in 1937.

D 450 Standard Specification for Coal-Tar Pitch for Roofing, Dampproofing and Waterproofing. Defines three types of coal-tar pitch suitable for use in the construction of built-up roofing, dampproofing and membrane waterproofing systems. Type I is suitable for use in built-up roofing, dampproofing and membrane waterproofing systems. Type II is suitable for use dampproofing and membrane waterproofing systems. Type III is suitable for use in built-up roofing, dampproofing and membrane waterproofing systems, but having less volatile components than Type I or II. First published in 1937.

D 1056 Standard Specification for Flexible Cellular Materials — Sponge or Expanded Rubber. Covers two types of rubber:

Type I open and Type II closed cell. There are four classes: Class A is not oil resistant, Class B is low swell from oil and Class C is medium swell. Class D is resistant to temperature extremes. Each Class is available in three grades with various compression deflection ranges. They range in increments from 0 - .5, 0.5 - 2 and 5 - 17 psi. First published in 1949.

D 1327 Standard Specification for Bitumen Saturated Woven Burlap Fabrics Used in Waterproofing. Defines the composition of woven burlap cloth saturated with either asphalt or refined coal-tar. First published in 1954.

D 1668 Standard Specification for Glass Fabrics (Woven and Treated) for Roofing and Waterproofing. Covers three types of glass fabrics composed of woven glass cloth treated with either asphalt or coal-tar pitch or an organic resin. Type I is asphalt-treated, Type II is coal-tar pitch-treated and Type III is organic resin treated. First published in 1959.

D 1752 Standard Specification for Preformed Sponge Rubber and Cork Expansion Joint Fillers for Concrete Paving and Structural Construction. Covers three types: Type I sponge rubber, Type II cork and Type III self-expanding cork. First published 1960.

D 2178 Standard specification for Asphalt Glass Felt Used in Roofing and Waterproofing. Covers three types of glass felts impregnated with asphalt, Types III (8.4 lb/110 sq. ft.), IV and VI (both 6.0 lb/100 sq. ft.). Types III and IV contain pinholes. Type VI is perforated with 1/8 in. dia. holes. First published in 1963.

D 3083 Specification for Flexible Poly (Vinyl Chloride) Plastic Sheeting for Pond, Canal and Reservoir Lining.

D 4397 Specification for Polyethylene Sheeting for Construction, Industrial and Agricultural Applications. Covers polyethylene sheets of 10 mils or less in thickness. Physical characteristics include color and finish, impact resistance, mechanical properties, reflectance, luminous transmittance, water vapor transmission from .014 to 1.4 grains/ 24 hr/ 100 sq. ft. and permeance from .076 to .76 perms.

D 4434 Standard Specification for Poly(Vinyl Chloride) Sheet Roofing. Covers reinforced flexible sheet made form poly (vinyl chloride) resin for use in single-ply roofing membranes exposed to the weather. Type II, Grade 1 is internally reinforced. Type II, Grade 2 is externally reinforced with fabric. Type III is internally reinforced with fabric and may also have a fabric backing. Type IV is internally reinforced with fabric and may also have a fabric backing of minimum 0.036 in.). Types II and III are 0.45 in. thick. Type IV is 0.91 in. thick. First published in 1985.

D 4637 Standard Specification for EPDM Sheet Used in Single-Ply Roof Membrane. Covers non-reinforced, fabric or scrim-reinforced and fabric-backed vulcanized rubber sheet made from EPDM for use in roofing. Type I is non-reinforced; Type II is scrim (or fabric) internally reinforced; Type III is fabric-backed. First published in 1987.

D 5295 Standard Guide for Preparation of Concrete Surfaces for Adhered (Bonded) Membrane Waterproofing Systems. Provides recommendations for the preparation of new concrete surfaces prior to the application of adhered (bonded) waterproofing. Discusses adhesion inhibitors, repair of surface defects, surface preparation and evaluation by field tests. First published in 1992.

D 5385 Standard Test Method for Hydrostatic Pressure Resistance of Waterproofing Membranes. Provides a laboratory test for the hydrostatic resistance of a waterproofing membrane and can be used to compare the hydrostatic resistance between different membranes. First published in 1993.

D 5474 Standard Guide for Selection of Data Elements for Ground-Water Investigations. Covers the selection of data elements for documentation of ground-water sites. Excellent list of documents relating to subsurface investigations of soil, rock and ground-water. First published in 1993.

D 5665 Standard Specification for Thermoplastic Fabrics Used in Cold-Applied Roofing and Waterproofing. Covers thermoplastic fabrics such as polyester, polyester/polyamide bicomponent, or composites with fiberglas or polyester scrims for use in cold-applied waterproofing. Type I is polyester spunbonded without resin, un-needled; Type II is polyester spunbonded without resin, needled; Type III is Polyester mat plus fiber glass scrim with resin; Type IV is polyester core/polyamide sheath bicomposite spunbonded; Type V is polyester mat with polyester stitching; and Type VI is polyester mat plus polyester scrim with resin. First published in 1995.

D 5726 Standard Specification for Thermoplastic Fabrics Used in Hot-Applied Roofing and Waterproofing. Covers thermoplastic fabrics such as polyester, polyester/polyamide bicomponent, or composites with fiberglas or polyester scrims for use in hot-applied waterproofing. Type I is polyester spunbonded with resin, un-needled; Type

II is polyester spunbonded with resin, needled; Type III is Polyester mat plus fiber glass scrim and resin; Type IV is polyester core/polyamide sheath bicomposite spunbonded. First published in 1995.

D 5843 Standard Guide for Application of Fully Adhered Vulcanized Rubber Sheets Used in Waterproofing. Provides information for the application and protection of fully adhered EPDM, butyl and neoprene vulcanized rubber sheets to be installed on concrete substrates. First published 1996.

D 5898 Standard Guide for Standard Details for Adhered Sheet Waterproofing. Illustrates details for typical conditions encountered in adhered sheet waterproofing membranes on below-grade structures and plazas. Contains drawings and explanatory notes for detailing terminations, penetrations, expansion joints and drains. First published in 1996.

D 5957 Standard Guide for Flood Testing Horizontal Waterproofing Installations. Describes a method for testing the watertightness of waterproofing installations applied to horizontal surfaces having a slope not greater than 2%. The membrane is dammed and covered with 1 to 4 inches of water for 24 hours. First published in 1996.

D 6134 Standard Specification for Vulcanized Rubber Sheets Used in Waterproofing Systems. Covers two types of rubber, Type I, EPDM and Type II, Butyl (IIR). First published in 1998.

D 6135 Standard Practice for Application of Self-Adhering Modified Bituminous Waterproofing. Outlines general procedures for the application of self-adhering modified bitumen waterproofing systems for new installations. First published 1998.

E 154 Standard Test Methods for Water Vapor Retarders Used in Contact with Earth Under Concrete Slabs, on Walls or as a Ground Cover. Describes various test methods for determining the properties of flexible membranes to be used as vapor retarders. Properties include water vapor transmission, tensile strength, low temperature bending, resistance to puncture, plastic flow deterioration from soil organisms and substances, soil poisoners, UV exposure and flame spread. First published in 1959.

E 946 Test Method for Water Absorption of Bentonite by the Porous Plate Method First Published in 1983. Discontinued 1996.

E 1643 Standard Practice for Installation of Water Vapor

Retarders Used in Contact with Earth or Granular Fill Under Concrete Slabs. Covers procedures for installing flexible, prefabricated sheet membranes under concrete slabs on ground. Describes placement and protection. Contains a field check list and illustrations. Appendix covers pre-design considerations for landscaping and irrigation, subgrade design and specification, base and protection courses. First published in 1994.

E 1745 Standard Specification for Water Vapor Retarders Used in Contact with Earth or Granular Fill Under Concrete Slabs. Covers non-bituminous flexible, preformed sheet materials to be used as vapor retarders under concrete slabs on ground. Lists three classes with values for permeance, tensile strength, puncture resistance and flame spread. First published in 1996

E 1907 Standard Test Methods for Determining Moisture Related Suitability of Concrete Floors to Receive Vapor Retardant Finishes. Covers the acceptance of concrete slabs to receive vapor retardant finishes by six tests: polyethylene-sheet test, mat test, electrical-resistance test, RMA test, primer or adhesive strip test, and humidifier test. First published in 1998.

Waterproofing Selection Procedure

The seven flow charts in this appendix demonstrate the formalizing of the design process. Reprinted from the U.S. Navy publication NAVFAC DM-1.4 Earth-Sheltered Buildings, Design Manual 1.4, each algorithmic flow chart represents one of the following stages:

- Evaluation of groundwater conditions
- Occupancy parameters
- Soil contaminants
- Structural requirements
- Construction procedures
- Product reliability
- Product performance

These successive algorithms constitute a highly detailed elimination process, converging on the solution to the waterproofing problem. The first five charts (F-1 through F-5) deal with technical problems. The last two charts, F-6 and F-7, focus on product liability, contractual relationships, and product performance.

Fig. F-6 is of particular interest. This algorithm puts the manufacturer through a rigorous investigation. The answers to one set of questions tells the designer whether he needs to re-evaluate or test the product. The answers to another set of questions tell the designer if, for example, the manufacturer "endorses" the applicator's work, thus implicitly accepting responsibility for it. If not the task of assigning responsibility in event of a failure will be complicated, as each party seeks to escape blame and attribute the failure to others. Mindful of the professional malpractice risks in our super-litigious society, prudent designers will find Figures F-6 and F-7 a big help in evaluating waterproofing products and their manufacturers.

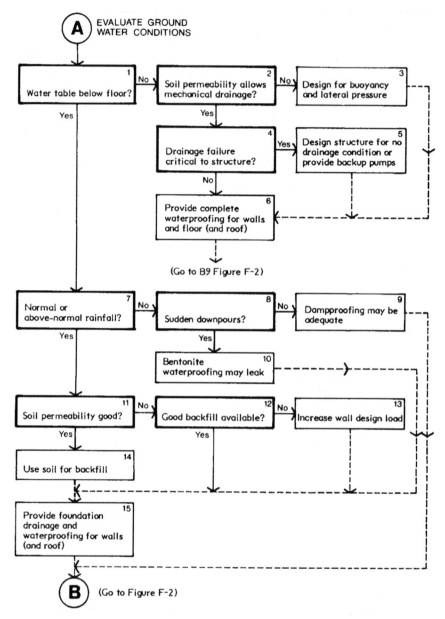

Fig. F-1 Waterproofing Flowchart--Ground-Water Conditions.

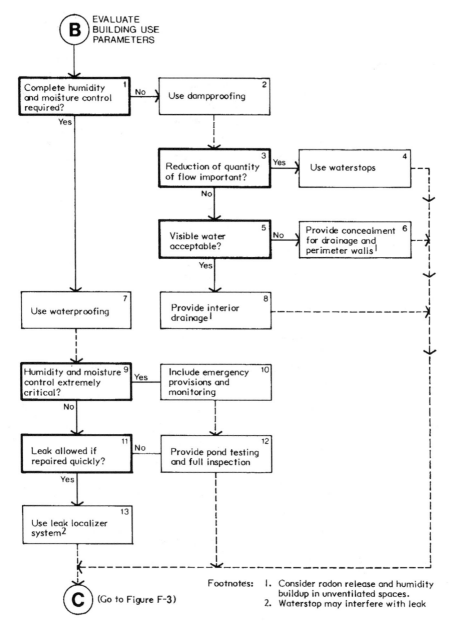

Fig. F-2 Waterproofing Flowchart--Building Use Parameters.

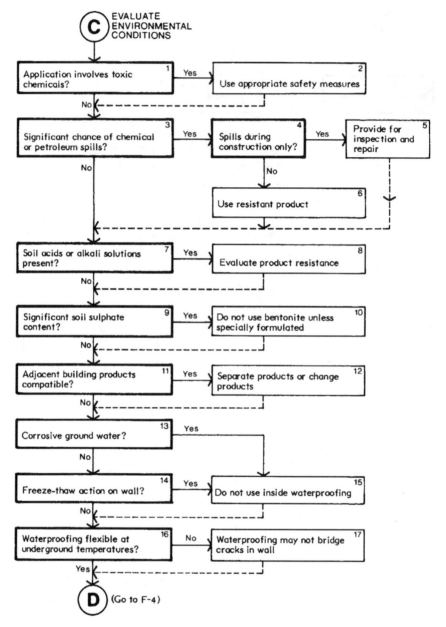

Fig. F-3 Waterproofing Flowchart--Environmental Conditions.

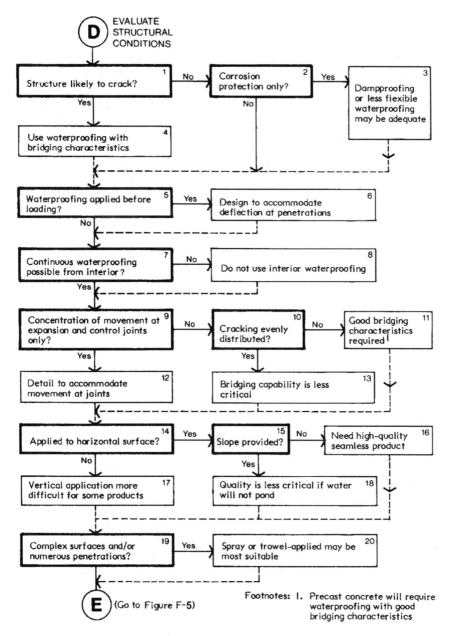

Fig. F-4   Waterproofing Flowchart--Structural Conditions.

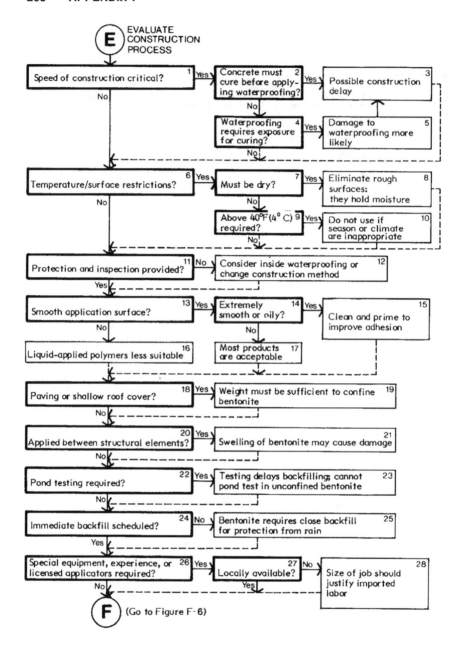

Fig. F-5 Waterproofing Flowchart--Construction Process.

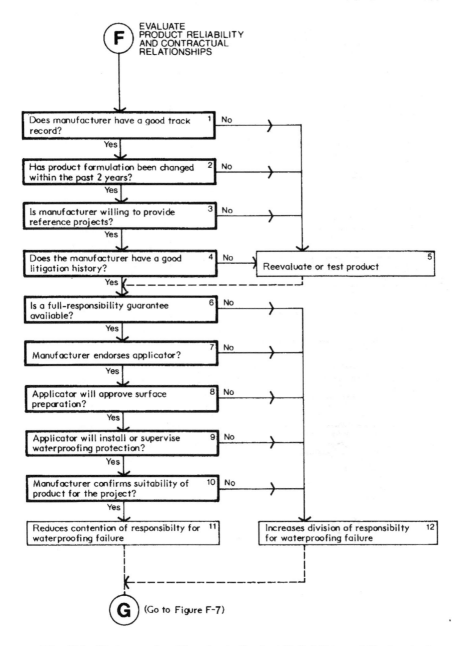

Fig. F-6 Waterproofing Flowchart--Product Reliablitiy and Contractual Relationships.

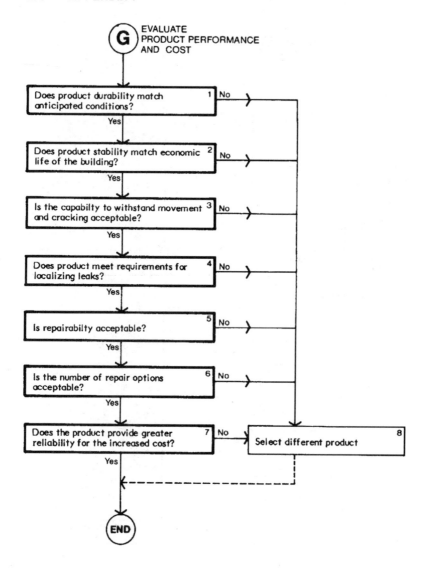

Fig. F-7 Waterproofing Flowchart--Product Performance and Cost.

Bibliography

[1]   ACI Guide 515, 1R79 *A Guide to the Use of Waterproofing, Dampproofing, Protective and Decorative Barrier Systems for Concrete*, American Concrete Institute, Detroit, MI (Revised 1984

[2]   Anderson, Brent, *Underground Waterproofing,* 1982.

[3]   Anderson, Brent, *Waterproofing & The Design Professional*, The Construction Specifier March 1986.

[4]   Babcock, Warner K. *Cementitious Membranes: Understanding the True Scope*, The Construction Specifier, April 1982

[5]   *Building Foundation Design Handbook,* K. Labs, J. Carmody, et al. Underground Space Center, University of Minnesota, Minneapolis, MN, ORNL/Sub/86-72143/1, May 1988

[6]   Cornell, Russell W. *Waterproofing is as Waterproofing Does*, The Construction Specifier December 1970

[7]   Construction Specifications Institute *Spectext*

[8]   Dworkin, Joseph F. *Waterproofing Below Grade — Materials, Methods and Controls,* Construction Specifier, 1990, March pp. 44-52

[9]   Engel, Joseph, *Cold Applied Fluid Elastomeric Waterproofing Membranes,* Building Deck Waterproofing, ASTM STP 606, J. Panek, Ed., ASTM, Philadelphia, 1976, pp. 204-217

[10]   Estenssoro & Perenchino, *Failures of Exterior Plazas,* Construction Specifier, January, 19911/91 pp 87-92

[11]   Friedberg, M. Paul *Roofscape,* Architectural Engineering News December 1969

[12]   Garden, G. K. *Roof Terraces,* Canadian Building Digest CBD 75, National Research Council, March 1966

[13]   Gaul, Robert W. *Preparing Concrete Surfaces for Coatings*, Concrete International July 1984

[14]   Griffin, C.W. and Fricklas, R.L., *The Manual of Low-Slope Roof Systems*, McGraw Hill, 3rd ed., 1996

[15]   Grimm, Clayford T. *Delamination of Masonry Pavements*, TMS Journal February 1994

[16]   International Concrete Repair Institute *Guide for Selecting and Specifying Materials for Repair of Concrete Surfaces* , Technical Guidelines, Sterling, VA 1996

[17]   Kanarowski, Stanley M. *Evaluation of Bentonite Clay for Waterproofing Foundation Walls Below Grade*, CERL Technical Report M-93, May, 1975

[18]   Kessi, Alfred *Negative Side Waterproofing*, Concrete Repair Bulletin, International Concrete Repair Institute, Sterling, VA. September/October 1996

[19]   Kidder-Parker *Architects' and Builders' Handbook*, Waterproofing For Foundations pp. 2123-2131, John Wiley & Sons, Eighteenth Edition, 1945

[20]   Kubal, Michael K. *Waterproofing the Building Envelope*, McGraw-Hill, Inc. New York, NY, 1993

[21]   Lawrence, Dorothy. Lecture in California October 24, 1990 and April 24, 1995

[22]   Lawrence, Dorothy and Pratt, Charles O, *Chapter 4 Waterproofing Barrier Systems,* Revised February 21, 1994 from ACI Guide 515, 1R79 A Guide to the Use of Waterproofing, Dampproofing, Protective and Decorative Barrier Systems for Concrete, American Concrete Institute, Detroit, MI

[23]   Laaly, H.O. *The Science and Technology of Traditional and Modern Roofing Systems*, Griffin Printing, Glendale, CA, Chapter 23, 1993

[24]   Maslow, Philip *Chemical Materials for Construction*, Structures Publishing Co. Famington, MI, 1974

[25]   Merriman-Wiggin *American Civil Engineering Handbook*, John Wiley, 5th Edition, February 1930. p. 1643

[26]   Monroe, D.C. *Reflective Cracking and Cold, Liquid-Applied Elastomeric Deck Coating and Membrane Systems: Practical Considerations from Field Observations*, Building Deck Waterproofing, ASTM STP 1084, L.E. Gish, Ed., ASTM, Philadelphia, 1990, pp. 121-130

[27]   National Roofing Contractors Association *The NRCA Roofing & Waterproofing Manual*, Third Edition, 1989, Rosemont, IL

[28]   NAVFAC DM-1.4 *Earth Sheltered Buildings*, Dept. of the Nay, Alexandria, VA Government Printing Office, Washington, DC, March 1984

Oak Ridge National Laboratory, United States Department of Energy, Fact Sheet # 04 ORNL/SUB-7849/04

[29]   Parise, C.J. *Architectural Considerations in Plaza Membrane Waterproofing Systems*, Materials and Research Standards, ASTM Vol 11, No. 5, May 1971 pp. 19-22

[30]   Pashina, Keith, *Coating Concrete,* The Construction Specifier, December, 1993 pp. 86

[31]   Pratt, Charles O. *Waterproofing — Problems in Terminology,* Building Deck Waterproofing, ASTM STP 1084, L.E. Gish, Ed., ASTM, Philadelphia, 1990, pp. 137-142

[32]   Ruggiero, Stephen S. and Rutila, Dean A. *Plaza Waterproofing Design Fundamentals*, The Construction Specifier, January 1991

[33]   Ruggiero, Stephen S. *Buried Buildings*, Progressive Architecture, June 1993

[34]   Ruggiero, Stephen S. and Rutila, Dean A. *Principles of Design and Installation of Building Deck Waterproofing,* Building Deck Waterproofing, ASTM STP 1084, L.E. Gish, Ed., ASTM, Philadelphia, 1990, pp. 5-28

[35]   Simmons, H. Leslie, *Repairing and Extending Weather Barriers*, Van Nostrand Reinhold, New York, 1989

[36]   Stilling, Robert G. *Waterstops - Materials and Configurations with Illustrated Test Results*, Meeting Association of Conservation Engineers, North Platte, NE, November 8, 1967

[37]   *Technics: Roofs for Use,* Progressive Architecture, July 1990

[38]   U. S. Army Corps of Engineers *Method of Test for Water Permeability of Concrete,* CRD-C 48-73, Revised December 1973

Index

About the Author

Justin Henshell, AIA, CSI, FASTM, is a partner in Henshell & Buccellato, Consulting Architects, based in Red Bank, New Jersey. He has been practicing architecture since 1952 and has specialized in moisture-related problems in the building envelope nationwide since 1974.

Among the more than 50 below-grade waterproofing projects on which he has consulted are: Seattle Art Museum, Wharton School of Business at the University of Philadelphia, Smith Barney Headquarters, New York City; Suffolk County Courthouse, Long Island, New York; Guam Legislature, and New York Public Library Book Stacks.

Mr. Henshell is chairman of the ASTM sub-committee on Roofing Membrane Systems and serves on the sub-committee on Waterproofing and Dampproofing Systems where he was the principal author for the ASTM Guide for Standard Details for Adhered Sheet Waterproofing.